STUDIES IN MILTON

BY

S. B. LILJEGREN

BY DUE PERMISSION OF THE PHILOSOPHICAL FACULTY OF LUND
TO BE PUBLICLY DISCUSSED IN ENGLISH IN LECTURE HALL VI
APRIL 5TH, 1918, AT 10 O'CLOCK A. M. FOR THE DEGREE
OF DOCTOR OF PHILOSOPHY

LUND
C. W. K. GLEERUP

ders. Ethisches und Literaturanalytisches zur Milton-Frage.
Ebd. 56, 59 - 68

STUDIES IN MILTON

BY

S. B. LILJEGREN

LUND
C. W. K. GLEERUP

LUND 1918
PRINTED BY AKTIEBOLAGET SKÅNSKA CENTRALTRYCKERIET

PREFACE.

The changed attitude of recent research towards the Stuart period seems to have affected the conception of Milton very little, perhaps because it has set in principally on points likely to be overlooked by the strict historian of literature. Masson's industrious and monumental Life still offers the starting-point for the study of the poet, though it has grown out of the appreciative position of Macaulay, Carlyle, and Taine, now apparently rejected in other respects.

The origin of this treatise will, I think, be clear to anyone acquainted with these facts; as to extent, it was limited to some points long in dispute, or dealt with insufficiently or not at all elsewhere.

Concessions to historical detail, the pivot of the treatise, have required many and at times lengthy quotations. This reason also explains e. g. my retaining some accents, p. 14 and pass. (verified from Add. MS. 36354), reprinting Francini's ode from ed. pr. (based upon his MS.) in accordance with the fresh light thrown on this person, and the like. When not otherwise indicated, the quotations from Milton are to be found in Fletcher's (prose) or Beeching's (poetry) ed.

The present situation abroad has delayed publication. First by rendering access to England difficult; then by causing my MS. to lie in vain for half a year in Germany, where the editor of "Anglistische Forschungen" had kindly promised to publish it in that series. On both occasions I received effective assistance from the Royal Swedish Department for Foreign Affairs, on the former also from Sir Gilbert Murray, for which I here beg leave respectfully to express my gratitude.

I likewise wish to thank my teacher, Prof. E. Ekwall; F. J. Fielden M. A., my chief helper in revising style and proofs; and the officials of the British Museum, the Public Record Office, Stationers' Hall, and similar institutions to which recourse has been had.

Lund

S. B. Liljegren.

INTRODUCTION

It is a well-known fact that conflicting principles in society, political, religious, etc., whether defined as liberalism — conservatism, progress — reaction, or otherwise, are mirrored in historians of different ages and nations, however disguised by name and apparel. And not only in such a manner as to show contemporary events in the recorder's colours, consciously or unconsciously individual; but even so as to illuminate the past principally by side-light and to foreshadow the future on anything but general lines.

As regards the past, one of the most highly esteemed historians of England thinks the history of his country more exposed to the consequences of this fact than that of other nations. And the explanation he finds in the peculiar relations of English institutions and English society to their origin and development: —

"The historical literature of England has indeed suffered grievously from a circumstance which has not a little contributed to her prosperity. The change, great as it is, which her polity has undergone during the last six centuries, has been the effect of gradual development, not of demolition and reconstruction. The present constitution of our country is, to the constitution under which she flourished five hundred years ago, what the tree is to the sapling, what the man is to the boy. The alteration has been great. Yet there never was a moment at which the chief part of what existed was not old. A polity thus formed must abound in anomalies. But for the evils arising from mere anomalies we have ample compensation. Other societies possess written constitutions more symmetrical. But no other society has yet succeeded in uniting revolution with prescription, progress with stability, the energy of youth with the majesty of immemorial antiquity.

This great blessing, however, has its drawbacks: and one of those drawbacks is, that every source of information as to our early history has been poisoned by party spirit. As there is no country where statesmen have been so much under the influence of the past, so there is no country where historians have been so much under the influence of the present. Between these two things, indeed, there is a natural connection. Where history is regarded merely as a picture of life and manners, or as a collection of experiments from which general maxims of civil wisdom may be drawn, a writer lies under no very pressing temptation to misrepresent transactions of ancient date. But where history is regarded as a repository of titledeeds, on which the rights of governments and nations depend, the motive to falsification becomes almost irresistible. A Frenchman is not now impelled by any strong interest either to exaggerate or to underrate the power of the kings of the house of Valois. The privileges of the States General, of the States of Brittany, of the States of Burgundy, are now matters of as little practical importance as the constitution of the Jewish Sanhedrim, or of the Amphictyonic Council. The gulph of a great revolution completely separates the new from the old system. No such chasm divides the existence of the English nation into two distinct parts. Our laws and customs have never been lost in general and irreparable ruin. With us the precedents of the middle ages are still valid precedents, and are still cited, on the gravest occasions, by the most eminent statesmen. Thus, when King George the Third was attacked by the malady which made him incapable of performing his regal functions, and when the most distinguished lawyers and politicians differed widely as to the course which ought, in such circumstances, to be pursued, the Houses of Parliament would not proceed to discuss any plan of regency till all the examples which were to be found in our annals, from the earliest times, had been collected and arranged. Committees were appointed to examine the ancient records of the realm. The first precedent reported was that of the year 1217: much importance was attached to the precedents of 1326, of 1377, and of 1422: but the case which was justly considered as most in point was that of 1455. Thus in our country the dearest interests of parties have frequently been staked on the results of the researches of antiquaries. The inevitable consequence was, that our antiquaries conducted their researches in the spirit of partisans.

It is therefore not surprising that those who have written concerning the limits of prerogative and liberty in the old polity of England should generally have shown the temper, not of judges, but of angry and uncandid advocates. For they were discussing, not a speculative matter, but a matter which had a direct and practical connection with the most momentous and exciting disputes of their own day.

From the commencement of the long contest between the Parliament and the Stuarts down to the time when the pretensions of the Stuarts ceased to be formidable, few questions were practically more important than the question whether the administration of that family had or had not been in accordance with the ancient constitution of the kingdom. This question could be decided only by reference to the records of preceding reigns. Bracton and Fleta, the Mirror of Justice and the Rolls of Parliament, were ransacked to find pretexts for the excesses of the Star Chamber on one side, and of the High Court of Justice on the other. During a long course of years every Whig historian was anxious to prove that the old English government was all but republican, every Tory historian to prove that it was all but despotic.

With such feelings, both parties looked into the chronicles of the middle ages. Both readily found what they sought; and both obstinately refused to see anything but what they sought. The champions of the Stuarts could easily point out instances of oppression exercised on the subject. The defenders of the Round-heads could as easily produce instances of determined and success-ful resistance offered to the Crown. The Tories quoted, from ancient writings, expressions almost as servile as were heard from the pulpit of Mainwaring. The Whigs discovered expressions as bold and severe as any that resounded from the judgement seat of Bradshaw. One set of writers adduced numerous instances in which Kings had extorted money without the authority of Parliament. Another set cited cases in which the Parliament had assumed to itself the power of inflicting punishment on Kings. Those who saw only one half of the evidence would have concluded that the Plantagenets were as absolute as the Sultans of Turkey; those who saw only the other half would have concluded that the Plantagenets had as little real power as the Doges of Venice; and both conclusions would have been equally remote from the truth." (Macaulay, History of England I, pp. 27—29).

Very characteristically, the author singles out the Great Rebellion for a demonstration when discussing the traces of party spirit in English historical writings. This is all but inevitable. Being the most violent clash of conflicting interests in the past history of the country, this event stirred passions that have toned down too slowly not to affect deeply every rising generation. Hence the zeal and industry bestowed by Tory as well as Whig on even insignificant details of the period, which in a special case led Hume to the quaint expression that he felt thoroughly convinced by either party's arguments to the exclusion of the other's. Hence the singular position, side by side, of the chief figures in the conflict, Charles and Cromwell, as, perhaps, the most severely censured as well as the most idolized figures in English history; the one occupying a day in the Common Prayer Book as a saint, the other placed by Carlyle's England among Old Testament prophets.

Roughly speaking, we may assert that, in the 17th and 18th centuries, this bias appeared in favour of the reactionary principles, as may be measured in the above special case by the excessive praise of Charles and the marked aversion towards Cromwell. The 19th century, however, brought a change. The considerable enthusiasm for "the martyr" became less prominent when Carlyle began apostrophizing his hero in the abrupt and ecstatic language of a Delphian prophetess and Macaulay extolled Milton with the volubility of a merchant marketing inferior goods. Between the two extremes represented by the above names there was, in fact, room for no middle course. Hume dearly paid for his attempt at impartiality by reproof even from Hallam.

But when the scales in this manner had changed position by violent ups and downs, the time seemed ripe for a more even balance. The last-mentioned name marks a step in this direction, but more especially so that of Gardiner, the standard modern author on Stuart History.

The impartiality attained by him, however, is of a rather curious kind; hardly that of a fair-minded judge. For the relations of both parties are given and sentence is often pronounced from either party's point of view. Hence the incompatibility and confusion existing between the different parts of his History pointed out by Usher, which makes it principally retain the value of a copious, not too faithful collection of facts and documents from the period covered.

One of the characteristics of Gardiner's method was to leave aside evidence belonging to a later stage of the course of events, in order not to let fore-knowledge disturb his view of the actual moment described. In this respect, too, he seems dimly to realize a point energetically urged in modern treatment of the revolution, viz. the chronology of ideas, perhaps most aptly stated by Maitland in his Doomesday Book [1]).

Gardiner, it is true, failed to attain results which would have accrued from this principle if duly extended beyond the limits of Maitland's subject. He faithfully continued the tradition of the existence at the time of the revolution of a modern, politically trained English nation, of a similar parliament, etc., without perceiving the differentiated sense acquired by certain expressions and denominations since Clarendon, — with no inconsiderable detrimental consequences to his work. It was reserved for successors to arrive at important discoveries about the Stuart period by this method, which has, in fact, proved one of the best means of removing deeply rooted misconceptions. The admirable works of McIlwain, Usher, Jenks, etc., on constitution, jurisdiction, church, and other matters are constructed on these lines.

Beyond impartiality and strict observance of the chronology not only of facts but also of ideas, a third point has asked for attention. It is no longer possible to let this part of English history — any more than other history — turn on occasional incidents and persons, as if it was the result of a few score years and momentous for as long afterwards. Charles I., Cromwell, Laud, the Petition of Right, Tonnage and Poundage, do not exhaust the event, though they are mostly represented as doing so. Regarding another important period this point of view is successfully worked out by McKechnie [2]), but for the present one it has mostly been left out of consideration.

---

[1]) Cambridge 1897, p. 356.
[2]) Magna Carta, p. 3 ff.

The ideal Stuart History on these lines, however, remains unwritten or is at least scattered in numerous fragments. Whence the student attacking that period will, if intent on a comprehensive understanding, have to survey the field for himself on the principles laid down, suspending valuation and attending to the main features of the actual course of events and thoughts as displayed before the eyes of contemporaries and fermented in their brains; and to the corresponding segment of the forces that, non-incidental and irresistible, moved underneath, covered by a motley surface of men and actions.

*　　　*

*

If, as is the present aim, we wish as a preliminary to examine some ethical aspects in an individual living in 17th cent. England, we must, since these aspects seem to point beyond the limits of an individual, and to be conditioned also and to some extent brought to play by the then stage of developing English society — we must, I think, call to mind this stage of society and its provenience, more especially in immediately pertinent respects, as presented by modern research. We must recall the Great Charter, as a class document involving repetition of the constitutional situation after the disintegration of feudal society in consequence of the rise of money economy, the feudal wars, and the age of the inventions; the interdependence of feudalism and natural economy and of commutation and money economy; the impetus given to the latter by declining agriculture and villeinage and by increasing enclosures after the Black Death; the displacement of the world trade in favour of England — all of them conditioning factors of the new anti-thesis culminating in 1649, of the re-orientation of English society which thrust the remnants of feudalism on the hands of the king, their old enemy, where not (as was the case with most of the gentry) economically grown consolidate with the new elements.

We remember also the clerical side of the problem. From its feudal opposition to the king, complicated through the backing of Rome in accordance with the general European situation, the mediæval clergy in England weakened, as with the barons it grew more and more unfit to meet the demands of the changed aspects of society. These demands, on the contrary, were satisfied by religious currents from the Continent, of a new structure and an essence specially adapted to the creation-mastering spirit setting in (Weber, Protestantische Ethik, Archiv f. Sozialwissenschaft, 1905). With the main body of the substitute, Calvinism, the extreme Reformation radicalism, after its frustrated attempt to rise for air in Munster, flowed on by way of Holland to England [1]) now strained with fundamental divergencies in its social structure, and here

---

[1]) Troeltsch, Bedeutung d. Prot., p. 62; Gesch. d. Christl. Rel., p. 589. Cf. also van Schelven, Vlucht. kerken.

became at least co-responsible for the violent character of the contest, where the fate of the mediæval religion and its social embodiment merged in that of the barons and the king.

The violence of the precipitation of the established order, however, was not due to these extreme Reformation elements only.

Calvinism itself will account for a part in face of the consideration that it had, like the other movement, absorbed a ferment not originating in or strictly consubstantial with either of them [1]). Two situations in the Middle Ages, the frequent antithesis between the pope and the king and that between the king and his subjects, resulted in an identical answer to the question as to the provenience of the king's power when arrived at from the point of view of the pope or the people. By its nature acceptable to the latter, it also coincided with the interests of the pope — in order to get assistance from the people against an unmanageable king — to accentuate the "contract of sovereignty", the voluntary conferment by the people of the sovereignty belonging to it on one person, which contract in the light of the growing influence of Roman law partook of the nature of a legally enforceable obligation.

As long as not raising the contract of sovereignty above the legal obligation by constituting the conferment of power irrevocable, this theory of the Monarchomachists', with its consequences followed up even to the killing of the monarch, brought a solution of the mediæval state dualism quite opposite to that offered by the actual tendency towards monarchical absolutism whose abstraction and motivation the Divine Right. Here the difficulty was only about the embodiment of the sovereignty after the elimination of the king, a mainly spatial difficulty unknown to the model constitutions of Antiquity based on the πόλις, and of course insurmountable e. g. in Germany or France, but not so in England since the rise of the House of Commons.

For from the principally judicial origin of the parliament, its Lower House, by reaping the fruits of the quarrel between the King and the nobility as a forced, to-be-made-much-of ally of the former, developed practical taxing and legislative supremacy and a construction seemingly representative of the Monarchomachist's theoretically sovereign people though really of the rising social strata [2]).

※   ※

※

---

[1]) Cf. Calvin, Opera, XXIX, p. 306; XXXI, p. 746; XXXII, p. 160; XXXVIII, p. 588; XXXIX, p. 158; XL, p. 657; XLI, p. 415; XLII, p. 311; XLVIII, pp. 109, 398, 505; XLIX, p. 250; Troeltsch, Gesch. d. Christl. Rel. pp. 507, 09.

[2]) As to the facts here recalled and their importance for the changed aspects of England dwelt upon in the following pages, see Weber, Op. cit.; Maitland, Const. Hist.; Treumann, Die Monarchomachen; McIlwain, High Court of Parl.; Jellinek, Allg. Staatslehre; Usher, High Commission; Windelband, Gesch. d. n. Phil. (Kult. d. Gegenwart); Traill, Social England; Cunningham, Western Civilization; Mantoux, Révolution industrielle, etc.

The needs of the mediæval church and society tended in many respects to effect uniformity and belief in authority and tradition, and to create men that seem to us to have existed less as individuals, in a manner, than sorted into certain groups of different social position within which individual activity — political, economical, intellectual, religious — was determined rather closely. The single craftsman had his life and views of the world limited by the initiative-hating craft-guild; the peasant by his lord and fellow-peasants, whose joint farming excluded individual enterprise; the intellectual and religious aspects were narrowed by the church's compressing society at large in the bonds of a paralysing creed whose intended or unintentional result was the establishment of tradition, authority, uniformity, inactivity, so far as it administered salvation to followers by a common means, the sacraments, which practically required no other action from the recipient than opening the mouth for the eucharist or bowing the head for the anointment.

Society did not rest, however, but new experiences created new situations and to the pioneers in the virgin regions, practical or theoretical, they themselves and their world gradually changed colour and significance. An enemy to authority and tradition rose in the individualism of the dawning time with its determined hunger and yearning for activity and enterprise, fostered by as well as fostering the new conditions of life.

In the history of trade and industry now emerge the most distinct traces of originating capitalism, social degradation of the workman, and birth of the employer looking at society not as a collection of beings with uniform, corporatively regulated shares in work and profit, but as a field intended for exploration by the fittest, without regard to the consequences for fellow-explorers.

Politically the result was the theory of the people as the source of power, the social contract, and the Monarchomachist movement.

Whatever the importance of the Renaissance and the New Learning, whether they were really a return to the founts and models of Antiquity or only continued unconsciously the currents of the Middle Ages, the fact is that its leaders and masses apparently felt like innovators, that they intended the overthrow of tradition and authority, were part of the movements already mentioned, expressions of the yearning for activity and enterprise, causes and effects of individualism [1]). In the case of England a confirmation of this fact is, to seize upon one instance only, offered in a sermon preached by one of the original introducers of Italian humanistic atmosphere in this country, Colet [2]).

---

[1]) It is evident that I here follow Windelband, Weber, Troeltsch, Pio, etc., also in abstaining from definitions of such denominations and conceptions as may appear ambiguous or vague to the reader. Because, when the general trend of thought has become familiar, the denominations will convey the sense intended.

[2]) Cambr. Hist. Engl. Lit. III, pp. 8, 9.

Turning to the religious movements we are aware that in Luther the Reformation already betrays its origin by substituting for the Catholic church's salvation of the passive object through an external common means the salvation by the active struggle for belief of the individual placed singly and immediately before his God. Troeltsch analyses Luther's position thus: —

"Das Wunder der Religion besteht ihm nicht darin, dass wir uns den wunderbaren Gnadenergiessungen der Kirche unterstellen, sondern darin, dass wir den Gedanken an Gottes Gnade und heiligen Liebeswillen fest und unerschütterlich fassen können. Die Erlösung findet ihm nicht statt durch einen passiv erlittenen Zauber, sondern durch die Befestigung in jener immer von neuem intensivierten Erkenntnis." .... "Aber eine Religion, die nicht im Sakrament, sondern in der aus der Überlieferung zu schöpfenden Erkenntnis und im Gedanken besteht, bedarf keines Priesters. Hier ist jeder sein eigener Priester und steht jeder selbst vor seinem Gott ohne andere Vermittelung als die der geschichtlichen, die Erkenntnis an uns heranbringenden Kräfte. Geschichtliche Überlieferung und Heranbringung der Religion im Leben, eigenes Herausgreifen und Bejahen des religiösen Gedankens in persönlicher Tat und Gewissheit, das ist alles und weiter bedarf es nichts." .... "Mit diesem Ersten ist nun untrennbar das Zweite verbunden. Jede solche Erkenntnis ist nur möglich in eigener persönlicher Überzeugung, als eine völlig individuelle Gewissheit, die jeder nur auf seine Weise und auf seine eigene Rechnung hat. Es ist die Einsetzung des religiösen Individualismus in sein prinzipielles Recht. Wenn jeder Gedanke einen überzeugenden Sinn hat, nur wenn er ein eigener und selbständiger Gedanke ist, so gilt das auch von der Religion. Jedes Individuum steht nicht bloss unmittelbar in Geist und Gedanken seinem Gott gegenüber, sondern es steht auch auf eigene Weise und in eigenem Sinne Gott gegenüber." (Luther und die moderne Welt, pp. 79—81).

Accordingly, with Luther the range of the new elements seems limited mainly to the inner continuous struggle for obtaining or retaining grace, without extending into the external world any more than is required for an honest, contented Christian living. Calvinism is, in this respect, fundamentally different. As in the elect the grace proceeds irresistibly, the contrast with mediæval passivity here manifests itself in outward action. Or as Troeltsch expresses the matter: —

"Die Irresistibilität und Perseveranz der Gnade gibt ihm (dem calvinistischen Glauben) seinen Charakter; einmal aktualisiert steigt er notwendig von Stufe zu Stufe; er braucht nicht Rückfälle zu fürchten, keine Werkheiligkeit zu scheuen, nicht mit allerhand Unterbrechungen sich auf seine Bewahrung oder Wiedergewinnung vor allem zu konzentrieren. So hat der Glaube nicht, wie im Luthertum, lediglich in sich selbst seinen Zweck, sondern in der sittlichen Auswirkung und Betätigung. Nicht Seligkeitsgefühle, sondern Ak-

tivität sind sein Charakter. Für die populäre Denkweise tritt gerade-
zu in den Vordergrund, dass man in dieser Aktivität seiner Er-
wähltheit gewiss wird, und so steigert dann ein Gedanke den
anderen. Für die feinere begriffliche Betrachtung liegt im Gottes-
begriff selbst die Nötigung zu einer derartigen entscheidenden und
zentralen Betonung des tätigen Handelns. Der Gott, der in die
Gnadengemeinschaft aufnimmt, ist ein tätiger Wille und kann
auch in der begnadeten Menschheit nicht ruhen. Der Gott-Mensch
Jesus Christus, unter den als Haupt die Gemeinde gesammelt und
von dem sie regiert werden soll, ist eine tätige Kraft und ein
spornendes Vorbild, ein regierender Herrscher." (Geschichte der
christlichen Religion, p. 576).

Not only here, however, is Calvinism accentuated in a singular
manner against the position of Luther, but also as regards individualism. The consequence of the doctrine of predestination would
naturally be a very intense feeling of personal worth in the elect,
of elevation above his fellow-beings. "Unter diesen Umständen tritt
im Calvinismus die Persönlichkeit ganz anders hervor als im Luthertum. Nicht demütige Selbstaufgebung gegen Gott und liebevolle
Selbstaufgebung gegen den Nächsten, sondern stärkster persönlicher Wert, das Hochgefühl einer göttlichen Mission in der Welt,
einer gnadenvollen Bevorzugung vor Tausenden und einer unermess-
lichen Verantwortung erfüllen die Seele des Menschen, der völlig
einsam und in sich selbst die ihn erwählende Gnadenwirkung emp-
findet und auswirkt. Hierin liegt ein ungeheurer Individualismus,
eine ausserordentliche Selbständigkeit der Person, mit der die Re-
naissancestimmung und die grössere Differenziertheit der westlichen
Kultur sich leicht vereinigen konnte." (E. Troeltsch, Geschichte
der christlichen Religion, p. 577).

As hinted at already, the actual advantage of Calvinism in
these respects made it *the* religion for the new England because
it furnished the spiritual stamina for practical, economical, self-relying
purposes within the boundaries of earth. Max Weber has made
this salient by pointing at Dante's

> "Tal era io a quella vista nuova:
> Veder voleva, come si convenne
> L'imago al cerchio, e come vi s' indova;
> Ma non eran da ciò le proprie penne;
> Se non che la mia mente fu percossa
> Da un fulgore, in che sua voglia venne.
> All' alta fantasia qui mancò possa;
> Ma già volgeva il mio disiro e il *velle,*
> Si come ruota che igualmente è mossa,
> L'amor che muove il sole e l'altre stelle."

and comparing these concluding strains of the greatest mediæval poem
with their characteristic passive-contemplative ideals of life with
the finale of Paradise Lost,

"onely add
Deeds to thy knowledge answerable, add Faith,
Add Vertue, Patience, Temperance, add Love,
By name to come call'd Charitie, the soul
Of all the rest: then wilt thou *not be loath*
To leave this Paradise, but shalt possess
A Paradise within thee, happier farr."
. . . . . .

"They looking back, all th' Eastern side beheld
Of Paradise, so late thir happie seat,
Wav'd over by that flaming Brand, the Gate
With dreadful Faces throng'd and fierie Armes:
Som natural tears they drop'd, but wip'd them soon;
The World was all before them, where to chooʒe
Thir place of rest, and Providence thir guide:" —
the renunciation of the contemplative paradise for the wide world [1]).

As we saw, Calvinism's active, imperious mastering of
external things and beings proceeded from Calvin's peculiar conception of God as an imperious, unscrupulous will, "freier Macht-
wille," whose characteristic is "die unermessliche Selbstverherrlichung
durch die freie Offenbarung seiner durch kein Gesetz gebundenen
Freiheit." (E. Troeltsch, Gesch. d. christl. Rel., pp. 518, 519;
cf. also Weber in Archiv f. Soz.wiss. u. Soz.pol. XXI, p. 9 n.)
It was to be expected that this conception, evidently conditioned by individual qualities in Calvin, together with the exagge-
rated self-esteem at the cost of fellow-beings growing out of the idea
of predestination, would manifest itself in the ethics of Calvin and
similarly predisposed followers in their relations to the "sinners"
over which they were called to reign. Because predestination
"bedeutet die Berufung der Besten und Heiligen, der Minorität,
zur Herrschaft über die Sünder, die Majorität;" (Troeltsch, Gesch.
d. christl. Rel., p. 577).

And, in fact, such the case proved. When Calvin found it
necessary, he resorted to the use of (according to Christian ethics)
more expedient than strict means against his enemies, "Anwendung
aller Mittel politischer Klugheit und Intrige . . . die er um der
Ehre Gottes willen gegen so gottlose Hunde für erlaubt hielt"
(Troeltsch, Gesch. d. christl. Rel., p. 524), — with the result that,

---

[1]) Here evidently belongs the unexpected ending of Lycidas, the elegy on
the death of Edward King: —

"Thus sang the uncouth Swain to th'Okes and rills,
While the still morn went out with Sandals gray,
He touch'd the tender stops of various Quills,
With eager thought warbling his Dorick lay:
And now the Sun had stretch'd out all the hills,
And now was dropt into the Western bay;
At last he rose, and twitch'd his Mantle blew:
To morrow to fresh Woods, and Pastures new."

sometimes, it may prove difficult from without to distinguish his behaviour from that of an ordinary criminal [1]).

Directing for a moment our attention towards such a follower of Calvinism as Cromwell, we remember the eager controversy about his ethical principles. That they are in no way exhausted by the strictly Christian system seems certain. According to Burnet he had one standing principle, viz, "that moral laws were only binding on ordinary occasions, but that upon extraordinary ones they might be superseded; so that when his own designs, or anything extraordinary did not lead him out of the way, he was a great lover of justice and virtue, but upon the interposition of anything of this nature he fell into all the practices of the vilest falsehood and cruelty."

Leaving aside the censure, Burnet's words, whence ever supported, seem to cover the case. The testimonies of Ludlow, Lilburne, Hutchinson, and others cannot be rejected unconditionally. There apparently arose occasions when Cromwell could show his cards to no one and when his policy became identical with that of Calvin as stated by Troeltsch. We recall his anxious excuses after the massacre of Drogheda. "I am persuaded that this is a righteous judgment of God upon these barbarous wretches, who have imbrued their hands in so much innocent blood; and that it will tend to prevent the effusion of blood for the future. Which are the satisfactory grounds to such actions *which otherwise cannot but work remorse and regret.*" (Letters II, p. 51).

Altogether it seems impossible to deny that here is an ethical element hardly to be derived from the primary sense of the Gospel. The element in view stands out the better when Cromwell is approached to such a contemporary as e. g. Gustavus Adolphus. Probably no one will claim precedence for the latter as to religious feeling or elevation of purpose, but, allowance being made for temperament, position, etc., a difference in ethics will nevertheless become plain.

I should like here to compare Burnet's characterization of Cromwell with a passage in the most widely studied statesman's primer of the period. The 18th chapter of Macchiavelli's Prince tells in what manner princes ought to keep faith. "Quanto sia laudabile in un principe mantenere la fede e vivere con integrità, e non con astuzia, ciascuno lo intende. Nondimeno, si vede per esperienza ne' nostri tempi, quelli principi aver fatto gran cose, che della fede hanno tenuto poco conto, e che hanno saputo con astuzia aggirare i cervelli degli uomini, ed alla fine hanno superato

---

[1]) Cf. e. g. the case of Servet whom Calvin caused to be denounced to the otherwise abhorred Catholic Inquisition. When even this institution hesitated, Calvin furnished proofs of Servet's identity. Later on he nevertheless denied having done so. (See the documents offered by D'Artigny, Nouveaux Mémoires d'histoire, de critique et de littérature II, Paris 1749 ff.; Auguste Dide, Michel Servet et Calvin [2], Paris 1907; Pey-Ordeix, Miguel Servet, Madrid 1911).

quelli che si sono fondati in su la lealtà. Dovete adunque sapere come sono due generazioni di combattere; l'una con le leggi, l'altra con le forze: quel primo modo è degli uomini, quel secondo è delle bestie; ma perchè il primo spesse volte non basta, bisogna ricorrere al secondo," etc.

If the coupling together of Cromwell and Macchiavelli is somewhat unexpected, another, apparently cogent connection turns out even more surprising. In his Discorsi sopra la prima deca di Tito Livio, Macchiavelli relates how Numa invented the religion of Rome and to get it obeyed pretended that it was from God. He continues: — "Et veramente mai non fù alcuno Ordinatore di leggi straordinarie in uno popolo che non ricorresse a Dio, perchè altrimente non sarebbero accettate; perchè sono molti beni conosciuti da uno prudente, iquali non hanno in se ragioni evidenti, da potergli persuadere ad altri. Però gli huomini savi che vogliono torre questa difficultà, ricorrono à Dio. Cosi fece Licurgo, cosi Solone, cosi molti altri che hanno havuto il medesimo fine di loro." (Cap. XI, Della religione de'Romani).

Compare with this Milton's Reason of Church Government, Chapter I. "And therefore all the ancient lawgivers were either truly inspired, as Moses, or were such men as with authority enough might give it out to be so, as Minos, Lycurgus, Numa, because they wisely forethought that men would never quietly submit to such a discipline as had not more of God's hand in it than man's."

Even if Milton's Commonplace Book did not show his knowledge of Macchiavelli, this passage does. And also, that in at least one case Milton had made the famous ethics of the Italian his own, viz. that great men may be right in misleading the people.

Considering the importance of the Stoa in its Roman form for the making of the modern world; that Macchiavelli was the chief transmitter of this element as regards the Roman will of power and ethics of power [1]); and that the traditions of Macchiavelli were continued by the French Renaissance jurisprudence, the atmosphere of the sometime student of law from Noyon, it seems natural that even if a system which, though ultimately determined by quite other aims, nevertheless accorded with some aspects of the teachings of Macchiavelli in earthly matters, did not from the beginning consciously remedy certain weak points in its position by means of the Italian, later development should, at least occasionally, bring the currents together.

*　　　*　　　*

These preliminaries will prove useful to us as we pass on to pay more undivided attention to the poet whom we have already

---

[1]) For the importance of Stoicism at the formation of the modern world see Dilthey, Auffassung und Analyse des Menschen im 15 und 16 Jhdt. The reception of M. in England may be seen e. g. in Bacon's Advancement of Learning or Nashe's Works (see e. g. vol. I, p. 220).

mentioned in passing. An examination of Milton's Works must undoubtedly start from the point of view offered. An individualist, self-respecting even to the point of self-complacency, deeply contemptuous of disagreeable fellow-beings, active, an innovator, revolutionary, caste-hating, facing the future, he exhibits the features pointed out [1]).

It is the spontaneous outcome of the sense of unique personal importance that makes him, when taunted with deformity by adversaries, rise, address mankind, and with apparent satisfaction give an account of his own good looks. "Deformis quidem a nemine, quod sciam, qui modo me vidit, sum unquam habitus; formosus necne, minus laboro; statura fateor non sum procera: sed quæ mediocri tamen quam parvæ propior sit: sed quid si parva, qua et summi sæpe tum pace tum bello viri fuere, quanquam parva cur dicitur, quæ ad virtutem satis magna est. Sed neque exilis admodum, eo sane animo iisque viribus ut cum ætas vitæque ratio sic ferebat, nec ferrum tractare, nec stringere quotidiano usu exercitatus nescirem; eo accinctus, ut plerumque eram, cuivis vel multo robustiori exæquatum me putabam, securus quid mihi quis injuriæ vir viro inferre posset. Idem hodie animus, eædem vires, oculi non iidem; ita tamen extrinsecus illæsi, ita sine nube clari ac lucidi, ut eorum qui acutissimum cernunt: in hac solum parte, memet invito, simulator sum. In vultu, quo «nihil exsanguius» esse dixit, is manet etiamnum color exsangui et pallenti plane contrarius, ut quadragenario major vix sit cui non denis prope annis videar natu minor; neque corpore contracto neque cute." (Prose Works ed. Fletcher, p. 713).

On other occasions his intensely heightened self-confidence found expression even to the point of later on laying him open to the charge of exorbitant vanity. Before having achieved anything above the ordinary, he openly declared that he would do things worthy of the "choicest wits" of the world.

"I began thus far to assent both to them and divers of my friends here at home, and not less to an inward prompting which now grew daily upon me, that by labour and intense study, (which I take to be my portion in this life) joined with the strong propensity of nature, I might perhaps leave something so written to after times, as they should not willingly let it die. These thoughts at once possessed me, and these other; that if I were certain to write as men buy leases, for three lives and downward, there ought no regard be sooner had than to God's glory, by the honour and instruction of my country. For which cause, and not only for that I knew it would be hard to arrive at the second rank among the Latins, I applied myself to that resolution, which Ariosto followed against the persuasions of Bembo, to fix all the industry

---

[1]) Of course, this does not affect his position as advanced beyond Puritanism. Cf. Weber, Archiv XXI, p. 8 n., whose conception of Milton, however, has to be complemented.

and art I could unite to the adorning of my native tongue; not
to make verbal curiosities the end, (that were a toilsome vanity,)
but to be an interpreter and relater of the best and sagest things
among mine own citizens throughout this island in the mother dia-
lect. That what the greatest and choicest wits of Athens, Rome,
or modern Italy, and those Hebrews of old did for their country,
I, in my proportion, with this over and above, of being a Christian,
might do for mine; not caring to be once named abroad, though
perhaps I could attain to that, but content with these British Island
as my world; whose fortune hath hitherto been, that if the Athe-
nians, as some say, made their small deeds great and renowned
by their eloquent writers, England hath had her noble achievements
made small by the unskilful handling of monks and mechanics."
(Prose Works ed. St. John, vol. II, pp. 477—78).

If something like this might be instanced in others of the
period, hardly even Aretino in his most arrogant moods could
have felt so supremely majestical, so elevated above peoples and
kings of all times as Milton did when on the first page in his treatise
De Doctrina Christiana he addressed mankind in exactly the same
language as a sovereign his subjects. "Joannes Miltonus Anglus
Universis Christi Ecclesiis nec non Omnibus Fidem Christianam
ubicunque Gentium Profitentibus Pacem et Veritatis Agnitionem
Salutemque in Deo Patre, ac Domino Nostro Jesu Christo Sem-
piternam." If the prototype of this greeting is apostolically humble,
such a character is hardly traceable in the above passage.

In this intense feeling of majesty and elevation above the
human race at large Milton evinced sentiments and a mode of
reasoning towards fellow-creatures that seem as absolute and arbitrary as those which he censured so severely in Charles I. It would
hardly have been possible for the latter to punish one of his subjects because he, Charles, chose to regard him as guilty of a crime
proved to have been committed by another. But this sublimely
oriental autocratic character Milton played to perfection. When, in
answer to Milton's onslaught on Salmasius, there appeared an anonymous pamphlet (written by Peter Du Molin) against Milton and
the Commonwealth and the author could not be found out, Milton
determined to fasten the authorship upon a friend of Salmasius',
Alexander More, protestant preacher in Holland, who had probably helped to forward the publication of the book. In vain
More furnished Milton with testimonies of his innocence. Milton
declared, "De te, More, dictum hoc volo: quem ego (quamvis tu
nunc, quasi insons omnium atque insciens falso te accusari voci-
fereris) nefandi illius clamoris vel esse authorem, *vel esse pro
authore haud injuria habendum statuo*." (Prose Works ed. Fletcher,
p. 734).

After having declared his determination that More shall
be held the criminal, Milton no less imperturbably proceeded to
the punishment. And the voluminous defamation that followed

was as majestically indifferent to truth or untruth, fact or gossip. "Est Morus quidam, partim Scotus, partim Gallus; ne tota hominis infamia, gens una, aut regio nimium laboraret; homo improbus, et cum aliorum, tum, quod gravissimum est, amicorum, quos ex intimis inimicissimos sibi fecit testimoniis quamplurimis infidus, mendax, ingratus, maledicus, et virorum perpetuus obtrectator et foeminarum, quarum nec pudicitiæ plus unquam parcere, quam famæ consuevit." (P. W. ed. Fletcher, p. 710).

In this manner More was dissected, his private life followed up and laid bare, his amorous pursuit of some maid-servants described in detail, his religious views denounced. Finally, at a passage in More's supposed libel about "making exceptions to Milton's expiatory folly" (piacularem vesaniam excipere), an allusion to the Defence of the English People, Milton seems literally to choke with resentment at the disrespect shown him. "Tu excepisses, furcifer? cujus nefaria flagitia si ecclesia illa Middelburgensis, te pastore infamis et infelix, pro meritis excepisset, jamdudum te Satanæ mandasset; si pro meritis excepisset magistratus, jamdudum adulteria patibulo pendens luisses; Et luiturus propediem sane videris; evigilavit enim, ut audio nuper, tua illa ecclesia Middelburgensis, suæque famæ consuluit, teque caprimulgum pastorem, immo hircum potius olentissimum, ablegavit ab se in malam crucem; hinc et magistratus Amsterodamensis, pulpitum quoque interdixit tibi, orchestram tuam; tuumque illud os impudicum eo ex loco ad summam omnium bonorum offensionem conspici, illam impiam vocem vetuit in sacro publice audiri: restat jam tibi sola Græcarum literarum professio et hæc quoque brevi eripienda, præter unam illam literam, cujus non professor, sed discipulus mox pensilis merito futurus es." (Prose Works ed. Fletcher, pp. 726—27).

Not only More, however, was in this effective manner punished for the "crimen læsæ majestatis" committed against Milton. The unfortunate printer, Vlac, was also addressed, his whole life inquired into, vituperated, and defamed.

"Est Vlaccus unde gentium nescio, vagus quidam librariolus, veterator atque decoctor notissimus; is Londini aliquandiu bibliopola fuit clancularius; qua ex urbe, post innumeras fraudes, obæratus aufugit. Eundem Parisiis fide cassum et male agendo insignem, vita tota Jacobæa cognovit: unde olim quoque profugus ne multis quidem parasangis audet appropinquare; nunc si cui opus est balatrone perditissimo atque venali, prostat Hagæcomitis typographus recoctus." etc. (Prose Works ed. Fletcher, p. 711). When More and Vlac dared to protest publicly against Milton's allegations, they were once more crushed with abuse, once more Milton filled pages with gossip telling how More had convened with Claudia in a garden, how the gardener had seen them, what the neighbours told, how Vlac had run away for debt, his iniquities, etc. He now and then interrupts himself to ridicule and vituperate one Doctor

Krantz who had dared to testify in favour of More against Milton's accusations.

I hardly think a more typical example could be afforded of the fact that Milton's adversaries in taking up a position against him became *ipso facto* outlawed, deprived of their right to be treated as human beings. "Hominem an dicam hæreo, purgamentum potius hominis," he says of More. Altogether, the reader is reminded of the Oriental despot's conception of himself as God among animal subjects.

This arbitrary supremacy thus established by Milton over his fellow-beings apparently did not always admit of identical ethics for the ruler and the ruled. In fact, it is rather curious to observe how a moral commandment repeatedly inculcated as indispensable in others was sinned against by Milton in the very act of punishing the criminal.

As the chief aim of contemporary religious controversialists was to found their theories on Scripture, the hunt for Scriptural quotations became intense. The more conscientious authors naturally worked according to the rule that the quotations should be full, literal, and contextual; those, however, who wanted to be in the right rather than to advance the question often resorted to corrupting the sense in several ways. "Wresting the Scripture" was a device that Milton resented very much in his antagonists. One of his treatises, e. g., with the title "Brief Notes upon a late Sermon titled 'the Fear of God and the King' preached and since published by Matthew Griffith, D. D. wherein many notorious Wrestings of Scripture, and other Falsities, are observed," is hardly more than an exposure of Griffith as a wrester of Scripture and the language used by Milton against him seems rather severe. It is therefore somewhat surprising to find that Milton's own handling of Scripture seems to exceed anything he has disapproved of in the other. Instances of this are rather numerous and are sufficiently illustrated by Allison, who points out that when "the plain sense of the text or incident is against him (Milton), he does not hesitate to wrest the Scripture to his purpose as unscrupulously as any of his opponents. When he quotes Deut. 17.14, "I will have a king set over me", he interprets these words as referring solely to the people's right of choice, thus deliberately ignoring the words in the next verse, "Thou shalt in any wise set him king over thee, whom the Lord thy God shall choose". The Royalist argument from Psalm 51 ("Against thee onely have I sinn'd," from which the royalists concluded that the king was responsible to God only), though it seems absurd to the modern mind, was hard to meet with a direct answer, so Milton brushes it aside with the remark that, after all, these are only "the patheticall words of a Psalme". The New Testament texts are also treated with a high degree of ingenuity. He cannot get round the simple words of 1 Pet. 2. 13, 16, where Christians are enjoined to obey superior powers, so he adds the phrase 'as free men', a refinement used by Christopher Goodman in 1558. Paul's dictum in Rom. 13. 1, 'For there is no power but of God', is explained as referring not to tyrannical, but to just power only", etc. (Yale Studies in English XL, p. XXIX).

Though Cromwell, as is known, established a despotism even more rigorous than the one so eagerly denounced by Milton, the latter did not protest. On the contrary, when Cromwell had dissolved the parliament and remained sole sovereign, Milton censured the parliament and extolled Cromwell somewhat extravagantly. "Parlamentum aliud convocatur novum; concessa iis duntaxat, quibus par erat, eligendi potestate; conveniunt electi; nihil agunt; cum se invicem dissidiis et altercationibus diu defatigassent, animadvertentes plerique se rebus tantis exequendis, neque pares esse, neque idoneos, ipsi sese dissolvunt. Deserimur Cromuelle; tu solus superes, ad te rerum summa nostrarum rediit; in te solo constitit; insuperabili tuæ virtuti cedimus cuncti, nemine vel obloquente, nisi qui aut æquales inæqualis ipse honores sibi quærit, aut digniori concessos invidet, aut non intelligit nihil esse in societate hominum magis vel Deo gratum, vel rationi consentaneum, esse in civitate nihil æquius, nihil utilius, quam potiri rerum dignissimum. Eum te agnoscunt omnes, Cromuelle, ea tu civis maximus et gloriosissimus, dux publici consilii, fortissimorum exercituum imperator, pater patriæ gessisti: sic tu spontanea bonorum omnium et animitus missa voce salutaris: alios titulos te dignos tua facta non norunt, non ferunt, et superbos illos, vulgi licet opinione magnos, merito respuunt. Quid enim est titulus, nisi definitus quidam dignitatis modus? tuæ res gestæ cum admirationis, tum certe titulorum modum omnem excedunt; et velut pyramidum apices coelo se condunt, populari titulorum aura excelsiores. Sed quoniam summis etiam virtutibus, qui honos habetur, humano quodam fastigio finiri ac terminari, non dignum est, sed tamen expedit, assumpto quodam titulo patris patriæ simillimo, non evehi te quidem, sed tot gradibus ex sublimi descendere, et velut in ordinem cogi, publico commodo, et sensisti et sustinuisti; regium nomen majestate longe majore aspernatus." etc. (Prose Works ed. Fletcher, p. 729).

When Cromwell was dead, however, and the power returned into the hands of the parliament, Milton censured the former and praised the latter. "To the Parliament of the Commonwealth of England, with the Dominions Thereof! — Owing to your protection, Supreme Senate! this liberty of writing, which I have used these eighteen years on all occasions to assert the best rights and freedoms both of church and state, and so far approved, as to have been trusted with the representment and defence of your actions to all christendom against an adversary of no mean repute; to whom should I address what I still publish on the same argument, but to you, whose magnanimous councils first opened and unbound the age from a double bondage under prelatical and regal tyranny; above our own hopes heartening us to look up at last like men and

Christians from the slavish dejection, wherein from father to son we were bred up and taught; and thereby deserving of these nations, if they be not barbarously ingrateful, to be acknowledged, next under God, the authors and best patrons of religious and civil liberty, that ever these islands brought forth? The care and tuition of whose peace and safety, *after a short but scandalous night of interruption,*[1]) is now again, by a new dawning of God's miraculous providence among us, revolved upon your shoulders. . . . Neither do I doubt, seeing daily the acceptance which they find who in their petitions venture to bring advice also, and new models of a commonwealth, but that you will interpret it much more the duty of a Christian to offer what his conscience persuades him may be of moment to the freedom and better constituting of the church: since it is a deed of highest charity to help undeceive the people, and a work worthiest your authority, in all things else authors, assertors, *and now recoverers of our liberty,*[1]) to deliver us, the only people of all protestants left still undelivered, from the oppressions of a simonious decimating clergy, . . ." etc. (Prose Works ed. Fletcher, p. 423).

This and many other encomiums addressed by Milton to the Long Parliament from its commencement to the Restoration assume, however, a curious aspect when the reader is acquainted with the fact that, during these decades, Milton was writing his History of Britain and that here he tenders the Long Parliament testimonials of hypocrisy, greed, corruption, stupidity, etc, vying with the most zealous royalist in applying black colours.

"To other causes therefore, and not to the want of force, to warlike manhood in the Britons, both these, and these lately, we must impute the ill husbanding of those fair opportunities, which might seem to have put liberty so long desired, like a bridle, into their hands. Of which other causes equally belonging to ruler, priest, and people, above hath been related: which, as they brought those ancient natives to misery and ruin, by liberty, which, rightly used, might have made them happy; so brought they these of late, after many labours, much bloodshed, and vast expense, to ridiculous frustration: in whom the like defects, the like miscarriages notoriously appeared, with vices not less hateful or inexcusable.

For a parliament being called, to address many things, as it was thought, the people with great courage, and expectation to be eased of what discontented them, chose to their behoof in parliament, such as they thought best affected to the public good, and some indeed men of wisdom and integrity; the rest, (to be sure the greater part,) whom wealth or ample possessions, or bold and active ambition (rather than merit) had commended to the same place.

But when once the superficial zeal and popular fumes that

---

[1]) Ital. by me. S. B. L.

acted their New magistracy were cooled, and spent in them, strait every one betook himself (setting the commonwealth behind, his private ends before) to do as his own profit or ambition led him. Then was justice delayed, and soon after denied: spight and favour determined all: hence faction, thence treachery, both at home and in the field: every where wrong, and oppression: foul and horrid deeds committed daily, or maintained, in secret, or in open. Some who had been called from shops and warehouses, without other merit, to sit in supreme councils and committees, (as their breeding was,) fell to huckster the commonwealth. Others did thereafter as men could sooth and humour them best; so he who would give most, or, under covert of hypocritical zeal, insinuate basest, enjoyed unworthily the rewards of learning and fidelity; or escaped the punishment of his crimes and misdeeds. Their votes and ordinances, which men looked should have contained the repealing of bad laws, and the immediate constitution of better, resounded with nothing else, but new impositions, taxes, excises; yearly, monthly, weekly. Not to reckon the offices, gifts, and preferments bestowed and shared among themselves: they in the mean while, who were ever faithfullest to this cause, and freely aided them in person, or with their substance, when they durst not compel either, slighted and bereaved after of their just debts by greedy sequestrations, were tossed up and down after miserable attendance from one committee to another with petitions in their hands, yet either missed the obtaining of their suit, or though it were at length granted, (mere shame and reason ofttimes extorting from them at least a shew of justice,) yet by their sequestrators and subcommittees abroad, men for the most part of insatiable hands, and noted disloyalty, those orders were commonly disobeyed: which for certain durst not have been, without secret compliance, if not compact with some superiours able to bear them out. Thus were their friends confiscate in their enemies, while they forfeited their debtors to the state, as they called it, but indeed to the ravening seizure of innumerable thieves in office: yet were withal no less burdened in all extraordinary assessments and oppressions, than those whom they took to be disaffected: nor were we happier creditors to what we called the state, than to them who were sequestered as the state's enemies.

For that faith which ought to have been kept as sacred and inviolable as any thing holy, "the Public Faith", after infinite sums received, and all the wealth of the church not better employed, but swallowed up into a private Gulf, was not ere long ashamed to confess bankrupt. And now besides the sweetness of bribery, and other gain, with the love of rule, their own guiltiness and the dreaded name of Just Account, which the people had long called for, discovered plainly that there were of their own number, who secretly contrived and fomented those troubles and combustions in the land, which openly they sat to remedy; and would continually find such work, as should keep them from being ever brought to that Terrible Stand of laying down their authority for lack of new business, or not drawing it out to any length of time, though upon the ruin of a whole nation. (Here Milton passes on to heavy charges against the presbyterians, their teachers, and then proceeds).

And well did their disciples manifest themselves to be no better principled than their teachers, trusted with committeeships and other gainful offices, upon their commendations for zealous, (and as they sticked not to term them,) godly men; but executing their places like children of the devil, unfaithfully, unjustly, unmercifully, and where not corruptly, stupidly. So that between them the teachers, and these the disciples, there hath not been a more ignominious and mortal wound to faith, to piety, to the work of reformation, nor more cause of blaspheming given to the enemies of God and truth, since the first preaching of reformation." (Prose Works ed. Fletcher, pp. 502—3).

It may be regarded as certain that, if Milton had detected these apparently contrasting attitudes in another, he would have severely condemned him, as he actually did e. g. in the case of Salmasius. —

"I had said, that because the Remonstrant was so much offended with those who were tart against the prelates, sure he loved toothless satires, which I took were as improper as a toothed sleekstone. This champion from behind the arras cries out, that those toothless satires were of the Remonstrant's making; and arms himself here tooth and nail, and horn to boot, to supply the want of teeth, or rather of gums in the satires. And for an onset tells me, that the simile of a sleekstone "shews I can be as bold with a prelate as familiar with a laundress." *But does it not argue rather the lascivious promptness of his own fancy,* who, from the harmless mention of a sleekstone, could neigh out the remembrance of his old conversation among the viraginian trollops?" (P. W., p. 87)

To get a fair idea of how far Milton himself evinced "a lascivious promptness of fancy" some passages may be adduced from his writings.

In the controversy with More the latter once said that if the cause defended had been his own only he might have kept silent. "Si mea proprie tantum res ageretur, imponere fibulam ori meo et obmutescere poteram exemplo Domini mei:"

Remembering More's love-affairs, Milton rejoins: — "O scortum et ganearum antistes! cujus non ori magis, quam inguini fibulam impositam oportuit;" (P. W. ed. Fletcher, p. 747).

Here belong also Milton's jokes when he related some gossip about More's meetings with a maid-servant in a certain garden. "Hospitis ancillam quandam forte adamaverat; eam paulo post etiam alteri nuptam sectari non destitit; tuguriolum quoddam intrare hortuli, solum cum sola, vicini sæpe animadverterant. Citra adulterium, inquis; poterat enim quidvis aliud: sane quidem; poterat

confabulari, nimirum de re hortensi, prælectiones quasdam suas
sciolæ fortasse foeminæ et audiendi cupidæ expromere de hortis,
Alcinoï puta vel Adonidis; poterat nunc areolas laudare, umbram
tantummodo desiderare, liceret modo ficui morum inserere, com-
plures inde sycomoros quam citissime enasci, ambulationem amoenis-
simam; modum deinde insitionis mulieri poterat monstrare: hæc et
plura poterat, quis negat?" (P. W. ed. Fletcher, p. 710),

With such samples may be compared the passage about this
supposed occurrence as more explicitly stated later on, and Milton's
jocular rendering of the gardener's testimony.

"Est Claudia Pelletta quædam, pellicem posthac nominemus
licet, nescio an tuam solum; quæ cum ancilla in eadem domo ho-
nestissimi viri Genevensis esset, in qua tu hospes eras turpissimus,
cum calone et rhedario communis tibi fuit. Ea muliercula, post-
modum nupta, quod stupri tecum habuerat commercium adulterio
continuavit. Cedo "testes", inquis, et "argumenta". Nugator! quid
tu testes ex me ubi non sunt, quæris, quas ubi erant, fugisti?
Genevam revertere, ubi horum criminum jamdiu reus factus es.
Dic velle te modo abolendæ calumniæ causa judicium his de rebus
legitimum fieri; invenies qui tecum libentissime his de criminibus
experiri lege velint; qui vadari, qui sponsionem facere non recusent.
Nec testes deerunt. Aderit imprimis Hortulanus ille qui te vidit,
cum in illud tuguriolum cum fœmina solus intrares; vidit, cum illa
Claudia tua clauderet fores; vidit postea egressum te, amplexantem
palam cum muliere impudica, et usque eo petulantem, ut illum
veterem hortorum custodem obscoenum, non ex ficu, ut olim, sed
ex moro factum conspexisse existimaret." (P. W. ed. Fletcher,
p. 746).

It is evident that, compared with Milton's own imagination
as manifested above, the "lascivious fancy" he censured seems
rather chaste and innocent. The circumstance was even observed
by contemporaries, so that Milton felt the necessity of defending
his practice which he did by addressing his accuser as "propu-
dium et prostibulum hominis" and citing some instances, not of
cynicism but of naturalism, from classical authors and the Bible.

The person who felt justified in thus spurning the laws he
wanted others to obey must, as hinted, have entertained no
low opinion of himself and not only absolutely or as against
antagonists. Indeed, it is very interesting to trace his secret
thoughts as they seem to betray how more than once he consciously
compared himself with the most illustrious persons of the century,
and not to his own disadvantage.

The relative worth of human activity was thus conceived by
Milton: — that *he only is to be termed great who performs, teaches,*
or with dignity describes great achievements. "Is solus magnus
est appellandus, qui res magnas aut gerit, aut docet, aut digne
scribit: res autem magnæ sunt solæ, quæ vel vitam hanc nostram
efficiunt beatam, aut saltem cum honestate commodam atque jucun-

dam, vel ad alteram ducunt beatiorem." (P. W. ed. Fletcher,
p. 716).

As to the precedence among these, Milton, apostrophizing
the Swedish queen, states that wisdom is by far superior to force,
peaceful achievements to those of the war. "Dicerem Adolphi
filiam invicti atque inclyti regis unicam prolem, nisi tu illi, »Christina«,
tantum præluceres, quantum viribus sapientia, belli artibus pacis
studia præcellunt." (P. W. ed. Fletcher, p. 717).

This pronounced depreciation of Gustavus Adolphus in favour
of Christina hardly leaves any doubts in the reader as to Milton's
estimation of his own pursuits (identical with those of Christina)
as against e. g. Cromwell's, the equal of the Swedish king.

In this light we must apparently read the encomium Milton
bestows on himself and the part played by him in the revolution.

Neque enim militiæ labores et pericula sic defugi, ut non alia
ratione, et operam, multo utiliorem, nec minore cum periculo
meis civibus navarim, et animum dubiis in rebus neque demissum
unquam, neque ullius invidiæ, vel etiam mortis plus æquo metuentem
præstiterim. Nam cum ab adulescentulo humanioribus essem studiis,
ut qui maxime deditus, et ingenio semper quam corpore validior,
posthabita castrensi opera, qua me gregarius quilibet robustior
facile superasset, ad ea me contuli, quibus plus potui; ut parte
mei meliore ac potiore, si saperem, non deteriore, ad rationes
patriæ, causamque hanc præstantissimam, quantum maxime possem
momentum accederem. Sic itaque existimabam, si illos Deus res
gerere tam præclaras voluit, esse itidem alios a quibus gestas
dici pro dignitate atque ornari, et defensam armis veritatem, ratione
etiam, (quod unicum est præsidium vere ac proprie humanum),
defendi voluerit. Unde est, ut dum illos invictos acie viros admiror,
de mea interim provincia non querar; immo mihi gratuler, et
gratias insuper largitori munerum cœlesti iterum summas agam
obtigisse talem ut aliis invidenda multo magis, quam mihi ullo
modo poenitenda videatur. Et me quidem nemini vel infimo
libens confero; nec verbum de me ullum insolentius facio; ad causam
vero omnium nobilissimam, ac celeberrimam, et hoc simul defensores
ipsos defendendi munus ornatissimum, ipsorum mihi suffragiis
attributum atque judiciis, quoties animum refero, fateor me mihi
vix temperare, quin altius atque audentius quam pro exordii ratione
insurgam: et grandius quiddam, quod eloqui possim, quæram:
quandoquidem oratores illos antiquos et insignes, quantum ego ab
illis non dicendi solum, sed et loquendi facultate, (in extranea
præsertim, qua utor necessario, lingua, et persæpe mihi nequa-
quam satisfacio), haud dubie vincor, tantum omnes omnium ætatum,
materiæ nobilitate et argumento vincam. Quod et rei tantam
expectationem ac celebritatem adjecit, ut jam ipse me sentiam
non in foro aut rostris, uno duntaxat populo, vel Romano, vel
Atheniensi circumfusum; sed attenta, et confidente quasi tota pene
Europa, et judicium ferente, ad universos quacunque gravissimorum

hominum, urbium, gentium, consessus atque conventus, et priore defensione, dixisse, et hac rursus dicturum. Jam videor mihi, ingressus iter, transmarinos tractus et porrectas late regiones, sublimis perlustrare: vultus innumeros atque ignotos, animi sensus mecum conjunctissimos." etc. (P. W. ed. Fletcher, p. 708).

Truly there is less exaggeration than would seem at first sight in Milton's "feeling nearly superior to the Gods" at the praise of Christina. "Quod si mihi quidem hæc scribere adolescenti contigisset, et oratoribus idem quod poëtis liceret, haud dubitassem profecto sortem meam deorum sorti nonnullorum anteferre: quippe illos de forma duntaxat aut de musica deos, humano sub judice, contendisse; me hominem in certamine longe omnium præclarissimo, dea judice, superiorem discessisse." (P. W. ed. Fletcher, p. 726).

Altogether it would be difficult for any human being to emulate the self-respect, the quiet, condescending majesty towards mankind with which this poet later on told "things unattempted yet in Prose or Rhime" before a world-wide auditory where born and future generations alike were to him present, attentive, and reverent. —

Milton's Satan has been termed an imperious, Cæsarian temperament. "Satan gehört zu den cäsarischen Naturen, die alles oder nichts, und lieber das Regiment in der Hölle als die zweite Stelle im Himmel haben wollen." (Kræger, Byronsche Heldentypus, p. 5). This key apparently unlocks also the inmost recesses of Milton's character. Originally destined for the church, he seems to have given up this calling principally on account of the subordinate position entailed, as may be inferred from several spontaneous utterances in his writings. In his attack on Episcopacy he says:

"I endure to interrupt the pursuit of no less hopes than these, and leave a calm and pleasing solitariness, fed with cheerful and confident thoughts, to embark in a troubled sea of noises and hoarse disputes, put from beholding the bright countenance of truth in the quiet and still air of delightful studies, to come into the dim reflection of hollow antiquities sold by the seeming bulk, and there be fain to club quotations with men whose learning and belief lies in marginal stuffings, who, when they have, like good sumpters, laid ye down their horse-loads of citations and fathers at your door, with a rhapsody of who and who were bishops here or there, ye may take off their packsaddles, their day's work is done, and episcopacy, as they think, stoutly vindicated. Let any gentle apprehension that can distinguish learned pains from unlearned drudgery, imagine what pleasure or profoundness can be in this, or what honour to deal against such adversaries. But were it the meanest under-service, if God by his secretary conscience enjoin it, it were sad for me if I should draw back; for me especially, now when all men offer their aid to help, ease, and lighten the difficult labours of the church, to whose service, by the intention of my parents and friends, I was destined of a child, and in mine own resolutions: till coming to some maturity of years, and perceiving what tyranny had invaded the church, that he who would take orders must subscribe slave, and take an oath withal, which, unless he took with a conscience that would retch, he must either straight perjure, or split his faith, I thought it better to prefer a blameless silence before the sacred office of speaking, bought and begun with servitude and forswearing. Howsoever thus church-outed by the prelates, hence may appear the right I have to meddle in these matters, as before the necessity and constraint appeared." (P. W. ed. Fletcher, pp. 44—45).

In this passage it may be observed that Milton did not object to the "meanest under-service" of denouncing (in his opinion) ignorant and contemptible bishops, but that he *did* object to entering the church because of the "servitude" implied. What Milton here meant more definitely by servitude seems plain from another passage written in this controversy, maintaining that to oppose and expose the vileness of the bishops contracts severe consequences for the lover of truth, as Milton often styled himself. The passage seems strongly autobiographical: "they that seek to discover and oppose their false trade of deceiving, do it not without a sad and unwilling anger, not without many hazards; but without all private and personal spleen, and without any thought of earthly reward, whenas this very course they take *stops their hopes of ascending above a lowly and unenviable pitch in this life.*" (P. W. ed. Fletcher, p. 55).

Significantly enough, with Milton the considerations of a "lowly and unenviable pitch" in life rank first, his conscience second. And even so, the tenderness of the latter seems open to question. For at his departure from the university, when his conscience was said to have prevented his entering the Church because he was unable truthfully to subscribe to the established creed, it did not hinder him from doing this very thing in subscribing to the 39 articles, an act accompanying the obtaining of the M. A. degree.

Milton's ambition even takes the somewhat curious form that, when, occasionally, he counts the items that he thinks will forward his high aims, he includes the quality of being a Christian, a mode of reasoning to be explained from the general premises of Calvinism (see above). "That what the greatest and choicest wits of Athens, Rome, or modern Italy, and those Hebrews of old did for their country, I, in my proportion, with this over and above, of being a Christian, might do for mine;" (P. W. ed. Fletcher, p. 43).

Discoursing on virtue he does not mention it as something intrinsically good to be exercised for its own sake, but, in the first place, as productive of fitness for his high aims. "And long it was not after, when I was confirmed in this opinion, that he who would not be frustrate of his hope to write well hereafter in laudable things, ought himself to be a true poem; that is, a

composition and pattern of the best and honourablest things;"
(P. W. ed. Fletcher, p. 81).

This passion which burnt in his core to lord it over and look
down on a worshipping world at his feet, this passion which he
mostly took care to veil in seemly words when publicly professed,
was apparently his deepest source of emotion and therefore irresistibly broke forth in the creation of a congenial mind, Satan,
commonly felt as the consummation of Milton's creative power.
It is no mere chance that the first lines composed of Paradise
Lost were Satan's address to the sun, the unrivalled utterance of
thwarted yet invincible ambition.

> "O thou that with surpassing Glory crownd,
> Look'st from thy sole Dominion like the God
> Of this new World; at whose sight all the Starrs
> Hide thir diminisht heads; to thee I call,
> But with no friendly voice, and add thy name
> O Sun, to tell thee how I hate thy beams
> That bring to my remembrance from what state
> I fell, how glorious once above thy Spheare;
> Till Pride and worse Ambition threw me down
> Warring in Heav'n against Heav'ns matchless King:
> Ah wherefore! he deservd no such return
> From me, whom he created what I was
> In that bright eminence, and with his good
> Upbraided none; nor was his service hard.
> What could be less then to afford him praise,
> The easiest recompence, and pay him thanks,
> How due! yet all his good prov'd ill in me,
> And wrought but malice; lifted up so high
> I sdeind subjection, and thought one step higher
> Would set me highest, and in a moment quit
> The debt immense of endless gratitude,
> So burthensome, still paying, still to ow;
> Forgetful what from him I still receivd,
> And understood not that a grateful mind
> By owing owes not, but still pays, at once
> Indebted and dischargd; what burden then?
> O had his powerful Destiny ordaind
> Me some inferiour Angel, I had stood
> Then happie; no unbounded hope had rais'd
> Ambition. Yet why not? som other Power
> As great might have aspir'd, and me though mean
> Drawn to his part; but other Powers as great
> Fell not, but stand unshak'n, from within
> Or from without, to all temptations arm'd.
> Hadst thou the same free Will and Power to stand?
> Thou hadst: whom hast thou then or what to accuse,

But Heav'ns free Love dealt equally to all?
Be then his Love accurst, since love or hate,
To me alike, it deals eternal woe.
Nay curs'd be thou; since against his thy will
Chose freely what it now so justly rues.
Me miserable! which way shall I flie
Infinite wrauth and infinite despaire?
Which way I flie is Hell; my self am Hell;
And in the lowest deep a lower deep
Still threatning to devour me opens wide,
To which the Hell I suffer seems a Heav'n.
O then at last relent: is there no place
Left for Repentance, none for Pardon left?
None left but by submission; and that word
Disdain forbids me, and my dread of shame
Among the spirits beneath, whom I seduc'd
With other promises and other vaunts
Then to submit, boasting I could subdue
Th'Omnipotent, Ay me, they little know
How dearly I abide that boast so vaine,
Under what torments inwardly I groane:
While they adore me on the Throne of Hell,
With Diadem and Scepter high advancd
The lower still I fall, onely Supream
In miserie; such joy Ambition findes.
But say I could repent and could obtaine
By Act of Grace my former state; how soon
Would highth recal high thoughts, how soon unsay
What feign'd submission swore: ease would recant
Vows made in pain, as violent and void.
For never can true reconcilement grow
Where wounds of deadly hate have peirc'd so deep:
Which would but lead me to a worse relapse,
And heavier fall: so should I purchase deare
Short intermission bought with double smart.
This knows my punisher; therefore as farr
From granting hee, as I from begging peace:
All hope excluded thus, behold in stead
Of us out-cast, exil'd, his new delight,
Mankind created, and for him this World.
So farwel Hope, and with Hope farwel Fear
Farwel Remorse: all Good to me is lost;
Evil be thou my Good; by thee at least
Divided Empire with Heav'ns King I hold
By thee, and more then half perhaps will reigne;
As Man erelong, and this new World shall know."

(P. L. IV, 32—113; cf. with this passage Weber, Archiv
XXI, p. 11 ff., and notes).

The tone and language, the fierce and haughty scorn exhibited in Milton's self-assertions against his opponents, though very peculiar and *sui generis*, no doubt sound familiar to the reader acquainted with Milton's poetical works. Anyone will recall the passage in Paradise Lost where Ithuriel surprises Satan,

> "Squat like a Toad, close at the eare of *Eve;*
> Assaying by his Devilish art to reach
> The Organs of her Fancie," (IV, 800—02)

and the controversy following.

> "Him thus intent *Ithuriel* with his Spear
> Touch'd lightly; for no falshood can endure
> Touch of Celestial temper, but returns
> Of force to its own likeness: up he starts
> Discoverd and surpriz'd. As when a spark
> Lights on a heap of nitrous Powder, laid
> Fit for the Tun som Magazin to store
> Against a rumord Warr, the Smuttie graine
> With sudden blaze diffus'd, inflames the Aire:
> So started up in his own shape the Fiend.
> Back stept those two fair Angels half amaz'd
> So sudden to behold the grieslie King;
> Yet thus, unmovd with fear, accost him soon.
> Which of those rebell Spirits adjudg'd to Hell
> Com'st thou, escap'd thy prison, and transform'd,
> Why satst thou like an enemie in waite
> Here watching at the head of these that sleep?
> Know ye not then said *Satan*, filld with scorn
> Know ye not me? ye knew me once no mate
> For you, there sitting where ye durst not soare;
> Not to know mee argues your selves unknown,
> The lowest of your throng; or if ye know,
> Why ask ye, and superfluous begin
> Your message, like to end as much in vain?"
> (IV, 810—833).

Or Satan's snarl at Abdiel before the battle.

> "Ill for thee, but in wisht houre
> Of my revenge, first sought for thou returnst
> From flight, seditious Angel, to receave
> Thy merited reward, the first assay
> Of this right hand provok't, since first that tongue
> Inspir'd with contradiction durst oppose
> A third part of the Gods, in Synod met
> Thir Deities to assert, who while they feel
> Vigour Divine within them, can allow
> Omnipotence to none. But well thou comst

Before thy fellows, ambitious to win
From me som Plume, that thy success may show
Destruction to the rest: this pause between
(Unanswerd lest thou boast) to let thee know;
At first I thought that Libertie and Heav'n
To heav'nly Soules had bin all one; but now
I see that most through sloth had rather serve,
Ministring Spirits, trained up in Feast and Song;
Such hast thou arm'd, the Minstrelsie of Heav'n,
Servilitie with freedom to contend,
As both thir deeds compar'd this day shall prove."
(VI, 150—170).

The clue to this character is also repeatedly given with the compelling logic and persuasive force emanating from the work of art when the essence of the artist has sprung into verses, strains, marble, or colours.

"that fixt mind
And high disdain, from sence of injur'd merit,
That with the mightiest rais'd me to contend,
And to the fierce contention brought along
Innumerable force of Spirits arm'd
That durst dislike his reign, and me preferring,
His utmost power with adverse power oppos'd
In dubious Battel on the Plains of Heav'n,
And shook his throne. What though the field be lost?
All is not lost; the unconquerable Will,
And study of revenge, immortal hate,
And courage never to submit or yield:
And what is else not to be overcome?
That Glory never shall his wrath or might
Extort from me. To bow and sue for grace
With suppliant knee, and deifie his power
Who from the terrour of this Arm so late
Doubted his Empire, that were low indeed,
That were an ignominy and shame beneath
This downfall:" (I, 97—116).

"Hail horrours, hail
Infernal world, and thou profoundest Hell
Receive thy new Possessor; One who brings
A mind not to be chang'd by Place or Time.
The mind is its own place, and in it self
Can make a Heav'n of Hell, a Hell of Heav'n.
What matter where, if I be still the same,
And what I should be, all but less then hee
Whom Thunder hath made greater? Here at least
We shall be free; th'Almighty hath not built

Here for his envy, will not drive us hence:
Here we may reign secure, and in my choyce
To reign is worth ambition though in Hell:
Better to reign in Hell, then serve in Heav'n."
(I, 250—263).

When inquiring, in the light of the preceding, somewhat more closely into the nature of the subject treated in Paradise Lost, we are led to the following observations.

In the cosmogony underlying and pervading the Christian religion the first action of God was a "tour de force", the creation of the world, the first action of Satan one of intelligence, viz. seducing Eve. These notions of God and the devil as representatives, the one primarily of power, the other primarily of intelligence, seem to have played a part in Christianity at large, however timidly and dimly. This seems quite natural, because in accordance with that conception of overwhelming power which, as we know, even the Jews had been anxious to accentuate in their God [1]), the devil would have small chance of capturing souls if he were not more intelligent than God, an anthropomorphic conclusion which, though necessarily excluded from the theological systems, must — when anthropomorphism was otherwise admitted into every part of Christian belief — have been drawn or felt unconsciously from the common experience that the stronger of two combatants ought to be outwitted by his adversary if the latter wants to win his game at all. In mediæval literature the intelligence was sometimes personified by the devil and, as the chief way from God to mankind was the way of faith, so that from Satan was frequently the reason, which accordingly at times enjoyed no high repute among plain Christians [2]).

There are traces, too, tending to show that conjectures about the fate of the dead created a certain deference for the intellectual standard of hell as compared with that of heaven. Observe that even in primitive religion there exists a notion that defective understanding predestinates to heaven but intelligence to hell, and that a man of parts going to heaven would not be at ease there [3]).

---

[1]) Jülicher, Kult. d. Gegenwart I, 4, p. 67.
[2]) Cf. e. g. Harnack, Lehrbuch d. Dogmengesch.[4] III, p. 259 and n. 3.
[3]) Cf. Aucassin et Nicolette, VI: —
"En paradis qu'ai jë a faire? Je n'i quier entrer, mais que j'aie Nicolete, ma tresdouce amie que j'aim tant. C'en paradis ne vont fors tex gens, con je vous dirai. Il i vont ci viel prestre et cil viel clop et cil manke, qui tote jor et tote nuit cropent devant ces autex et en ces viés creutes, et cil a ces viés capes ereses et a ces viés tacelés vestures, qui sont nu et decauc et estrumelé, qui moeurent de faim et d'esçi et de froit et de mesaises. Icil vont en paradis, aveuc ciax n'ai jou que faire, mais en infer voil jou aler. Car en infer vont li bel clerc, et li bel cevalier qui sont mort as tornois et as rices gueres et li bien sergant et li franc home. Aveuc ciax voil jou aler. Et s'i vont les beles dames cortoises, que eles ont II amis ou III avoc leur barons, et s'i va li ors et li argens

It seems quite superfluous to refer to the fact that, during the Middle Ages, most men intellectually in advance of their time were reported and believed even by serious historians to derive their superiority from the devil and to join him after their death. We remember Pope Sylvester II., Roger Bacon, Albertus Magnus, Paracelsus, and the many stories circulated about them [1]).

This state of things seems, curiously enough, to be reflected in Paradise Lost, and not only in such a manner as to leave on the reader a general impression of God as less gifted and of Satan as a genius, but Milton even *states* the thing more clearly than was to be expected from a Christian. As readily as Satan concedes God's superior might, as implicit and self-evident seems his own intellectual superiority. Even such a concession as this is significant.

> "Be it so, since hee
> Who now is Sovran can dispose and bid
> What shall be right: fardest from him is best
> *Whom reason hath equald, force hath made supream*
> *Above his equals."* (P. L. I, 245—49).

But the thought underlying the following passages tells more.

> "If then his Providence
> Out of our evil seek to bring forth good,
> Our labour must be to pervert that end,
> And out of good still to find means of evil;
> Which oft times may succeed, so as perhaps
> Shall grieve him, if I fail not, *and disturb*
> *His inmost counsels from their destind aim."*
> (P. L. I, 162—68).

> "Henceforth his might we know, and know our own
> So as not either to provoke, or dread
> New warr, provok't; *our better part remains*
> *To work in close design,* by fraud or guile
> What force effected not: that he no less
> At length from us may find, who overcomes
> By force, hath overcome but half his foe."
> (P. L. I, 643—49).

It is evident that when Milton makes God send an angel to warn Adam and the latter nevertheless falls, God is placed in the position of wanting something he is prevented from getting on account of the cleverness of his adversary.

---

et li vairs et li gris, et si i vont harpeor et jogleor et li roi del siecle. Avoc ciax voil jou aler, mais que j'aie Nicolete, ma tresdouce amie, aveuc mi."

Of course, the character of Aucassin dominates here.

[1]) See e. g. Graf, Il diavolo, pp. 236—9, 260.

Thus much granted, we recall the fact that to the impatient, iconoclastic individualism of those centuries — exuberant, innovating, active, inventive — whether clothed in the guise of Renaissance, Monarchomachism, or Science, the settled state of things grounded on tradition and traditional rights and power would naturally appear identical with mental inferiority, their own battle as that of long oppressed genius against the ruling powers of stupidity, and that every other similar war whether realized as such or not would become a source of sympathetic, conscious or unconscious, emotion.

These circumstances, I feel thoroughly persuaded, lie at the bottom of something in Milton that has been till now mostly a cause of astonishment and has remained without much attempt at explanation, viz. that the real hero, even the only dramatic person, in Paradise Lost is Satan, the proud genius, conscious of immense superiority, gnashing his teeth at the shadow of a challenge, waging war against a Lord secure in unlimited power and possession, established in eternity.

> "But he who reigns
> Monarch in Heav'n, *till then as one secure*
> *Sat on his Throne, upheld by old repute,*
> *Consent or custome,* and his Regal State
> Put forth at full, but still his strength conceal'd,
> Which tempted our attempt, and wrought our fall."
> (P. L. I, 637—42).

This does not at all amount to anything like a suggestion that, consciously, Milton thought God inferior or wrong and Satan superior or right, but only that, with the choice of the subject, the position of God as the conservative, traditional, authoritative ruler and of Satan as the oppressed, admirable, though criminal genius was given, though not necessarily clearly realized by Milton, and that, however faithfully he may have meant to work along lines befitting a Christian, his irresistible sympathy with a personality, mind, cause, and fate all but identical with his own and those of his time elicited, in spite of his reason, the passion that centuries after his death emanates fresh from the mouth of Satan, gripping and impressing the reader with the hateful hands, high head, burning eyes, and scorching breath of the indomitable oppressed [1].

The case is enforced by most of Milton's writings. Opening the sequel to Paradise Lost, unanimously declared as arid and destitute of dramatic power as Paradise Lost is endowed with it, the reader perceives at once that the ambitious, aspiring Satan has vanished and with him the force of the poem. The devil of Paradise

---

[1] Cf. the case of Tasso and his Gerusalemme liberata.

Regained is very poorly conceived. What dramatic interest is left centres round Christ, but the shock is rather great at detecting that this Christ has a most unfamiliar look. To us the saviour of the poor and miserable in the world, the love incarnate of the Gospel, *Milton's* Christ, on the contrary, does not want to save mankind out of love. He simply wants to achieve a splendid career and the means to do so is the feat of saving a few valuable souls, but mankind at large, the "miscellaneous rabble", he despises.

> "what the people but a herd confus'd,
> A miscellaneous rabble, who extol
> Things vulgar, & well weigh'd, scarce worth the praise,
> They praise and they admire they know not what;
> And know not whom, but as one leads the other;
> And what delight to be by such extoll'd,
> To live upon thir tongues and be thir talk,
> Of whom to be disprais'd were no small praise?
> His lot who dares be singularly good.
> Th' intelligent among them and the wise
> Are few," (P. R. III, 49—59).

It is difficult to imagine the Christ who speaks thus as willing to die for publicans, shoemakers, and tailors. This Christ does not at all seem inclined to forget himself for the sake of others. With visible satisfaction he recalls the admiration his learning aroused in the Temple, but at the same time he professes higher ambition.

> "e're yet my age
> Had measur'd twice six years, at our great Feast
> I went into the Temple, there to hear
> The Teachers of our Law, and to propose
> What might improve my knowledge or their own;
> *And was admir'd by all, yet this not all*
> *To which my Spirit aspir'd,* victorious deeds
> Flam'd in my heart, heroic acts, one while
> To rescue *Israel* from the *Roman* yoke,
> Thence to subdue and quell o're all the earth
> Brute violence and proud Tyrannick pow'r,
> Till truth were freed, and equity restor'd:"
> (P. R. I, 209—20).

Even the devil perceives the real character of Milton's Christ. He tells him: —

> "all thy heart is set on high designs,
> High actions: but wherewith to be atchiev'd?
> Great acts require great means of enterprise,
> . . . . .

Which way or from what hope dost thou aspire
To greatness?
. . . . .
Therefore, if at great things thou wouldst arrive,
Get Riches first," (P. R. II, 410—27).

Christ's answer implies that his sole aim in the world is to
satisfy his ambition. He will be able to do so by means of "Virtue,
Valour, Wisdom," but the riches offered by the devil he rejects.

"To whom thus Jesus patiently reply'd;
Yet Wealth without these three is impotent,
To gain dominion or to keep it gain'd.
Witness those antient Empires of the Earth,
In highth of all thir flowing wealth disolv'd:
But men endu'd with these have oft attain'd
In lowest poverty to highest deeds;
. . . . . .
For I esteem those names of men so poor
Who could do mighty things, and could contemn
Riches though offer'd from the hand of Kings.
And what in me seems wanting, but that I
May also in this poverty as soon
Accomplish what they did, perhaps and more?
Extol not Riches then, the toyl of Fools,
The wise mans cumbrance if not snare, more apt
To slacken Virtue, and abate her edge,
Then prompt her to do aught may merit praise."
(P. R. II, 432—56).

Looking back we may perhaps consider it made good that,
in the manner indicated, the force of Milton's inspiration was
supplied by the passions dominating his soul[1]) and his surroundings. And so it becomes quite intelligible that Satan's revolt,
the battle of hate for mastery, would conform admirably to his
purpose whereas the violence he must do to the Gospel to make
hateful, exclusive, and intellectual ambition — Christ is even made
an intellectualist — out of submissive, universal, levelling love lost
him his Paradise Regained.

Two points are here brought home to the reader. First
that Milton's writings unconditionally presuppose the anthropology
of which Petrarch is commonly held to be the first typical representative. To "descend into himself" (P. R. II, 111), to study the contents
of the soul in himself and in others was Milton's practice from his
youth, a practice which developed in him to a pronounced science

---

[1]) Cf. Thompson who says: "He (Milton) is always at his best when his
thoughts turn to self", without following up the thought.

and art of life. Cf. e. g. his Reason of Church-Government, where, actually inspired by Petrarch's heir in the above respect, Macchiavelli, he says that law-making demands an intimate study of man's internal life: — "if it be at all the work of man, it must be of such a one *as is a true knower of himself,* and in whom contemplation and practice, wit, prudence, fortitude, and eloquence, must be rarely met, both to comprehend the hidden causes of things, and *span in his thoughts all the various effects, that passion or complexion can work in man's nature."* (P. W. ed. Fletcher, p. 30). The importance of this fact for the soul-dissecting character of his prose and poetry is evident.

Second, that the Christ of Paradise Regained, fully as Cæsarian as his predecessor, Satan, reveals Milton as less of a Christian than a disciple of Roman Stoicism whose revival proved very momentous to developing individualism in those centuries. When Christ first says,

> "canst thou not remember
> *Quintius, Fabricius, Curius, Regulus?*
> For I esteem those names of men so poor
> Who could do mighty things, and could contemn
> Riches though offer'd from the hand of Kings."
>
> (P. R. II, 445—49)

and then, later on, condemns the Stoics,

> "The Stoic last in Philosophic pride,
> By him call'd vertue; and his vertuous man,
> Wise, perfect in himself, and all possessing
> Equal to God, oft shames not to prefer,
> As fearing God nor man, contemning all
> Wealth, pleasure, pain or torment, death and life,
> Which when he lists, he leaves, or boasts he can,
> For all his tedious talk is but vain boast,
> Or subtle shifts conviction to evade." (P. R. IV, 300—08)

the whole trend of the discourse shows that his censure originates rather from Christian afterthought than spontaneously.

Taking stand on this point in Milton's character, the Cæsarian trait and the inward, self-ward directed search for exclusive human worth — taking stand here when examining Milton's relations not only to his contemporaries and his poetry but also to the general currents of thought of his time, we are able to solve several much discussed incongruities between his theories and doings, or between the former themselves. Thus we are able to understand him when he in one place starts with a theory as wide and comprehensive as to include anyone, but then step by step qualifies it in other places so as, if worked out quite consistently, to exclude most men but himself. In his Tenure of Kings, his Defensio pro populo anglicano, etc, Milton looks quite unmistakeably a democrat. This is the case e. g. with the passage in the former treatise about the origin of the state, doubly interesting as a mirror of other favorite theories of the age, the social contract, Monarchomachism, the origin of parliaments, etc: —

"No man who knows ought, can be so stupid to deny that all men naturally were borne free, being the image and resemblance of God himselfe, and were by privilege above all the creatures, borne to *command*[1]) and not to obey: and that they livd so, till from the root of Adams transgression, falling among themselves to doe wrong and violence, and foreseeing that such courses must needs tend to the destruction of them all, they agreed by common league to bind each other from mutual injury, and joyntly to defend themselves against any that gave disturbance or opposition to such agreement. Hence came Citties, Townes and Common-wealths. And because no faith in all was found sufficiently binding, they saw it needfull to ordaine some authoritie, that might restraine by force and punishment what was violated against peace and common right. This authoritie and power of self-defence and preservation being originally and naturally in every one of them, and unitedly in them all, for ease, for order, and least each man should be his owne partial judge, they communicated and deriv'd either to one, whom for the eminence of his wisdom and integritie they chose above the rest, or to more then one whom they thought of equal deserving: the first was calld a King; the other Magistrates. Not to be thir Lords and Maisters (though afterward those names in som places were giv'n voluntarily to such as had bin authors of inestimable good to the people) but, to be thir Deputies and Commissioners, to execute, by vertue of thir intrusted power, that justice which else every man by the bond of nature and of Cov'nant must have executed for himselfe, and for one another. And to him that shall consider well why among free persons, one man by civill right should beare authority and jurisdiction over another, no other end or reason can be imaginable. These for a while governd well, and with much equitie decided all things at thir owne arbitrement: till the temptation of such a power left absolute in thir hands, perverted them at length to injustice and partialitie. Then did they, who now by tryall had found the danger and inconveniences of committing arbitrary power to any, invent Lawes either fram'd, or consented to by all, that should confine and limit the autority of whom they chose to govern them: that so man of whose failing they had proof, might no more rule over them, but law and reason abstracted as much as might be from personal errors and frailties. When this would not serve but that the Law was either not executed, or misapply'd they were constraind from that time, the onely remedy left them, to put conditions and take

---

[1]) Ital. by me, as is the case in all quotations from Milton illustrating the subject treated (except proper names). S. B. L.

Oaths from all Kings and Magistrates at thir first instalment to doe impartial justice by Law: who upon those termes and no other, receav'd Allegeance from the people, that is to say bond or Covnant to obey them in execution of those Lawes which they the people had themselves made, or assented to. And this oft times with express warning, that if the King or Magistrate prov'd unfaithfull to his trust, the people would be disingag'd. They added also Counselors and Parlaments, not to be onely at his beck, but with him or without him, at set times, or all times, when any danger threatn'd to have care of the public safety. . . . . .

It being thus manifest that the power of Kings and Magistrates is nothing else, but what is onely derivative, transferrd and committed to them in trust from the people, to the Common good of them all, in whom the power yet remaines fundamentally, and cannot be tak'n from them, without a violation of thir natural birthright, and seeing that from hence Aristotle and the best of Political writers have defin'd a king, him who governs to the good and profit of his people, and not for his owne ends," etc. (Tenure ed. Allison, pp. 9—12).

For an autocrat Milton here looks very fair-minded towards the people. It is difficult, however, to perceive an intimate relation between this passage and his constant, contemptuous references to the "rabble", whence we feel inclined to regard it rather as a theory to fit the occasion, made up as it is out of common authors of the period (Allison, pp. 79—86) and not obviously assimilated to, much less born in, Milton's own thoughts and feelings. We rather accept as a piece of his mind his rejoinder on the accusation of the Revolution's being the work of the few and unsupported by the people, that, "very often, by far the greater part of the people consists of reprobates and rascals to be coerced by the few worthy citizens." "tu vero *perfugarum ac perditorum* voces populo attribuis; et quod agyrta peregrinus ad coronam solet, *vilissimorum duntaxat animalium* voces imitaris. Quis autem negat ea posse tempora sæpius accidere, in quibus *civium longe major numerus improborum* sit; qui Catilinam vel Antonium, quam saniorem senatus partem sequi malint; neque idcirco boni cives obniti contra, et fortiter facere non debebunt, sui magis officii, quam paucitatis rationem ducentes." (P. W. ed. Fletcher, p. 724).

It is evident that the exemplification of this part of the subject might be very much extended. We recall Milton's treatises on divorce, toleration, education, liberty of the press, and other general questions where his position, usually censured as shifty or explained at the cost of facts, becomes intelligible in this light. Completeness not being aimed at here, however, the matter offered ought to be sufficient for the present purpose.

I.

MILTON AND GALILEO

CHAPTER I.

Introductory.

Insufficient knowledge of Milton's Italy evinced by his biographers. La Tina. Il Malmantile racquistato and Milton's friends. Francini, Dati, Malatesti.

Beyond being a study of some points in Milton's ethical position the following pages have another aim, viz. to call attention to the circumstances of the Continental Journey. This event is rather worse off as to careful information. The best qualified historian, Alfred de Reumont, has paid but slight attention to the subject. Masson's knowledge of the Italian language seems unsatisfactory and he (as well as Stern) generally furnishes such common matter only as is to be found in encyclopedias and handbooks of literary history. The result is that, beyond many rather serious errors, they betray want of intimate acquaintance with the scenes and aspects of life that met the English traveller of the 17th century in France or Italy.

E. g. there are the sonnets inscribed to Milton by Malatesti with the title, *"La Tina:* Equivoci Rusticali di Antonio Malatesti, cōposti nella sua Villa di Taiano il Settembre dell anno 1637: Sonetti Cinquanta"*. This elicits from Masson the explanation that *La Tina* was evidently the pet name of some real or imaginary rustic mistress. Now, *Tina,* the abbreviation of *Caterina,* signified in the neighbourhood of Florence simply *lass* or *country woman.* An illustration is offered by *Lippi's Malmantile racquistato.*

> "Stanco già di vangar tutta mattina
> Il contadino alfin la va a risolvere,
> In fermar l'opre, ed in chiamar *la Tina*
> Col mezzo quarto, e il pentol dell'asciolvere;"
> (Dodicesimo cantare, stanza prima;
> cf. also the note to these lines.)

I think it has not as yet been observed that this poem has a very great interest for the Miltonist just because furnishing an intimate picture of Milton's Italy. Written by a Florentine not many years after Milton's visit it contains abundant information about every-day circumstances nowhere else recorded. It is a heroi-comic epos describing how citizens of every kind went out to conquer an old castle, Il Malmantile, near Florence. Anagrammatic names conceal many of Milton's friends, as Carlo Dati (Alticardo), Malatesti (Amostante Laton), Francini (Franconio Inganna-vini), etc.

Real help towards elucidating what sort of men Milton saw and associated with at Florence is offered here, an important fact, as it is known that they were such people as Milton liked best to mingle with, according to his own confession.[1]) Here we meet with Francini, the man who wrote that enthusiastic ode in Milton's honour:

> "Ergimi all' Etra ò Clio
> Perche di stelle intreccierò corona
> Non più del Biondo Dio
> La Fronde eterna in Pindo, e in Elicona,
> Diensi a merto maggior, maggiori i fregi,
> A'celeste virtù celesti pregi.
>
> Non puo del tempo edace
> Rimaner preda, eterno alto valore
> Non puo l'oblio rapace
> Furar dalle memorie eccelso onore,
> Su l'arco di mia cetra un dardo forte
> Virtù m'adatti, e ferirò la morte.
>
> Del Ocean profondo
> Cinta dagli ampi gorghi Anglia risiede
> Separata dal mondo,
> Però che il suo valor l'umano eccede:
> Questa feconda sà produrre Eroi,
> Ch'hanno a ragion del sovruman tra noi.
>
> Alla virtù sbandita
> Danno ne i petti lor fido ricetto,
> Quella gli è sol gradita,
> Perche in lei san trovar gioia, e diletto;
> Ridillo tu Giovanni e mostra in tanto
> Con tua vera virtù, vero il mio Canto.
>
> Lungi dal Patrio lido
> Spinse Zeusi l'industre ardente brama,
> Ch'udio d'Helena il grido
> Con aurea tromba rimbombar la fama,
> E per poterla effigiare al paro
> Dalle più belle Idee trasse il più raro.

---

[1]) It may be pointed out that a scrap of information about Milton in Italy might accrue from recent research about Manso. Bozzelli's *Giovan Battista Manso*, severely criticized in *Giornale Storico*, 1917, pp. 151—156, seems nevertheless to contain several undeniable facts, e. g. that Manso seems to have given out as one of his forefathers a renowned nobleman, whereas he was a silk merchant, and to have played several tricks to get fame as a Mæcenas, etc.

Cosi l'Ape Ingegnosa
Trae con industria il suo liquor pregiato
Dal giglio e dalla rosa,
E quanti vaghi fiori ornano il prato;
Formano un dolce suon diverse Chorde,
Fan varie voci melodia concorde.

Di bella gloria amante
Milton dal Ciel natio per varie parti
Le peregrine piante
Volgesti a ricercar scienze, ed arti;
Del Gallo regnator vedesti i Regni,
E dell'Italia ancor gl'Eroi più degni.

Fabro quasi divino
Sol virtù rintracciando il tuo pensiero
Vide in ogni confino
Chi di nobil valor calca il sentiero;
L'ottimo dal miglior dopo scegliea
Per fabbricar d'ogni virtù l'Idea.

Quanti nacquero in Flora
O in lei del parlar Tosco appreser l'arte,
La cui memoria onora
Il mondo fatta eterna in dotte carte,
Volesti ricercar per tuo tesoro,
E parlasti con lor nell'opre loro.

Nell'altera Babelle
Per te il parlar confuse Giove in vano,
Che per varie favelle
Di se stessa trofeo cadde su'l piano:
Ch 'Ode oltr' all Anglia il suo piu degno Idioma
Spagna, Francia, Toscana, e Grecia e Roma.

I più profondi arcani
Ch'occulta la natura e in cielo e in terra
Ch'a Ingegni sovrumani
Troppo avara tal'hor gli chiude, e serra,
Chiaramente conosci, e giungi al fine
Della moral virtude al gran confine.

Non batta il Tempo l'ale,
Fermisi immoto, e in un ferminsi gl'anni,
Che di virtù immortale
Scorron di troppo ingiuriosi a i danni;
Che s'opre degne di Poema o storia
Furon gia, l'hai presenti alla memoria.

Dammi tua dolce Cetra
Se vuoi ch'io dica del tuo dolce canto,
Ch'inalzandoti all'Etra
Di farti huomo celeste ottiène il vanto,
Il Tamigi il dirà che gl'è concesso
Per te suo cigno pareggiar Permesso.

Io che in riva del Arno
Tento spiegar tuo merto alto, e preclaro
So che fatico indarno,
E ad ammirar, non a lodarlo imparo;
Freno dunque la lingua, e ascolto il core
Che ti prende a lodar con lo stupore."
(Ed. pr.)

This Francini tried to learn the art of painting from the
author of the Malmantile, the poet-painter Lorenzo Lippi, who
entertained a very poor opinion of the endowments of his disciple. As
might be guessed from that ode, he found him a rather shallow fellow
who talked nonsense very confidently on every occasion offered. In the
poem he is depicted in such a situation. He is one of the chaplains of
the army directed against the Malmantile, is summoned to make a
speech to comfort the people, and proffers one out of which neither
head nor tail can be made, so that his audience cries "Mercy."

27.

'L'Armata avea tra gli altri un Cappellano
Dottor, ma il suo saper fu buccia buccia;
Perocch'egli studiò col fiasco in mano:
Ed era più buffon d'una bertuccia.
Faceva da Pittor, da Tiziano;
Ma quant'ei fece mai, n'andava a gruccia.
Ebbe una Chiesa, e quivi a bisca aperta
Si giuocò fino i soldi dell'offerta.

28.

Franconio si domanda Ingannavini:
E fu pregato, come il più valente,
Perch'egli sapea leggere i Latini,
A far quattro parole a quella gente.
Egli, che aveva in casa il Coltellini
Già fatta una lezione, e salla a mente,
Subito accetta, e siede in alto solio
Senza mettervi su nè sal nè olio.

29.

Sale in Bigoncia con due torce a vento,
Acciò lo vegga ognun pro tribunali:
Ove, mostrar volendo il suo talento,

Fece un discorso, e disse cose tali,
Che ben si scorse in lui quel fondamento,
Che diede alla sua casa Giorgio Scali:
E piacque sì che tutti di concordia
Si messero a gridar misericordia.

30.

Il tema fu di questa sua lezione,
Quand' Enea, già fuori del suo pollajo,
Faceva andare in fregola Didone,
Come una gatta bigia di Gennajo:
E che se i Greci, ascosi in quel ronzone,
In Troja fuoco diedero al pagliajo:
E in man d'Enea posero il lembuccio,
Ond' ei fuggì col padre a cavalluccio;

31.

Cosi, dicea, la vostra e mia Regina
Qui viva e sana, e della buona voglia,
Cacciata fu dall'empia concubina
Tre dita anch'ella fuor di questa soglia;
Però, se un tanto ardire e tal rapina
Parvi, che adesso gastigar si voglia,
V'avete il modo, senza ch'io lo dica.
Io ho finito: Il Ciel vi benedica.

32.

Poichè da esso inanimite furo
Le schiere, si portarono a'lor posti:"...
(Terzo cantare).

Carlo Dati is mentioned many times and represented as a somewhat innocent young man. He is one of the leaders of a troop characterised by drinking a very weak wine and thence expectorating copiously.

"Nanni Russa del Braccio, ed Alticardo
Conduce quei di Brozzi e di Quaracchi,
Che, perchè bevon quel lor vin gagliardo,
Le strade allagan tutte co'sornacchi.
Hanno a comune un lor vecchio stendardo,
Da farne a'corvi tanti spauracchi:
E dentro per impresa v'hanno posto
Gli Spiragli del dì di Ferragosto."
(I, 47).

Later on his deeds in the battle are described.

"Dalle diacciate bombole e guastade
Il vino sprigionato bianco e rosso
Fugge per l'asse, e da un fesso cade
Giù, dove è Piancianteo, e dagli addosso.
Ei, che nel capo ha sempre stocchi e spade,
A quel fresco di subito riscosso,
Pensando sia qualche spada o coltello,
Si lancia fuora, e via sarpa, fratello.

Ma il fuggir questa volta non gli vale,
Perch'Alticardo, ch'al passo l'attende,
Il gozzo gli trafora col pugnale,
E te lo manda a far le sue faccende:
Così dal gozzo venne ogni suo male;
Per lui fallì, per lui la vita spende:
E vanne al diavol, che di nuovo piantalo
A ustolare a mensa appiè di Tantalo.

Era suo camerata un tal Guglielmo,
Ch'ha la labarda, e i suoi calzoni a strisce:
Un bigonciuolo ha in capo in vece d'elmo,
E tutto il resto armato a stocchefisce.
Alemanno è costui berneiter scelmo,
E con quel dir, che brava ed atterrisce,
Sbruffi fetenti scaricando e rutti,
In un tempo spaventa e ammorba tutti.

Costui, che a quel ghiottone a tutte l'ore
Fu buon compagno a ber la malvagia;
Per non cadere adesso in qualche errore,
E fare un torto alla cavalleria,
Pur anco gli vuol far, mentre ch'ei muore,
Con farsi dar due crocchie, compagnia:
E non durò molta fatica in questo,
Ch'ei trovò chi spedillo bene e presto.

Perchè voltando il ferro della cappa
Verso Alticardo a vendicar l'amico,
Quei gliele scansa, e gli entra sotto, e il chiappa
Colla spada nel mezzo del bellico;
Ond'il vin pretto in maggior coppia scappa,
Che non mesce in tre dì l'Inferno e il Fico;
Ma non va mal, perch'ei caduto allotta,
Mentre boccheggia, tutto lo rimbotta."
(XI, 33—37.)

The witty and vivacious Malatesti, who ridiculed Milton's
severe chastity by dedicating those highly immoral sonnets to him,

is true to his temperament in the poem. As a commanding general he tolerates no laziness.

"È general di tutta questa mandra
Amostante Laton, poeta insigne:
Canta improvviso, come una calandra:
Stampa gli enigmi, strologa e dipigne.
Lasciò gran tempo fa le polpe in Fiandra
Mentre si dava il sacco a certe vigne.
Fortuna, che l'avea matto provato,
Volle, ch'ei diventasse anche spolpato.

Passati tutti con baule e spada,
Serransi in barca, come le sardelle.
Gli affretta il Duca; e chi lo tiene a bada,
O ferma un passo, guai alla sua pelle;
Ch'ei lo bistratta, e comecchè ne vada
Giù la vinaccia, e il sangue a catinelle:
E benchè lesto ciaschedun rimiri,
Non gli dà tanto tempo ch'ei respiri."
(I, 61—62).

In another place he is taxed with cultivating astrology.

". . . già sdrajato ognun, lasso e maturo
In grembo al sonno gli occhi aveva posti;
Quando a un tratto le trombe ed il tamburo
Roppe i riposi e i sonni appena imposti;
Ma svanì presto così gran fracasso,
Che il fiato ai trombettier scappò da basso.

E questo cagionò, che incollerito
Il Generale di cotanta fretta,
Con occhi torvi minacciò col dito,
Mostrando voler farne aspra vendetta:
Seguì, che un Uffizial suo favorito,
Che più d'ogn'altro meno se l'aspetta,
Toccò la corda con i suoi intermedi
De'tamburini e trombettieri a'piedi.

Alla corda così vuol che s'attacchi,
Perchè d'arbitrio e senza consigliarsi,
Facea venir all'armi, allorchè stracchi
Bisogno avevan più di riposarsi:
Ed eran mezzo morti, e come bracchi
Givano ansando inordinati e sparsi:
E con un fuor di lingue e orrenda vista
Soffiavan, ch'io ho stoppato un Alchimista.

Amostante non solo era sdegnato,
Che di suo capo e propria cortesìa,
Senza lasciar che l'uom riabbia il fiato,
Ei volesse attaccar la batterìa;
Ma perchè seco aveva concertato,
Ch'egli stesso, che sa d'astrologìa,
Vuol prima, che il nimico si tambussi,
Veder che in Cielo sien benigni influssi."
(III, 32—35).

His courageous behaviour in the battle is enlarged upon in several places, with many little touches adding to the confirmation and understanding of his personality.

"Il Principe d'Ugnano, ed Amostante
Da toccatori fan col brandistocco,
Perocchè della morte almen cessante,
Se non prigion si fa chi è da lor tocco.
All'incontro ritrovasi Sperante,
Che fa menando la sua pala, il fiocco:
E se già le sustanze ha dissipate,
Or manda male gli uomini a parlate.

Maso di Coccio a questo e quel comanda,
Ed all'un danne, e a un altro ne promette:
La compagnia del Furba innanzi manda,
Che resti a'fianchi a Batiston commette,
Con Pippo, il quale sta dall'altra banda;
Ma egli in retroguardia poi si mette:
E mentr'ognun s'avanza, a gloria intento,
Ei siede a gambe larghe, e si fa vento.

Amostante all'incontro un nuovo Marte
Sembra fra tutti avanti alla testata:
Lo segue Paol Corbi da una parte,
E da quell'altra Egeno alla fiancata.
Vengonsi intanto a mescolar le carte,
E vien spade e baston per ogni armata;
E chi dà in picche, e a giuocar non è lesto,
Vi perde la figura, e fa del resto."
(IX, 31—33).

An invitation to negotiate follows.

"A questo il General, ch' ha un po'd'ingegno,
Ritiene il colpo, e indietro si discosta:
Che si fermino i suoi, dipoi fa segno
Passa parola, e manda gente a posta:

Nè badò molto a fargli stare a segno;
Che la materia si trovò disposta:
Ciascun d'ambe le parti stette saldo;
Ch'ognun cerca fuggire il ranno caldo."
(IX, 37).

Peace is concluded and the assailants are invited to the palace.

"Giunta a palazzo Bertinella intanto
In Amostante e in Celidora incappa:
E vuol, che (gli odj omai posti da canto)
Stien seco; ma ciascun ricusa e scappa:
Pur finalmente ne li prega tanto,
Ch 'e' non si fanno poi stracciar la cappa,
Va innanzi il General dentro al palagio:
Chi dà spesa, dic' ei, non dia disagio."
(IX, 47).

In the renewed tussle Malatesti takes a conspicuous part.

"Sperante per di là gran colpi tira
Con quell'infornapan della sua pala:
Ne batte in terra, sempre ch'ei la gira,
Otto o dieci sbasiti per la sala;
Talchè ciascuno indietro si ritira,
O per fianco schifandolo fa ala:
E chi l'aspetta, come avete inteso,
Ha (come si suol dir) finito il peso.

Amostante, che vede tal flagello
D'un' arme non usata più in battaglia,
Alza la spada, e quando vede il bello,
Tira un fendente, e in mezzo gliela taglia.
Riman brutto Sperante, e per rovello
Il resto che gli avanza all'aria scaglia:
Vola il troncone, e il diavol fa, ch'ei caschi
Sulla bottiglieria tra vetri e fiaschi.
(XI, 31—32).

The poem ends with the marriage of Malatesti and the queen of the Malmantile.

As seen, every little trait given fits admirably and brings Milton's Florence nearer to us. To offer more details here, however interesting, would carry us beyond our purpose.

CHAPTER II.

Reliability of Milton's Statements.

*Legendary and real Milton in Italy. Foundations of the latter.
Milton's own picture not reliable on account of his high opinion of
himself. Relation in Defensio Secunda. Milton and the Jesuits.
Alleged cause of his return. Areopagitica and Galileo. Masson and
astronomy. Reumont. Allodoli. Mrs. Byse. Galileo and Descartes.
Galileo and Hobbes.*

"Quando la notte è nelle valli, e pende
Scolorata la luna, alle montagne
Mezzo velate, che gli fan corona,
L'insonne mandrian leva lo sguardo,
Come a concilio di giganti, e giura,
Se de' venti il romor taccia ne 'boschi
E nel burron non mormori il torrente,
Sotto le nubi dall' opposte cime
Udirle favellar. Milton divino
E divin Galileo, l'alte parole
Vostre, che in notte memoranda udiro
Le toscane pendici, se superba
La preghiera non è, dalle mie labbra
Con augurio di pace oda l'Italia.

Scende nell 'acque del Tirreno il Sole,
Nè quegli occhi il vedean che di spiarlo
Primi fur osi. Il carrezzevol fiato
Occidentale a respirar, sul colle
Sedea d'Arcetri l'Esule divino,
E le spente pupille al moribondo
Lume girava, un dì suo studio e vanto.
Presso gli stava di virginee bende,
Come a Suora s'addice, il crin velato,
Guardïana fedel, Maria, la dolce
Primogenita sua. Tra ramo e ramo
Gli ultimi raggi dardeggiava il Sole,
Imporporando del Vegliardo il capo
Meditante. Ei tenea sovra una sfera

La manca mano, e con la destra in aria
Scrivea cerchi su cerchi. A quali stelle
Eri volato allor? Quale seguivi
Rivolgimento di lontan pianeta,
Quando improvviso e per nascosti calli
Alla solinga collinetta asceso
Stette l'anglico Bardo al tuo cospetto?"

It is a curious fact that Milton's Italian journey has come to
be looked upon in a rather legendary light in England as well as
in Italy itself. At Domo d'Ossola there is a tradition that Milton
passed this place on his way home and even composed part of
Paradise Lost in its neighbourhood. At Vallombrosa the monks
showed to Wordsworth

"The Cell
Where our Milton was wont lonely vigils to keep."

According to a writer in "Notes and Queries" even the organ
on which Milton played was pointed out to the credulous visitor
in the monastery. And Florence, above all, has spun many an
imaginary incident round the visits paid to her by the poet. Few
additional details, in fact, Zanella needed to tell the melodious tale
of which we have just quoted the beginning as an adequate specimen
of the traditional Italian conception of Milton.

It is superfluous to point out that these legends cannot possibly be rooted in the actual journey of the poet, but are a later
effect of the fame of Paradise Lost. Indeed, the known facts underlying are peculiarly meagre, as the only sources are some
registers at Geneva, Florence, and Rome, and Milton's own relations,
especially the one in Defensio Secunda. But even the last-mentioned
information is liable to exception. There no longer exists any
doubt as to Milton's desire to impress his importance on the public.
This desire induced him to write to Deodati:

"Italorum in obscura re diu versati sumus sub Longobardis,
et Francis, et Germanis, ad illud tempus quo illis ab Rodolpho
Germaniæ rege concessa libertas est . . ." just as if he, as
Horwood remarks, had been working through most matter relating to the subject, when his commonplace book shows that
he had been reading Sigonius' History only, in one volume,
exactly covering the period indicated. Actuated by this same desire he wrote in Defensio Secunda: "Cum itaque tres omnino ani-
madverterem libertatis esse species, quæ nisi adsint, vita ulla
transigi commode vix possit, ecclesiasticam, domesticam seu privatam,
atque civilem, deque prima jam scripsissem, deque tertia magi-
stratum sedulo agere viderem, quæ reliqua secunda erat, domesticam mihi desumpsi; ea quoque tripartita, cum videretur esse, si
res conjugalis, si liberorum institutio recte se haberet, si denique philo-

sophandi potestas esset, de conjugio non solum rite contrahendo, verum etiam, si necesse esset, dissolvendo, quid sentirem explicui; ...

Institutionem deinde liberorum uno opusculo brevius quidem tractabam; ...

Postremo de typographia liberanda, ne veri et falsi arbitrium, quid edendum, quid premendum, penes paucos esset, eosque fere indoctos, et vulgaris judicii homines, librorum inspectioni præpositos, per quos nemini fere quicquam quod supra vulgus sapiat, in lucem emittere, aut licet aut libet, ad justæ orationis modum Areopagiticam scripsi." (Milton, Prose Works, ed. Fletcher, p. 720).

This sounds rather magnificent, but nevertheless it is not true, as is pointed out by several of Milton's biographers, the treatises evidentially rising out of his own personal affairs.

Such facts naturally impair the value of his autobiographical writings, and so the necessity has arisen of taking into account his most obvious mis-statements. As yet, however, a critical investigation of Milton's narratives of the Continental tour is wanting, though they contain some details that invite discussion.

As a preliminary to such discussion it seems apt to read through the complete version of the journey as Milton has given it in his <u>Defensio Secunda</u>; "Exacto in hunc modum quinquennio, post matris obitum, regiones exteras, et Italiam potissimum, videndi cupidus, exorato patre, uno cum famulo profectus sum. Abeuntem vir clarissimus Henricus Woottonus, qui ad Venetos orator Jacobi regis diu fuerat, et votis et præceptis, eunti peregrè sanè utilissimis, eleganti epistola perscriptis, me amicissimè prosequutus est. Commendatum ab aliis nobilissimus vir Thomas Scudamorus vicecomes Slegonensis, Caroli regis legatus, Parisiis humanissimè accepit; meque Hugoni Grotio viro eruditissimo, ab regina Suecorum tunc temporis ad Galliæ regem legato, quem invisere cupiebam, suo nomine, et suorum uno atque altero deducente, commendavit: Discedenti post dies aliquot Italiam versùs, literas ad mercatores Anglos, quà iter eram facturus, dedit, ut quibus possent officiis mihi præstò essent. Nicæa solvens, Genuam perveni; mox Liburnum et Pisas, inde Florentiam. Illa in urbe, quam præ cæteris propter elegantiam cum linguæ tum ingeniorum semper colui, ad duos circiter menses substiti; illic multorum et nobilium sanè et doctorum hominum familiaritatem statim contraxi; quorum etiam privatas academias (qui mos illic, cum ad literas humaniores, tum ad amicitias conservandas laudatissimus est) assiduè frequentavi. Tui enim Jacobe Gaddi, Carole Dati, Frescobalde, Cultelline, Bonmatthæi, Clementille, Francine, aliorumque plurium memoriam, apud me semper gratam atque jucundam, nulla dies delebit. Florentia Senas, inde Romam profectus, postquam illius urbis antiquitas et prisca fama me ad bimestre ferè spatium tenuisset, (ubi et Luca Holstenio, aliisque viris cum doctis tum ingeniosis, sum usus humanissimis) Neapolim perrexi: Illic per eremitam quendam, quicum Roma iter feceram, ad Joannem Baptistam Mansum, marchionem Villensem, virum nobilissimum atque gravissimum, (ad quem Torquatus Tassus insignis poeta Italus de amicitia scripsit) sum introductus; eodemque usus, quamdiu illic fui, sanè amicissimo; qui et ipse me per urbis loca et proregis aulam circumduxit, et visendi gratia haud semel ipse ad hospitium venit: Discedenti seriò excusavit se, tametsi multo plura detulisse mihi officia maxime cupiebat, non potuisse illa in urbe, propterea quod nolebam in religione esse tectior. In Siciliam quoque et Græciam trajicere volentem me, tristis ex Anglia belli civilis nuntius revocavit: Turpe enim existimabam, dum mei cives domi de libertate dimicarent, me animi causa otiosè peregrinari. Romam autem reversurum, monebant mercatores se didicisse per literas parari mihi ab Jesuitis Anglis insidias, si Romam reverterem; eò quod de religione nimis liberè loquutus essem. Sic enim mecum statueram, de religione quidem iis in locis sermones ultrò non inferre; interrogatus de fide, quicquid essem passurus, nihil dissimulare. Romam itaque nihilominùs redii: Quid essem, si quis interrogabat, neminem celavi; si quis adoriebatur, in ipsa urbe pontificis, alteros prope duos menses, orthodoxam religionem, ut antea, liberrimè tuebar: Deoque sic volente, incolumis Florentiam rursus perveni; haud minus mei cupientes revisens, ac si in patriam revertissem. Illic totidem, quot prius, menses libenter commoratus, nisi quod ad paucos dies Luccam excucurri, transcenso Apennino, per Bononiam et Ferraram, Venetias contendi. Cui urbi lustrandæ cum mensem unum impendissem, et libros, quos per Italiam conquisiveram, in navem imponendos curâssem, per Veronam ac Mediolanum, et Pæninas Alpes, lacu denique Lemanno, Genevam delatus sum. Quæ urbs, cum in mentem mihi hinc veniat Mori calumniatoris, facit ut Deum hic rursus testem invocem, me his omnibus in locis, ubi tam multa licent, ab omni flagitio ac probro integrum atque intactum vixisse, illud perpetuò cogitantem, si hominum latere oculos possem, Dei certè non posse. Genevæ cum Joanne Deodato, theologiæ professore doctissimo, quotidianus versabar. Deinde eodem itinere, quo priùs, per Galliam, post annum et tres plus minus menses in patriam revertor." (Milton, Prose Works, ed. Fletcher, p. 719).

In this narrative Milton's courageous behaviour in the close and dangerous atmosphere of Italy has received most attention and been commented upon. It has even excited some wonder that, with such conduct in those the most vigorous days of the Inquisition, he should escape unhurt, though, as he asserts, especially sought for by the English Jesuits in Rome. The wonder increases in face of the fact that according to an entry found in the Travellers' Book of the English Jesuit College at Rome, Milton even enjoyed the hospitality of these his enemies: "Octobris die 30, Pransi sunt in Collegio nostro Illustrissimus D. N. Cary frater baronis de Faukeland, Doctor Holdingus, Lancastrensis, D. N. Fortescuto, et Dominus Miltonus, cum famulo, nobiles Angli, et excepti sunt lautè." (Com. pl. book, p. XVI).

If the Jesuits' dinners were not of a piece with those of Pope

Alexander VI. and Cesare Borgia, — and this possibility is, of course, excluded, — their invitation presupposes friendly relations and reciprocal forbearance in religious matters. Even if we infer that a rupture took place between the above entry and the alleged persecution, this does not explain the inefficacy of the Inquisition, the peaceful presence of the Jesuithater among his foes, and the civilities of Barberini, which probably fall within the second Rome period.

That Milton, as natural, freely discussed religion among the Svogliati at Florence[1]) does not nearly amount to the situation implied by his narrative, and so we have probably here another instance of Milton's predilection for posing before the public.

The passage where Milton declares that, on gathering the news about the outbreak of the First Bishops' War, he turned homewards at Naples because he would not travel abroad for his pleasure, when, at home, his countrymen were contending for their liberty, — this passage has aroused much admiration. Simple chronology, however, shows that Milton's words conflict with facts. The negotiations between Charles and the Scots continued through 1638 and the first months of 1639. In March only, when Milton had been on his way home for three months and was staying at Florence, came the sudden outbreak of the Civil War.

Therefore, when we further compare his statement with the fact, that, contrary to expectation from such a sentiment, he returned even more leisurely than he went, staying for several months at Rome, at Florence, and making a long circuit to Venice, Verona, etc., we must explain the proclaimed cause as a somewhat showy afterthought intended for public exhibition. [2])

---

[1]) More than this need not be inferred either from the correspondence with Dati or the letter from Heinsius, as the latter evidently drew his information from his friend Dati. Vossius to Heinsius: —

"Salmasius totus est in responso ad Miltonum . . . Miltonum passim Catamitum vocat, aitque eum in Italia vilissimum fuisse scortum, & paucis nummis nates prostituisse." (Burmannii Sylloge III, p. 662).

Heinsius to Vossius: — "Miltonum mortuum credideram, sic certe nunciaras. Sed præstat in vivis illum esse, ut Sycophantæ cum Sycophantis committantur. Poëmata ejus mihi ostendit Holstenius. Nihil illa ad elegantiam apologiæ. In prosodiam peccavit frequenter. Magnus igitur Salmasianæ crisi campus hîc apertus. Sed qua fronte alienos iste versus notabit, cujus musis nihil est cacatius? Quod ait adversarium nates Italis vendidisse, mera est calumnia. Utinam ejus malæ tam tutæ fuissent a pugnis uxoriis, quam posticum Miltoni os a sicariis Hetruscis! Imo invisus est Italis Anglus iste, inter quos multo vixit tempore, ob mores nimis severos, cum & de religione libenter disputaret, ac multa in Pontificem Romanum acerbe effutiret quavis occasione." (Burm. Syll. III, p. 669).

In addition see Chauvet, Religion de Milton, pp. 60—62.

[2]) Note that Milton stated his return as coinciding with the outbreak of the Second Bishops' War. This war began in Aug. 1640, Milton arrived in England in the summer of 1639. Cf. Masson, Life II, 3 ff., who states Milton's return *at the beginning of the Second Bishops' War* and then fills more than 100 pages with the description of the two Bishops' Wars without perceiving the incompatibility of the statements. To me this is in accordance with Masson's, I may say superstitious, belief in Milton's words.

The instances of this propensity in Milton of disregarding the real occurrences for alleged ones apt to increase his importance with the public might be multiplied. I shall, however, draw attention to one more only.

In 1644, Milton alluded to his Italian journey as follows, when addressing to the Parliament his Areopagitica for unlicensed printing: — "And lest some should persuade ye, lords and commons, that these arguments of learned men's discouragement at this your order are mere flourishes, and not real, I could recount what I have seen and heard in other countries, where this kind of inquisition tyrannizes; when I have sat among their learned men, (for that honour I had) and been counted happy to be born in such a place of philosophic freedom, as they supposed England was, while themselves did nothing but bemoan the servile condition into which learning amongst them was brought; that this was it which had damped the glory of Italian wits; that nothing had been there written now these many years but flattery and fustian. There it was that I found and visited the famous Galileo grown old, a prisoner to the inquisition, for thinking in astronomy otherwise than the franciscan and dominican licensers thought". (Prose Works, ed. Fletcher, pp. 112—113).

This passage is very frequently cited. The meeting of, perhaps, the two most celebrated men of the time has appealed very strongly to the popular mind. Even as late as the 19th century an Italian poet chose this theme as seen above. To a closer scrutiny by his biographers, however, the passage has not as yet been subjected. Masson's account is unsuspecting and indicates ignorance of the circumstances. "Amid many rencontres of Milton with Florentine celebrities which must be left conjectural, he has himself recorded one, the most interesting of all. *There it was,* he says, *that I found and visited the famous Galileo, grown old, a prisoner to the Inquisition, for thinking in Astronomy otherwise than the Franciscan and Dominican licensers thought.* The words imply an excursion (perhaps more than one) to Galileo's villa at Arcetri, a little way out of Florence; an introduction to the blind sage by Malatesti, or Gaddi, or Buommattei, or some one else of the Florentine group; a cordial reception by the sage, according to his wont in such cases; a stroll, perhaps, under the guidance of one of the disciples in attendance, to the adjacent observatory, to see and handle the telescopes; a conversation, perhaps, on returning, with the assembled little party, over some of the fine wines produced in welcome; and all the while, surely, a reverent attention by the visitor to the features and the mien of Italy's most famous son, judging reciprocally of *him* through courteous old mind and ear, but unable to return his visual glance. I know not whether the reader has observed, with me, in Milton's writings hitherto, a certain fascination of the fancy, as if by unconscious presentiment, on the topic of blindness. How in men like Homer and Tiresias

2

a higher and more prophetic vision had come when terrestrial vision was denied, and the eyes had to roll in a less bounded world within, was an idea, I think, vivid with Milton from the first, and cherished imaginatively by verbal repetitions. Be this as it may, the sight of Galileo, frail and blind, was one which he never forgot; and long afterwards, when his minor recollections of Florence and Tuscany had grown dim in the distance, it was with this central recollection of Galileo, as the great Tuscan, that he associated whatever remained." (Life of Milton I, pp. 736—37).

The passage is as good a specimen as any of Masson's notions of his subject. To a man watched by the Inquisition and allowed to receive but a few relatives and friends, and prohibited from holding discourse even with *them*, — to this man's villa a pleasure-trip is made, and the party is cordially received by one decrepit, who is known for boring visitors with endless complaints, and who during Milton's stay at Florence is verging on death; and by a disciple in attendance, an office which did not exist till after Milton's departure[1]), the latter is guided to the adjacent observatory built 195 years after his death,[2]) to see and handle the telescopes not as yet invented.[3]) And then the reader is asked to perceive in Milton a presentiment of his blindness on account of Galileo, about whose being blind Milton is so persistently silent in his writings that we can hardly believe he knew it.

However inaccurate in many respects, Stern[4]) has a more adequate conception of the Inquisition (Milton und seine Zeit I, pp. 275—80), and his relation was taken as the starting-point for some comments upon the subject by the best authority of the 19th century on Florentine history. *Alfred de Reumont* does not entertain

---

[1]) Viviani was admitted to Galileo in 1639, Evangelista Torricelli later on (Opere di Galileo, Carteggio).

[2]) The observatory at Arcetri was founded in 1869 (A. Abetti, Galilei in Arcetri, p. 40, n). The first observatory in the neighbourhood of Florence seems to have been the very primitive one erected by Ferdinand II. for Borelli on the hill of San Miniato, some twenty years after the death of Galileo. The latter made his observations from some hill in the open air, from the Torre del Gallo, or from Bello Sguardo. (Cf. Reumont, Geschichte Toscana's; E. Müntz, Florence et la Toscane). The *museo di fisica e d'istoria naturale,* founded in 1774, was used (but seldom) as an observatory till the new one at Arcetri was built.

[3]) Masson evidently imagines a rather modern observatory, unconscious of the facts that, at the time, astronomy was in its infancy; that, in 1638, there were, at most, two observatories worthy of the name in use in Europe, at Leyden and, perhaps, at Copenhagen, the earlier ones at Nuremberg (1472), Cassel (1561), and Uranienburg (1576) being already discontinued; that the astronomical telescope was invented by Newton, Galileo's optical instruments being very primitive ones and not requiring to be put up in a special room.

These latter instruments are not mentioned in the *inventario delle masserizie della villa d'Arcetri* after the death of Galileo. They were collected in the *Tribuna di Galilei* of the *museo di fisica e d'istoria naturale* at Florence, in 1840.

[4]) The hypothesis of Mitford's that Milton was acquainted with Vincenzio Galilei is accepted as a fact by Masson and Stern. Florence, however, was crowded with Galileis.

any doubts about the occurrence of the visit but at the same time dwells so strongly on the vigilance and severity of the Inquisition that, had he known the facts stated, his conclusion might have been another. "Il biografo tedesco del sommo poeta, saviamente riflettendo quanto fosse la severità del divieto, quale l'asprezza del Sant'Uffizio nel trattare il più illustre degli scienziati italiani, pone in dubbio, che la visita dal Milton rammentata abbia potuto aver luogo in città; [opinione la quale coincide colla tradizione sempre mantenutasi à Firenze . . .

Galilei . . . era di ritorno in villa dove ad ogni modo se non facile meno difficile era l'accesso presso l'uomo spiato da tanti occhi aguzzati dalla gelosia e dal livore dell'ignoranza caparbia. Visite di forestieri non cattolici erano proibite e Milton, contro al precetto Wottoniano non si è mai curato di far misterio delle sue opinioni religiose. La visita dunque sicuramente ebbe luogo a Arcetri dove più facile era farla passare inosservato . . .

Secondo il detto biografo avrebbe potuto essere, invece del 1638, durante il secondo soggiorno dell'Inglese in Toscana. Non lo credo. Milton in quel tempo erasi fatto troppo conoscere in Italia" . . . (Archivio storico italiano 1877, p. 427 ff; Cf. further Beiträge zur italiänischen Geschichte I, 405; Saggi di storia e letteratura, p. 395 ff; Geschichte Toscanas I, 554).

It is evident that, beyond this, nothing has been done to advance our knowledge of the matter in question. The latest authority on Milton among the Italians, Ettore Allodoli, writes as follows: — "La visita famosa a Galileo si deve porre in questo primo soggiorno a Firenze? Le relazioni storiche tra Milton e Galileo furono examinate brevemente ed efficacemente da Alfredo Reumont il quale sostenne che la visita deve essere posta in questo periodo, perchè Milton si creò poi à Roma una riputazione molto cattiva di acceso protestante e quindi più difficilmente poteva essere introdotto presso Galileo sorvegliato attentamente dall'autorità ecclesiastica. Che la visita sia avvenuta nell'autunno del 1638 o nella primavera del 1639, non ha per noi grande importanza: certo è che la visita avvenne, nonostante i grandi rigori dai quali era circondato Galileo per ordine dell'Inquisitione e nonostante che Milton fosse uno straniero, e, per di più, un protestante. Ma bisogna supporre che il desiderio di vedere in persona il grande scienziato fosse nel giovine entusiasta si ardente, da superare ogni ostacolo: d'altra parte si sa che molte persone di fede non cattolica trovarono il mezzo di fare omaggio a Galileo: alcuni mercanti tedeschi poterono offrirgli una catena d'oro in dono e dargli una lettera. Per questo mio lavoro, importa rilevare che Galileo fece sul Milton un' impressione straordinaria.[1])" (Allodoli, Miltone e l'Italia, pp. 18—19.)

---

[1]) Some lines further down Allodoli translates Paradise Lost V, 261—263,
As when by night the Glass
Of Galileo, less assur'd, observes
Imagind Lands and Regions in the Moon:

Apparently, the actual surroundings of Galileo are not known to Allodoli. The German merchants were Florentine citizens, probably Catholics. The visits will be examined later on.

There remains the latest result of research in England. This is even more disappointing than the Italian contributions. In fact, I doubt whether it is worth mentioning the publication of Mrs. Byse's *Milton on the Continent,* in 1903.[1]) The author undertakes to show that Milton's Il Penseroso and L'Allegro were a result of his Italian journey, not as is now believed written before that event. The theory is worked out in such a manner as to secure for the book a rather amused interest. The fact that in 1638—39 there existed certain persons and landscapes in France, Switzerland, and Italy means to her that Milton has seen and known them and foisted them into his two poems under the strangest disguise so as to defy discovery by human intellect. The visit to Galileo, of course, is gratefully accepted and properly used. "Here (at Florence), too, in flesh and blood, but aged and ill, was the great Galileo, condemned by the Inquisition and hopelessly blind.

What we now wish to suggest is that, when Milton wrote in Il Penseroso:

> *Where I may oft outwatch the Bear,*
> *With thrice-great Hermes,*

he was alluding to the astronomical studies of Galileo, whom he takes as a type of Melancholy." Etc.

It would be to no purpose here to cite the 9 pages of extravagancies which Mrs. Byse dedicates to the incident. The above is sufficient to show the unsatisfactory result.[2])

---

in the following strange manner: *Raffaello . . . vede . . . la Terra coll' Eden, come di notte Galilei col cannocchiale osserva "i poeti" e le regioni lunari.* Printer's error?

[1]) My copy, though not indicated as a reprint, contains additions dated 1909.

[2]) It would be unjust not to acknowledge the enthusiasm and care with which the author has followed Milton's route in Italy and collected legends, folklore, and geographical notes on the spot, but the merits of the book stop at this merely physical labour, as Mrs. Byse uses her material strangely. Maria Celeste, who died in 1634, tends her blind father who became blind in 1638. Adriana and Leonora Baroni were, between 1637 and 1641, the finest voices in the world and *moved Italy to madness.* As Adriana lost her voice before 1630, it may be that people went mad at her performances in 1637—41, especially in 1641, when she had been dead a year. For this erroneous information Masson is responsible, as well as for that of their being from Mantua instead of from Posilipo (cf. Milton's *Mutavit rauci murmura Pausilipi),* and Leonora's sister Catherine, the poetess, assisting at their performances, instead of their aunt Margherita.

Further Mrs. Byse thinks that Zanella describes dawn when he is dilating on the sunset; that the mention of knights and ladies and Hymen in Allegro applies directly to Parisian society because *What would be more natural than marriages between the knights and bright-eyed women?;* that Epitaphium Damonis, 12—13,

pastorem scilicet illum
Dulcis amor Musæ Thuscæ retinebat in urbe, means
for then that shepherd was absent,
Kept by the Muse's sweet love in the far-famed tower of the Tuscan,

This survey of the most representative authors on the subject exposes two faults common to all of them, more or less, viz. insufficient knowledge about Galileo's actual situation at the time, and too much fiction in the treatment. Our purpose, then, will be to get at the bare facts as they were in 1638—39. This will be possible by means of the exhaustive Galileo edition by the Italian government. Then Milton's works may be examined. Beforehand, however, two legends must be disposed of, often adduced as an explanation of the possibility of Milton's getting access to Galileo, viz. the alleged visits of Descartes and Hobbes to the Italian astronomer.

The latter never went out of Italy. Descartes visited Italy in 1623—25 only, when Galileo was not as yet watched by the Inquisition, and, had such an incident occurred *then,* it would have been of no importance as a proof of *Milton's* visit. But Descartes never saw Galileo, as he writes to Mersenne in 1638: — "Et première-ment, touchant Galilée, ie vous diray que je ne l'ay jamais vû, ny n'ay eu aucune communication avec luy," (Opere di Galilei, ed. naz., XVII, p. 391). The oldest biography of Hobbes, dated 1682, is in Latin and consists of three parts. No 1 is a *Life* composed from his own notes; No 2, one based upon other information; No 3, a versified autobiography. Now, Nos 1 and 3 contain no hint of a personal acquaintance with Galileo. Nor do Hobbes' Works. In the great Galileo edition where with utmost care is as far as possible collected all contemporary documents relating to Galileo there is no mention of Hobbes. As far as I can see the statement may be traced back to the following passage in the second part of the above-mentioned biography: — "Anno 1634 cum Domino in Galliam transiit, ubi Parisiis degens, præcipuam naturali Philosophiæ promovendæ operam impendit . . . Posthæc Hobbius in Italiam profectus, Pisis quotidiana consuetudine usus est Galilei Galilei Lyncei, Mediceorum Syderum & Solarium macularum inventione clari, qui etsi præ aliis ad res Astronomicas impetu quodam ferebatur, in Philosophiâ tamen naturali magnâ cum laude versatus est, & in naturam motûs (cui fidem faciunt scripta Cedro dignissima) supra Antiquos longissime penetravit. Amicitiam inter ipsos conciliavit idem studiorum cursus, & summa morum ac temperaturæ similitudo; quæ fortasse communis infortunii causa, ut uterque acerrimis Ecclesiasticorum censuris vexaretur; quo jure, quâve injuriâ, non est meum pronunciare. — Anno 1637. cum Patrono in patriam reversus," . . . (Magni Philosophi Thomæ

---

and recalls Galileo. But the climax in sagacious exegesis is reached when the lines from L'Allegro,

> *Sometimes with secure delight*
> *The upland hamlets will invite,* etc.

are referred to an Alpine shepherds' festival, and *secure* is taken to mean that *the bulls are shut up in the stable on these occasions.*

Hobbes Malmesburiensis Vita, London 1682, pp. 43—44). Now it should be noted that Galileo left his lectureship in Pisa when Hobbes was three years old, which makes the biographer's statement simply ridiculous. He then resided in Padua till 1610, and for the rest of his life — except the visits to Rome — in Florence. Nor is it possible that, at a later time, any friendship should have grown up without leaving traces among the countless papers of the Galileo edition. Or that Hobbes, whose timorous disposition has become proverbial, should try to gain access to a person watched by the Inquisition. It is evident that, as in the case of Descartes, this story is due to the biographer's desire to connect his hero with other celebrities of the time.

CHAPTER III.

Milton and Galileo.

Documents of the Continental Journey. Letters and records. Galileo before 1632. The order from Rome. The sentence. Siena. Il Gioiello and "ritiratezza". Blindness, illness, and the will. The States General. Castelli's visit. Milton's knowledge of Galileo. Improbability of the visit.

The Milton documents relating to the Continental Journey are comparatively few. First, a letter from Henry Lawes about the passport.

"Sir, I have sent you with this a letter from my Lord Warden of the Cinque Ports under his hand and scale, which wilbe a sufficient warrant to justify your goinge out of the King's Dominions; if you intend to wryte yourselfe you cannot have a safer convoy for both than from Suffolk House, but that I leave to your owne consideration and remaine your

faithfull friend and servant,
Henry Lawes.

(Address) . . . any waies Aprooved.

Mr. John Milton
haste these".

(Com. pl. book, p. XVI).

For date see Com. pl. book, l. c.

Further there is the well-known letter from Wootton prefixed to Comus, of April 13th, 1638, which refers to Milton's speedy departure for the Continent.

Among the Epistolæ Familiares there is a letter of Sept. 10th, 1638, at Florence and addressed to Buommattei. The purpose of this letter to a person in the same city on a subject better discussed orally is not clear.

Next comes an entry in the records of the Accademia degli Svogliati at Florence.

"A dì 16. di Settembre (1638).

I Signori Accademici ragunati in numero competente furono lette alcune composizioni e particolarmente il Giovanni Miltone Inglese lesse una poesia latina di versi esametri molto erudita."

. . . .

On October 30th Milton was at the Jesuit College in Rome (see above). In 1639 Milton is present in three entries at the Svogliati.
"A dì 17. di Marzo:
Nell Accademia si trovarono li Signori ... 10. Miltonio ...
Furon portati .... dal decimo ... e letti alcuni nobili versi latini."
"A dì 24. Marzo:
Si ragunò l'Accademia, nella quale furono li Signori ....
Miltonio ...
Il 4to (Milton) lesse et esplicò un cap. dell' etica, a cui fece alcuni estemporanei argomenti l'ultimo (Gaddi). Furon recitate ... diverse poesie latine del Signor Miltonio" ...
"A dì 31.
Nell Accademia si trovarono li Signori ... 10. G. Miltonio ..."
(The entries from the Svogliati are cited from Stern I, 2, p. 499).

A familiar epistle dated March 30th, 1639, at Florence, is extant.

The album of Camillus Cardonius at Geneva has the following note:

"if Vertue feeble were
Heaven itselfe would stoope to her.
Coelum non animum muto dum trans mare curro.

Junii 10. 1639.
                    Joannes Miltonius Anglus."

Now we should pay some attention to Galileo. Born at Pisa in 1564, he got a lectureship at the University there in 1589, which he changed for a similar position at Padua in 1592. Thence he moved to Florence in 1610 as first philosopher and mathematician to the Duke of Tuscany, and, but for visits to Rome and Siena, remained there till his death in 1642, either in his city house or at Arcetri, some way out of Florence, where he finally hired a villa, *il Gioiello*.

At first he was on good terms with the Pope and even went to Rome to demonstrate his improved optical instrument and its importance to astronomy. As early as 1611, however, the Inquisition secretly began spinning nets around him, and five years later he once more went to Rome, this time to receive a warning not to teach the Copernican system. But his real troubles date from 1632. The recent publication of his Dialogo sopra i due Massimi Sistemi del Mondo, in which Urban VIII., perhaps not without cause, thought himself ridiculed, brought about a peremptory summons from the Inquisition. Galileo was very much afraid, and tried to evade a journey to Rome by means of the intercession of the Duke of Tuscany, and of medical testimonies about his severe infirmities and illness, but it availed nothing. The brother of Urban, Antonio Barberini, Prime Minister during the absence of Francesco, wrote to Egidii, the inquisitor at Florence, that if Galileo tarried he would be fetched and put in irons. "Da questa Congregatione del Santo Off.° è stato molto male inteso che Galileo Galilei non habbi prontamente ubbidito al precetto fattogli di venire a Roma: et non deve egli scusar la sua disubbidienza con la stagione, perchè per colpa sua si è ridotto a questi tempi; et fa malissimo a cercar di paliarla con fingersi ammalato, poi che la Santità di N. S.ʳᵉ et questi Emin.ᵐⁱ miei SS.ʳⁱ non vogliono in modo alcuno tolerare queste fintioni, nè dissimular la sua venuta qui: che però V. R. gli dica, che se non ubbidisce subito, si manderà costì un Commissario con medici a pigliarlo, et condurlo alle carceri di questo supremo Tribunale, legato anco con ferri, poi che sin qui si vede che egli ha abusato la benignità di questa Congregatione; dalla quale sarà parimente condannato in tutte le spese che per tale effetto si faranno." (Opere di Galilei, XX, pp. 575—76).

A fortnight later, Jan. 15ᵗʰ, 1633, the Tuscan ambassador at Rome wrote to Cioli, first secretary to the Duke of Tuscany, that Galileo must go or there might be trouble: "Comparve alla Congrega-zione del S.ᵗᵒ Offizio la fede della poca salute del Sr. Galilei; et io ho procurato d'intender da Mons.ʳ Assessore se veniva appro-vata, come si poteva sperare, e se le sarebbe fatta grazia della proroga del suo rappresentarsi qua: et risponde confidentemente, che si fa poco caso della medesima fede, accennando, col girar del capo et anco in voce, che non sia piaciuta e che sia stata composta per farli servizio; e che non saprebbe dir altro se non che stimerebbe molto a proposito per il Sr. Galilei, e di suo ser-vizio, il risolversi di pigliarsi le comodità maggiori che possa, e di venire; perchè altrimenti dubita veramente di qualche stravagante risoluttione contro di lui. . . . ." (Opere, XV, p. 28).

Galileo went immediately and was confined in the house of Niccolini, where access to him was refused.

Niccolini to Cioli, Feb. 16ᵗʰ, 1633.

"Io vo continuando di servir il Sig.ʳ Galilei con tutti i mezzi possibili; et perchè il Sig.ʳ Card. Barberino ha dato per avverti-mento che non pratichi et che non si curi d'ammetter tutti quelli che venghino per visitarlo, le quali cose per diversi rispetti le potreb-bono essere di danno e di pregiudizio, se ne sta qui in casa riti-rato, ..." (Opere, XV, p. 41.)

Niccolini tried to procure permission for Galileo to take some exercise in the garden, but in vain.

Niccolini to Cioli, March 6ᵗʰ, 1633.

"Del Sig.ʳ Galilei non posso dir a V. S. Ill.ᵐᵃ più dello scritto con le passate, se non che vo procurando, se sarà possibile, che li sia permesso di poter qualche volta transferirsi al giardino della Trinità per poter far un poco d'esercizio, già che li è di molto nocumento lo star sempre in casa; ma per ancora non m'è stata data risposta alcuna, nè so quel che ce ne possiamo sperare. . . ." (Opere, XV, p. 61.)

Then Galileo was brought to the prison, examined, threatened with torture, and finally ordered to abjure. He behaved most abjectly, old and ill as he then was, and consented to everything required. The celebrated *Eppur si muove* belongs, of course, to fiction. He was sentenced to prison *arbitrio Sacræ Congregationis*, first confined at the ambassador's as before, and then in the house of the archbishop at Siena. A correspondent asked about the conditions of the confinement there.

Bocchineri to Galileo in Siena, July 28th, 1633. ". . . Mi favorisca di dire in che forma ella stia in casa di Mons.re Arcivescovo, et se le sono permesse visite et conversationi." (Opere, XV, p. 200).

The records of the Inquisition give the following information. ". . . illumque (Galileum) relegari tamen mandavit Senis, quo recto tramite se conferat, et in primo accessu se præsentet coram Archiepiscopo dictæ civitatis; et a dicta civitate non discedet sine licentia huius Sacræ Congregationis, sub poenis arbitrio." (Opere, XIX, p. 284).

At the end of 1633 he was allowed to return to Arcetri but with strong injunctions to live retired and to receive relatives and friends only, and even these sparingly.

"Feria V. Die p.ª Decembris 1633.

Fuit congregatio . . .

Galilei de Galileis Florentini, Senis relegati, lecto memoriali, S.mus oratorem habilitavit ad eius rurem, ubi vivat in solitudine, nec eo evocet aut venientes illuc recipiat ad collocutiones, per tempus arbitrio S. S.tis" (Opere, XIX. pp. 285—86).

As usual the ambassador tried to tell Galileo the decree in the mildest terms possible.

Niccolini to Galileo in Siena, Dec. 3rd, 1633.

"Molt' Ill.re Sig.r mio Oss.

Sua Santità essendo intervenuta nella Congregatione del S. Offitio di giovedì passato, si contentò di permettere a V. S. che da Siena ella se ne potessi passare alla sua villa, per starvi con ritiratezza e senza ammettervi molte persone insieme a discorsi nè a magniare, per levar ogn' ombra che ella faccia, per così dire, accademia o tratti di quelle cose che le posson tornare in pregiuditio, come io son sicuro che la farà per conseguire tra qualche tempo la grazia intera. Così m'ha fatto sapere S. B., acciò io l'avvisi a V. S.; la quale potrà muoversi a suo piacere senz 'aspettar altro decreto in questo proposito, soggiugnendole che non li son prohibite le visite de gl'amici e de'parenti, pur che non dien ombra, come sopra. . . ." (Opere, XV, pp. 344—5).

It is evident from these documents that Galileo was on very bad terms with the Inquisition. And the following years do not seem to have ameliorated his position. He sometimes tried to move the Pope to relaxation, but was enjoined to be silent as otherwise he might be remanded to the Inquisition at Rome.

On March 25th, 1634, the omnipotent nephew Francesco writes to the inquisitor at Florence. "Il Sr Galileo Galilei, non contento che si sia da questa S. Cong.[ne] con tanta benignità proceduto seco, viene con continui memoriali a dimandare altre gratie, particolarmente di ritornare alla patria, sotto pretesto di curarsi dalle infirmità che patisce; et perchè qui è nota la commodità dell'habitatione che egli ha, dove si ritrova, et la vicinanza di quel luogo alla città, sì che può haver medici e medicamenti senza veruno incommodo, quando ne habbia di bisogno, hanno ordinato questi Em.[mi] miei SS.[ri] che V. R. gli faccia intendere che cessi da queste sue dimande, perchè, non volendosegli concedere lo ritorno alla città, non venghi pensiero a questi miei Emin.[mi] di richiamarlo a queste carceri." (Opere, XX, pp. 578—79).

The time following is of minor importance for our subject. In the beginning of 1638, about half a year before Milton's arrival, Galileo became blind. He therefore implored the Pope to let him move into the city, in order to try to cure his disease. The Inquisitor at Florence was questioned about the matter and confirmed the fact that Galileo was in a very sad condition, totally and irremediably blind, ill, and helpless. Visits to him were not very frequent because of his endless complaints about his infirmities, whence there would be no risk in letting him move into the city.

"Firenze, 13 febbraio 1638.

Per sodisfare più interamente al comandamento della Santità di N. S., sono andato in persona all'improvviso, con un medico forestiero mio confidente, a riconoscere lo stato del Galileo nella sua villa di Arcetri, persuadendomi con questo non tanto di poter referire la qualità delle sue indisposizioni, che di penetrare et osservare gli studi a'quali è applicato e le conversazioni colle quali si trattiene, per aver luce di quanto se, venendo a Fiorenza, possa con radunanze e discorsi seminare la sua dannata openione del moto della terra. Io l'ho ritrovato totalmente privo di vista e cieco affatto; e sebbene egli spera di sanarsi, non essendo più di sei mesi che gli caderono le cateratte negli occhi, il medico però, stante l'età sua di 75 anni, ne' quali entra adesso, ha il male per quasi incurabile: oltre di questo ha una rottura gravissima, doglie continue per la vita, et una vigilia poi, per quello che egli afferma e che ne rifferiscono li suoi di casa, che di 24 hore non ne dorme mai una intiera; e nel resto è tanto mal ridotto, che ha più forma di cadavero che di persona vivente. La villa è lontana dalla città et in luogo anche scomodo, e perciò non può che di raro, con difficoltà e con molta spesa, havere le comodità del medico. Gli studi suoi sono intermessi per la cecità, sebbene alle volte si fa leggere qualche cosa, e la conversazione sua non è frequentata, perchè, essendo così mal ridotto di salute, non può per ordinario far altro che dolersi del male e discorrere delle sue infermità con chi talvolta va a visitarlo: onde, per questo rispetto ancora, credo che quando la Santità di N. S. usasse della infinita sua pietà verso

di lui, che concedendole che stasse in Fiorenza, che non avrebbe
occasione di far radunanze; e quando l'avesse, è mortificato in tal
guisa, che per assicurarsene credo che potrà bastare una buona
ammonizione per tenerlo in freno." (Opere, XVII, p. 290).

Galileo's supplication was granted rather ungraciously on the
condition that he was not to walk out into the city or receive
people in his house.

"Feria V. Die XXV Februarii MDCXXXVIII . . . .
Inquisitoris Florentiæ lectis literis, datis 13 huius, quibus significat adversam valetudinem Galilei de Galileis, relegati in villa Arcetri
prope Florentiam, et dicit suum sensum circa illius reditum Florentiam; S.mus mandavit, dictum Galileum habilitari ad domum suam
Florentiæ, ut curetur ab infirmitatibus, et cum hoc tamen, ne exeat
e domo per civitatem, nec minus domi suæ admittat publicas seu
secretas conversationes personarum, ad fugiendos discursus circa
olim illius damnatam opinionem de motu terræ, eique sub gravis-
simis poenis prohiberi ne de huiusmodi materiis cum aliquo tractet,
et eum observari." (Opere, XIX, p. 287).

Castelli and the inquisitor at Florence informed Galileo of
the favour obtained, but at the same time recommended prudence.
The Inquisitor had to write once more to Rome and dilate on the
innocuity of Galileo. His son was instructed to hinder visits in
various ways, and Galileo himself seems to have been afraid to do
anything that might endanger the recent favour.

"Io ho significato a Galileo Galilei la grazia fattale dalla
Santità di N. S. e dalla Sacra Congregazione, di potersi far portare
dalla villa d'Arcetri a sua casa in Fiorenza per curarsi delle sue
indisposizioni, e giontamente l'ho precettato di non uscire per la
città, e con pena di carcere formale in vita e di scomunica latæ
sententiæ, riservata a Sua Beatitudine, di non entrare con chi si
sia a discorrere della sua dannata openione del moto della terra.
Egli si ritrova dall 'età di 75 anni, dalla cecità, e da molte altre
indisposizioni e sinistri accidenti che lo travagliano, talmente mortificato, che si però facilmente credere, come ha promesso, che non
sia per trasgredire il comandamento che se li è fatto. Oltre di
questo, la sua casa è in uno de' più remoti luoghi e lontani dall'abi-
tato che forsi sia in città; e di più ha un figliuolo molto morigerato
e dabbene, che li assiste continuamente, e questo è avvisato da me
di non ammettere in modo alcuno persone sospette a parlare col
padre, e di far sbrigare presto quegli che alle volte lo visiteranno,
e son sicuro che invigilerà et eseguirà puntualmente, poichè, come
si confessa obbligatissimo a Nostro Signore et a V. E. per la grazia
fatta di poter essere in città a curarsi, così teme che ogni minima
cosa possa fargliela revocare, complendo assai all'interesse suo pro-
prio che il padre si governi e che campi assai, perchè con la morte di
esso si perdono mille scudi che le dà l'anno il Granduca. Con tutto
ciò invigilerò come devo, affinchè sia eseguito quanto viene imposto
da Sua Beatitudine e da V. E.: alla quale aggiongo che il medesimo

Galileo si raccomanda assai per poter farsi portare nei giorni di festa, per quanto le sarà permesso dalle sue indisposizioni, a sentir messa in una chiesa piccola, lontana da 20 passi dalla sua casa, e m'ha richiesto di supplicarne, come faccio, V. E." (Opere, XVII, pp. 312—13).

It is evident that the Inquisition had not forgotten him in 1638. On the contrary, there arose during the whole year repeated occasions of irritation against Galileo which led to stronger measures than previously. As the publication of his books was impossible in Italy, he tried in several ways to print them abroad without the knowledge of the Inquisition. When reproved he pretended to know nothing of the matter.

Another circumstance was of a graver nature. In 1636 Galileo had offered to the States General an invention of his for determining the longitude at sea. A resolution of the States in 1636 tells that a certain Laurens Reael "heeft aen Haer Hooch Mogende met de complimenten hiertoe dienende overgelevert seeckere remonstrantie in forme van een brieff, uyt den naem ende van weegen Galileus Galilei . . . bestaende de voors. remonstrantie principalick hierin, dat de voornoemde Galileus Galilei in een vrijwillige gifte opoffert aen Haer Hooch Mogende seecker groot werck, sijnde een beginsel om tot volmaeckheit te brengen seecker middel omme te cunnen weeten, als het tot perfectie sal sijn gebracht, soo wel de lengte als de breete op de groote aert- ende zeecloot, ende dat soo wel te water als te landt." (Opere, XIX, p. 538).

It is determined "dat men den voornoemden Galileus Galilei sal vereeren met een gouden kettingh" and that professor Hortensius is to be asked to go to Italy to treat with Galileo.

The inquisitor at Florence got wind of the matter and reported to Rome, where the following decree was issued. "Inquisitoris Florentiæ lectis literis, datis 26 Iunii, quibus significat, brevi ex Germania venturum Florentiam personam qualificatam, cum muneribus, ad alloquendum Galileum de Galileis mathematicum, pro habenda ab eo instructione circa modum navigationis per longitudinem poli; Em.i DD. mandarunt rescribi Inquisitori, quod si persona profectura ex Germania ad Galileum sit hæretica vel de civitate hæretica, non permittat accessum illius personæ ad alloquendum Galileum, eidemque hoc prohibeat; sed quando civitas atque persona esset Catholica, non impediat negociationem, dummodo non tractent de motu terræ, iuxta prohibitionem alias factam." (Opere, XIX, p. 288).

At this Galileo was very much afraid and tried to stay the negotiations by every means. In Aug. 1638 he wrote to Diodati:

"Continuando le mie gravi e noiose indisposizioni, non posso se non con brevità rispondere all' ultima sua de' 20 del passato, con dirle che già che la mala fortuna ha voluto che si scuopra al S. Offizio il trattato che tenevo con gl'Ill.mi e Potentissimi Sig.ri Stati circa la longitudine, il che mi poteva arrecare gran danno e pregiudizio, come già le accennai, m'è stato gratissimo che V. S.

molto Ill.^{re}, con avvisarne il Sig.^r Ortensio e distorlo dal pensiero del viaggio che intendeva fare, abbia ovviato a qualche sinistro accidente che mi soprastava." (Opere, XVII, p. 372).

Not even the gold chain sent him by the States General dare he accept. The inquisitor at Florence writes. "Ch'il personaggio destinato a Galileo Galilei non è comparso, nè meno, per quanto intende, è per comparire; ma che bene sono capitati in mano d'alcuni Tedeschi i regali, insieme con la lettera, sigillata col sigillo de gli Stati Olandesi, per detto Galilei, il quale ha ricusato di ricever gli uni e l'altera." (Opere, XIX, p. 398).

This happened just at the time when we must suppose that Milton arrived in Italy. The occasion for a visit really seems the worst possible, especially as Galileo was also taken ill, to a degree that is described very vividly in the following letter. He is in bed, utterly prostrated and prepared for death, and suffers very much from pains in the stomach and a violent dysentery acquired through a mistake by the person who gave him his medicin. Neither sleep nor appetite.

Galileo to Deodati, Florence, Aug. 1638.

"Trovomi da circa un mese in qua sommamente afflitto e prostrato in letto, consumato di forza e di carne, che dispero del tutto il più poterne risurgere con la vita. Alla cecità, infiammazione e flussione d'occhi s'è aggiunto l'essere io stato travagliato da dolori colici e finalmente da una grandissima e violentissima evacuazione, accadutami non per errore del medico, ma di chi mi somministrò alcuni bocconi di diaprunis, che per ordine del medico doveva esser lenitivo, ma per errore del ministro fu preso in quel cambio il solutivo, sì che doppo brevissimo tempo cominciò a tirarmi giù tutto quello che avevo non solo nello stomaco e ne gli intestini, ma credo in tutta la sustanza carnosa, cavandomi da dosso credo bene due fiaschi d'umori. Aggiungesi a questo una perpetua vigilia, per la quale a gran fortuna mi tocca a domire qualche quarto o mez 'ora sul far del giorno e tal volta un 'ora o due verso la sera. Disgustatissimo d'ogni cosa, il vino nimicissimo alla testa et a gli occhi, l'acqua a i dolori di fianco, sì che in questi ardori il mio bere si riduce a poche once tra vino e acqua et ad una totale astinenza di frutte di qualsivoglia sorte; l'inappetenza è grande, nessuna cosa mi gusta, e se alcuna mi gusterebbe m'è del tutto proibita. Questi, Sig.^r mio, sono a me travagli grandi; ma molto maggiori sono i fastidii che mi perturbano per molti versi la mente e la fantasia, che lunghissima cosa sarebbe il raccontarli, nè io posso dettare anco questo poco senza grave offesa della testa." ... (Opere, XVII, pp. 369—70).

This is confirmed in the correspondence between the State Secretary at Florence and the ambassador at Rome.

Cioli to Niccolini, Florence, Sept. 9th, 1638.

"Il Sigr. Galileo Galilei, per la sua grave età et per l'indisposizioni che lo travagliano, si trova in stato di andarsene fra poco

tempo nell'altro mondo; et benchè in questo sia per restare eterna
la memoria della sua fama et del suo valore, desidera però S. A.
grandemente che la sua morte apporti meno danno che sia possibile all'universale, et che non si perdono i suoi studii, ma si possino
ridurre, in benefizio publico, a quella perfezione che esso non potrà
dargli. Egli ha molte cose degne di lui nella mente, le quali non
conferirebbe mai ad altri che al Padre D. Benedetto Castelli, in
chi egli interamente confida. Vuole però S. A. che V. E. chiami
detto Padre, et lo induca a procurare licenza di venirsene a Fiorenza
per trattenersi un paro di mesi a questo effetto, in che S. A. ha
premura particolare; et ottenendo detta licenza, come S. A. spera,
V. E. gli somministrerà il danaro per il viaggio et quel che gli
occorra, purchè si incamini, acciò non sopravenga qualche accidente
che impedisca questa buona opera, in che V. E. s'impieghi pure
con ardore". (Opere, XVII, p. 374).

Before we turn to this visit of Castelli's some words may be
said about the interpretation of these documents. Not seldom the
conjecture has been made that Galileo's illness was feigned in order
to procure him the presence of Castelli. The conjecture is a very
unfortunate one. In his letter to Diodati Galileo had no cause to
dissimulate, much less Cioli in his letter. Further, there are two
wills of Galileo's, the first of Jan. 15th, 1633, very significantly
made when he was summoned to Rome by the Inquisition; the
second of August 21st, 1638. This proves beyond doubt that
Galileo was very ill just about the time of Milton's arrival at Florence.

Though their victim was dying the inquisitors did not feel
inclined to leniency. Castelli dared not ask leave to visit Galileo
as proposed by the secretary, but told he would go to Florence
only. The Pope, however, was not to be deceived and C. got
leave to call on Galileo on the condition only that a third person
should be present.

Niccolini to Cioli, Sept. 25th, 1638: "Il Padre Don Benedetto
Castelli venne domenica a participarmi d'haver dimandata la licenza
di potersene venir costà a S. B.ne medesima: la quale (dice lui)
entrò in sospetto che fusse procurata per abboccarsi col S.re Galilei;
e perchè egli disse che, mentre veniva costà, non poteva non
procurar d'esser seco, dice che li fu risposto che se li darebbe
licenza di vederlo, ma con l'assistenza di qualch'uno". (Opere,
XVII, p. 381).

Castelli went to Florence and saw Galileo, but was so much
hindered by the restrictions of the Pope that he wrote to Barberini
and begged leave to call on Galileo more freely, "Sono gionto in
Firenze sano e salvo, per grazia del Signore, ed hoggi sono stato
a fare riverenza a questi Ser.mi, da'quali tutti sono stato visto con
gran benginità; ma ho scoperto subito un poco di difficoltà in obe-
dire puntualmente V. Em.za ed il comandamento di Nostro Signore:
vivo però risolutissimo di non mancare mai, e più presto che

mancare ci lasciarò la vita. Il punto è che il Ser.^{mo} Gran Duca, vedendo che il Sig.^r Galileo va tuttavia mancando e che assolutamente non può durare molto, ha procurato e tuttavia procura che si prepari a questo ultimo passo per farlo da christiano e con quella devozione che è obligato; e non solo S. A. Ser.^{ma} ha procurato da sè medesima, con pietà singolare e carità benigna, di essortarlo a finire i suoi giorni honoratamente, ma con altri mezzi ancora l'ha incaminato in modo, che sta tutto rimesso nella volontà di Dio benedetto, e si è dato a devozioni ed a pensieri santi: hora, se bene io sono inettissimo per altro, in ogni modo S. A. desidera che ancora io vadia cooperando, come quello con il quale il Sr Galileo ha sempre hauta particolare confidenza. Per tanto vengo a supplicare V. Em.^{za} per amor di Dio che si compiaccia impetrarmi da Nostro Signore grazia più libera di poter visitare questo povero vecchio; e gli prometto di non trattare con esso lui se non di cose concernenti all'anima ed alla sua salute, ed al più di un altro particolare che non appartiene punto a cose controverse o dannate da S. Chiesa . . .

Mi sovviene dire che il Rev.^{mo} qua di Badia mi accompagnerà volontieri, conforme al comandamento di V. Em.^{za}, per le tre volte che io ho facoltà di fare la visita; ma se Nostro Signore allargarà il seno della paterna carità, ritrovandosi il Padre Abbate occupato nel governo del monasterio, sempre mantenuto in rigore di santa osservanza, supplico humilmente che il medesimo Padre Abbate mi possa assegnare un altro compagno, con il quale, e non altrimenti, io possa far quel tanto che Dio benedetto m'inspirarà che io faccia." (Opere, XVII, pp. 382—83).

To a modern reader it seems marvellous that the Inquisition at Rome should be able in this way to control and direct not only the most insignificant actions but also the speech of two persons at Florence, and, really, it does every honour to their system of espionage, as mentioned by Reumont. The control was so effective that seven days later Castelli had to write a fresh letter and repeat his supplication to be allowed intercourse with Galileo more freely. The answer was highly ungracious. The order was given and determined, and had to be obeyed. The irritation against Galileo is very markedly expressed through his being referred to as "quella persona". Barberini to Castelli, Rome, Oct. 16th, 1638.

"Rispondo brevemente alla lettera di V. R., perchè non ho tempo: et dico che S. S.^à si contenta ella faccia le visite per trattare con quella persona, quante volte li pare, di cose concernenti all'anima et alla sua salute, come V. R. mi scrive, ma non già di un altro particolare (per usar delle proprie di lei parole) che non appartiene punto a cose controverse o dannate da S. Chiesa. Forse può procedere dalla mia relatione ambigua, ma non dal scrivere di V. R.^{za}; ma tutto è uno, che o io non l'intenda, o ella non si lasci intendere. Basta, l'ordine preciso è come di sopra ho detto, et quello importa. Vuol perciò S. S.^{tà} che ella si faccia dare un compagno, riputato idoneo dal P. Abate per trovarsi in simili discorsi, acciò, quando il P. Abate non può venire, questo compagno possa assisterli: che tutto questo è stato concesso essendo nota la pietà di V. R.^{za} et che ella se ne valerà come ha promesso. Et io mi ricordo alle sue orazioni". (Opere, XVII, p. 393).

On the very day when Barberini wrote this angry letter at Rome the unhappy Castelli wrote another letter from Florence that repeated the supplication, for the third time within two weeks. A fourth letter followed before Barberini's answer had arrived. On November 25th, at last, it was determined to grant more liberty to Castelli in one particular, but with strong, very strong intimations to keep within the limits of the decree or an "excommunicatio latæ sententiæ" would follow from which not even the Penitentiary could liberate him. "S^{mus} iussit scribi Inquisitori Florentiæ, qui permittat D. Benedictum frequentius agere cum Galileo Galilei, ut possit instrui de periodis Planetarum Mediceorum ad investigandam artem navigandi per longitudinem, iuncto tamen præcepto, sub pœna excommunicationis latæ sententiæ, a qua non possit absolvi nisi a S. S.^{te}, etiam ablata facultate S. Penitentiariæ, ne audeat loqui cum eodem Galileo de opinione damnata circa terræ motum." (Opere, XIX, p. 396). It is superfluous to add that when Galileo in this same year sent up a petition for liberty it was peremptorily refused. Two documents of April 27th and 28th, 1638, read as follows. "Galilei de Galileis Florentini, abiurati de vehementi in hoc S. Officio, petentis libertatem, lecto memoriali, E.^{mi} et R^{mi} DD. decreverunt ut memoriale legatur coram S.^{mo}."

"Galilei de Galileis Florentini, Fratris Bernardi Besuzzii Mediolanensis, Min. Obs., Andreæ Labiæ Veneti, D. Octavii Baccii, petentium diversas gratias, lectis memorialibus, S.^{mus} nihil eis concedere voluit." (Opere, XIX, p. 290).

It has mostly been supposed that it was a singular case, that of Castelli's, and that the friends of Galileo, at least, could see him freely. The following letter of Galileo's tells to the contrary.

"Firenze, 7 gennaio 1639.
Illmo Sig.^{re} e P.^{ron}mio Col.^{mo}

La gratissima lettera di V. S. Illma mi fu resa hieri, insieme col suo libro Del moto, dal molto Rev. P. D. Clemente di S. Carlo delle Scole Pie, compagno del Rev. P. Francesco di S. Giuseppe: e perchè il mio infortunio di esser cieco del tutto da circa due anni in qua non mi permette il poter vedere nè anche il sole, non che oggetti tanto minori e privi di luce quali son le scritture o le figure geometriche, ho ottenuto questo giorno che il sopradetto P. D. Clemente sia venuto a trattenersi da me per molte hore, nel qual tempo haviamo di compagnia scorso il detto suo libro, veramente con mio gusto particolare, anchorchè io non habbia

3

potuto intendere distintamente le dimostrationi, non potendo in-
contrarle con le figure; ma per la pratica che ho della materia, e
per sentire buona parte delle sue propositioni incontrarsi con le
mie già scritte, ho penetrato i suoi sensi e concetti." (Opere,
XVIII, p. 11).

About this Padre Clemente there was now much ink wasted.
The result was that he got permission to go and see Galileo but not
to stay for the night habitually. As if it were an affair of State,
the ambassador wrote to Florence, April 16th, 1639: — "Ho rap-
presentato al P. Generale delle Scuole Pie il desiderio del Sr Galileo Galilei circa al valersi del P. Clemente di S. Carlo, col farlo
anche pernottare nella sua villa. Ma il P. Generale, doppo havermi
rimostrato che il medesimo Padre ha pernottato più volte fuori di
convento a instanza del medesimo Sr Galileo, ha procurato di
rendermi capace che la licenza in scritto di poterlo fare di con-
tinuo non è concedibile, non tanto perchè è Padre giovine, come
perchè questa introduttione è di cattivo esempio nella sua Religione,
che professa osservanza grande delle sue constitutioni, e che i
Padri più vecchi che sono costà se ne potrebbono lamentare;
soggiugnendomi che hora vengono le giornate lunghe, e che quando
non basti al Sr Galileo che il sudetto Padre si trasferisca alla
sua villa una volta la settimana, può farlo chiamare o ordinarle
che si vada più spesso. Dice bene che se qualche volta bisognerà
che si pernotti, potrà farlo, come è seguito sin qui, ma che la
continuatione di star fuori di convento a dormire non se li può
permettere;" (Opere, XVIII, p. 42).

It is evident that at the time of Milton's second visit to Florence the Inquisition kept as close a watch on the persons calling
on Galileo as the previous autumn. Nor was his health better.
He writes Jan. 15th, 1639: "Alla gratissima di V. S. molto Ill.[re]
delli 18 Xbre, comparsami tre giorni sono, rispondendo, dico lo
stato mio essere infelice et andare di giorno in giorno peggiorando
in tutte le mie indispositione, che sono molte, et sopra tutte la total
cecità mi affligge perpetuamente, privandomi del poter operare
nessuna cosa." (Opere, XVIII, p. 17).

The above documents relating to Galileo may be summed
up as follows: — Except for relatives and friends, Galileo was
prohibited from receiving people, especially in large numbers. In
1638, he was refused when petitioning for liberty; a person from
an heretical country was peremptorily denied access to him. Even
known friends had trouble, in some cases, to see him. The system
of espionage around him apparently worked to perfection. In the
summer of 1638, he fell so seriously ill that he found it necessary
to make his will and was himself sure that he would die very
soon.

If we turn to Milton's Works and try to make out his real
position in regard to Galileo, there are some facts that offer food
for thought. The Areopagitica, where the visit is mentioned, was

written in English five years after his Italian journey. Ten years later he wrote the *Defensio Secunda* in Latin, a language understood throughout the world at the time, and there, as seen above, he gave a full account of that journey. Here, if anywhere, we should expect to hear the visit to Galileo mentioned, but this is *not* the case, whereas Milton relates how he had seen Grotius at Paris etc. In the same treatise he defends himself against the taunts of his enemies on account of his blindness, and does so by enumerating great men from ancient and recent times, that have been blind. Here Galileo seems to be the most apt and celebrated instance, but his name is wanting.

These singular circumstances have already been noted by Bernhardi. "Es ist übrigens merkwürdig, dass Milton hier in der Darstellung seiner italiänischen Reise Galilei's gar nicht erwähnt, den er doch nach seiner Äusserung in der Schrift Areopagitica gleichfalls gesehen und besucht hatte und nicht weniger, dass er dieses Mannes nicht unter den Beispielen erblindeter Gelehrter gedenkt, die er sozusagen zur Verteidigung seiner eigenen Blindheit anführt da gerade Galilei, der, wie Milton, sein Gesicht im Dienste der Wissenschaft verlor, ein besonders passendes Beispiel gewesen wäre." (John Milton's Politische Hauptschriften, übersetzt von W. Bernhardi, II, pp. 215—16, n.)

That Milton had not forgotten Galileo but remembered him particularly well at the time when he wrote his Defensio Secunda we know, because just then he began seriously to occupy himself with his great epos and there the allusions to Galileo take a very conspicuous place from the very first. In Book I, 284 ff. he compares Satan's shield to the moon viewed by Galileo through his optical instrument.

> "his ponderous shield
> Ethereal temper, massy, large and round,
> Behind him cast, the broad circumference
> Hung on his shoulders like the Moon, whose Orb
> Through Optic Glass the Tuscan Artist views
> At Ev'ning from the top of Fesole
> Or in Valdarno, to descry new Lands,
> Rivers or Mountains in her spotty Globe."

Later on he alludes to the discovery of the solar spots claimed by Galileo. Satan makes for the sun on his way through the Universe.

> "There lands the Fiend, a spot like which perhaps
> Astronomer in the Sun's lucent Orb
> Through his glaz'd Optic Tube yet never saw."
> (Paradise Lost III, 588—90).

And finally he names him expressly. Raphael sees the earth from the gates of Heaven as Galileo the moon through his *"Glass"*.

> "From hence, no cloud, or, to obstruct his sight
> Starr interpos'd, however small he sees,
> Not unconform to other shining Globes,
> Earth and the Gard'n of God, with Cedars crownd
> Above all Hills.   As when by night the Glass
> Of Galileo, less assur'd, observes
> Imagind Lands and Regions in the Moon:"
> (Paradise Lost V, 257 ff.)

The common notions about Galileo throughout Milton's time were that he had invented the *Optic Tube,* discovered spots in the sun and landscapes in the moon, and was persecuted by the Inquisition for his opinions in astronomy.   His blindness never became widely known, as occurring shortly before his death.   Now, in Milton's writings Galileo is just what he was to the average contemporary.   If Milton had visited Galileo, he must have perceived that he was blind, and to him — especially when he became blind himself — this fact would probably have been more prominent in the memory than any of those above.

Under these circumstances it seems to me rather unlikely that Milton had seen Galileo. The possibility, as well as the cause, of his assertion to the contrary is, I think, easily understood.   In the intimate friend of those magniloquent Italians, Manso, Francini, Dati, etc., who were at such pains to appear remarkable (see Chapter I.), an unfounded display of acquaintance with a celebrity is natural.   In the Areopagitica, Milton evidently sees in himself one of the dignified statesmen of ancient Greece — the very title betrays his thoughts — wont to set forth their wisdom publicly and whose orations were generally intended to show the speaker's capability and worthiness of being entrusted with public affairs.   That it was Milton's ambition to obtain public employment and rise in the State nobody can doubt who has perceived his exultation and pride when he really had become Latin secretary.   It is clear though, that if any man could claim attention from the Parliament, it would be he who among his acquaintances counted Galileo, the most famous man of the century.

II.

MILTON AND THE PAMELA PRAYER

CHAPTER I.

Preliminary.

Unsatisfactory state of the case. Johnson. Evasiveness and futility of the apologies. Symmons. Masson. Charge against Milton wholly personal and unproved. Desirability of minute inquiry and its conditions.

There are many who have taken offence at Johnson's treatment of Milton. And surely, anyone who has read Paradise Lost and then constructed an image of its author out of some current biography, e. g. that by Macaulay, can hardly suppress a sense of disgust at the severe verdicts or the cold appreciation in Johnson's Life. Nothing, however, has roused so much indignation in Milton's admirers as the accusation of the interpolation in the case of the Eikon Basilike and the Pamela Prayer: —

"But as faction seldom leaves a man honest, however it might find him, Milton is suspected of having interpolated the book called Icon Basilike, which the Council of State, to whom he was now made Latin secretary, employed him to censure, by inserting a prayer taken from Sidney's Arcadia, and imputing it to the King; whom he charges, in his Iconoclastes, with the use of this prayer as with a heavy crime, in the indecent language with which prosperity had emboldened the advocates for rebellion to insult all that is venerable or great: 'Who would have imagined so little fear in him of the true all-seeing Deity as, immediately before his death, to pop into the hands of the grave bishop that attended him, as a special relique of his saintly exercises, a prayer stolen word for word from the mouth of a heathen woman praying to a heathen god?'

The papers which the King gave to Dr. Juxon on the scaffold the regicides took away, so that they were at least the publishers of this prayer; and Dr. Birch, who had examined the question with great care, was inclined to think them the forgers. The use of it by adaptation was innocent; and they who could so noisily censure it, with a little extension of their malice could contrive what they wanted to accuse".

It is to be regretted that Johnson's words, though showing that the case is very unclear and must be taken up for good to

do justice to him as well as to Milton, — that these words nevertheless have failed to bring forth anything but animosity towards
Johnson from Milton's admirers, and various excuses the inaccuracy
of which becomes apparent even on slight investigation. Symmons
very confidently demonstrates the fallacy of Hills's testimony, on
account of Royston, not Dugard, having printed the Eikon in
question.

"The disproportionate severity with which Milton has arraigned
this petty inadvertency rather than offence has exposed him to
the charge of having been its author in the first instance that he
might subsequently be its censurer. On the authority of Hills, the
Protector's printer, and who, afterwards, for the emolument of the
same office under James II, professed himself a Roman catholic,
Milton is accused of having prevailed, with the assistance of Bradshaw, on Du Gard, who was then printing an edition of the Icon
Basilike, to bring discredit on that publication by interpolating it
with this prayer from the Arcadia. If a moment's credit were due
to so idle a tale, we might confidently affirm that never before
did men descend so low from such heights of character for an
object so contemptibly minute: an eagle stooping from its proudest
wing to seize upon an earthworm would inadequately represent the
folly of Milton and Bradshaw in their condescension to forge, for
the purpose of casting a mere atom into the heavily charged scale
of the departed king. Fortunately, however, we possess the most
satisfactory evidence of their exemption from the imputed meanness.
By Royston, who was reported to have received the manuscript
from the King, and not by Du Gard, the printer to the Parliament,
was that edition of the Icon printed in which the controverted
prayer was originally inserted; and Royston's press was remote
from the suspicion of any contact with Milton or his supposed
accomplice. Notwithstanding this full though short confutation,
which was first adduced by Toland, of the testimony of the unprin-
cipled Hills, his calumny has been revived by the infamous Lauder,
admitted by Lauder's friend and coadjutor, Dr. Johnson, and only
faintly and timidly denied by the last compiler of our author's
life, Mr. Todd." (Life of Milton, Lond. 1806, pp. 279—281).

There is a mistake about this. Royston was a publisher,
Dugard a printer; the former employed the latter to print the
Eikon as will be seen later on. Thus, the confutation is not to
the point. Symmons proceeds, however, and tells that he possesses
the first edition of the Eikon and that the interpolated prayer is
there, whence it cannot have been put in by Milton.

"I have now in my possession the first edition of the Icon
Basilike printed in 1649 (for R. Royston at the Angel in Ivylane)
to which this prayer, called 'A Prayer in time of Captivity,' is
attached. Let us not then again be told by Milton's enemies of
his forgery in this instance, or be soothed by his friends with their
hopes and their belief that he was incapable of committing it."

The earliest editions of the Eikon were all of them dated 1648, as natural, because printed before March 25ᵗʰ, 1649. Symmons's edition, therefore, must really be rather late.

Next he states that Johnson is not speaking the truth in saying that the revolutionaries took away the King's papers or that Birch credited the story.

"As I have seldom, from the commencement of the present work, adverted to this libeller of Milton, my readers will, perhaps, pardon me, if I dedicate this note to his honour. Dr. Johnson tells us that 'the papers, which the King gave to Dr. Juxon on the scaffold, the regicides took away, so that they were at least the publishers of this prayer; and Dr. Birch, who examined the question with great care, was inclined to think them the forgers.' Fuller, who must have known and who would not have concealed the truth, shall refute the former part of this egregious paragraph: and Dr. Birch himself the latter. But 'faction, Dr. Johnson! seldom leaves a man honest, however it might find him'."

Even this is not satisfactory. It is proved by public records that Juxon really was kept in custody till after the execution, and that the papers were taken from him. As regards Birch, both Johnson and Symmons are right. In his first edition of Milton's Prose Works, Birch dedicated a fair space in the appendix to the present subject and then apparently *did* credit the story. In the second edition, however, this appendix was removed and some remarks to the contrary were inserted in the prefixed Life of Milton, though this does not seem to have been the effect of conviction but of external causes (see infra).

The chief authority in matters relating to Milton, David Masson, is not more fortunate in this question, which he, as was to be expected, treats rather superciliously, and with unaccustomed scarcity of details. He, too, furnishes proofs of the impossibility of the story that turn out to be rather fallacious on examination.

"I am not quite sure that the charge of having been himself the fabricator of the imposition was deliberately made against Milton by the Royalists as early as 1650; though I think it very likely. But in that strange stream of Restoration tradition, which seems to have choked all high honour out of the English literary conscience for some generations, the charge has actually come down to our day, and apparently with no more serious reflection in connection with it in some quarters than that the fabrication would have been a clever ruse de guerre. Even Dr. Johnson, in his Life of Milton, could write, 'As faction seldom leaves a man honest, however it might find him, Milton is suspected of having interpolated the book called Eikon Basilike, which the Council of State, to whom he was now made Latin Secretary, employed him to censure, by inserting a prayer taken from Sidney's Arcadia, and imputing it to the King, whom he charges, in his Eikono-klastes, with the use of this prayer, as with a heavy crime, in the indecent language with which prosperity had emboldened the advocates for rebellion to insult all that is venerable or great'. He adds that the interpolation was probably at least managed by the Regicides among them, and that, as *the use of the adaptation* by the King, had it been his, would have been *innocent,* so *they who could so noisily censure it, with a little extension of their malice, could contrive what they wanted to accuse.* This is pretty strong, though cautiously expressed; but what is to be thought of the repetition in 1812, without query or comment, in such a work as Nichols's Literary Anecdotes (Vol. I. pp. 525—6) of the direct charge against Milton in this form? — 'These [the editions of the Eikon Basilike through 1649] were first printed by Dugard, who was Milton's intimate friend, and happened to be taken printing an edition of the King's book. Milton used his interest to bring him off; which he effected by the means of Bradshaw, but upon this condition, that Dugard should add Pamela's prayer to the aforesaid book he was printing, as an atonement for his fault, they designing thereby to bring a scandal upon the book and blast the reputation of its authority. To the same purpose, Dr. Bernard, who, as well as Gill [one of the sources of the preceding legend], was physician to Hills, Oliver's printer, and told him this story: *That he had often heard Bradshaw and Milton laugh at their inserting this prayer out of Sir Philip Sidney's Arcadia.*' In another form of the legend it is Dugard's wife who consents, while her husband is in Newgate, to foist in the prayer.' — It is hardly worth while to point out that the first edition of Milton's Eikonoklastes, exposing the Pamela plagiarism, appeared in October 1649, and that Dugard was committed to Newgate four months afterwards, in Feb. 1649—50 (ante p. 152), and was not released, by Milton's or Bradshaw's intercession, till April 1650. But, if any Anti-Eikonoklast still wants to work out some profound solution of the Pamela Prayer mystery, on the assumption that the Eikon was really the King's and that the Regicides diabolically contrived the interpolation, have we not furnished means that may be converted to mischief (though *how* we cannot quite conjecture) in that unexplained and cancelled entry in the Stationers' Registers, under date March 16, 1648—9, of an edition of the Eikon as forthcoming from the shop of Matthew Simmons, one of the Commonwealth's printers, and who was the first printer of the Eikonoklastes (ante p. 148)? Could not a story be spun out of that? If only it could be ascertained that Simmons's edition of the Eikon did appear, and that it was the first that contained the Pamela Prayer? What then?" (Life, vol. IV, pp. 249—50).

Masson's relation offers food for thought. It is evident that the revolutionaries' taking away of the papers looks favourable for Johnson's view of the case. Masson does not cite this part of the passage from Johnson, nor the statement that the regicides must have published the prayer, nor Birch's examination. But he gives as Johnson's opinion that the interpolation was at least probably managed by the regicides among them, which seems to me incorrect.

Further he makes the prayer interpolation dependent on the King's authorship of the Eikon Basilike. As nobody can doubt that the King had *not* written the Eikon, it appears as if Masson wanted his readers to make the inference that the revolutionaries had *not* put in the prayer. It is clear to anyone, however, that the two questions have nothing to do with each other in this respect.

Some more research might have saved Masson the remark which he apparently thinks settles the matter; the fact that Dugard was committed to Newgate has nothing to do with the conjecture about Milton, Bradshaw, and the prayer, but according to Dugard's own statement was caused ultimately by his printing Salmasius's Defensio Regia [1]). From Nichols's Anecdotes as cited we need not infer that Dugard was committed when caught printing the Eikon, but only menaced with trouble in some way. The nature of this trouble we can probably trace in the following entries in the Journals of the Commons.

"Die Veneris, 16 Martii, 1648. . . .

Ordered, That the Serjeant at Arms be appointed to make stay of, and seize at the Press, all those Books now printing or printed under the Name of the Book of the late King.

Die Sabbati, 17 Martii, 1648.

The House being informed, that, according to the Order Yesterday, the Press hath been seized; and the Printer is at the Door;

Ordered, That it be referred to the Committee for scandalous Pamphlets, where Mr. Challoner hath the Chair, to examine the Business: And Mr. Dove, Mr. Lister, Mr. Smith, Alderman Atkins, Sir James Harrington, are added to that Committee."

Now, as Dugard was the first and chief printer of the Eikon and the one whose books most easily betrayed their maker on account of their singular ornaments and get-up, we may perhaps safely infer that he was the printer mentioned in the above entries, the more so as Dugard himself states in his Affidavit that he had troubles about this time too (April 28th), preventing him from printing a royalist book. As his citation coincides with the very day and week when, according to State records, the government took strong measures about the book and when Milton became attached to the Commonwealth and was ordered to answer the Eikon, it may very well have happened that Dugard was released on Milton's intervention and a promise to the effect handed down by tradition. More of this infra.

If the attitude of Milton's apologists towards the question seems unwarranted, the same is true of his accusers. With the ex-

---

[1]) Dugard's Affidavit in Almack's Bibliography.

ception of Birch, they bring forth their accusation with too much animosity to keep a clear judgment. Moreover, though the evidence, mostly hearsay, was collected forty or fifty years after the publication of the prayer, the witnesses display such minuteness as to time, persons, and circumstances as suggests less the exact knowledge of facts than the fruitful imagination peculiar to political partisans.

It is clear that a question which has been followed in its development by so many generations with the greatest interest and the details of which shed such intimate light on Milton's psychology as well as on the most important period of English history, ought not to remain in this state. But, if a satisfactory result is to be obtained, previous methods ought to be abandoned. It is necessary to keep out of view today's moral or political considerations; we want a legal inquiry into the case, with due attention paid to religious, ethical, political, and other circumstances of the time. The plan accordingly will be to state the case, follow the development in its earlier stages, with a summary of later opinions; then to inspect the *corpus delicti* and the place, hear the witnesses and the accused, sift and weigh the evidence, and see the result.

CHAPTER II.

The Origin of the Case.

Eikon Basilike, Eikonoklastes, and the Pamela Prayer. Milton's accusation. Its reception by contemporaries.

On January 30th, 1649, as we remember, Charles I. was executed. Not many days afterwards, perhaps on that very day, appeared a little pamphlet with the title: Εἰκὼν Βασιλική *The True Portraicture of His Sacred Majestie in his Solitudes and Sufferings.* This famous publication pretended to be written by Charles[1]) and

---

[1]) The close connection of the Eikon with the present matter makes a summary of the celebrated controversy about the authorship of the book indispensable; no easy task, in fact, as for more than two centuries literally thousands of pages have been written for and against the royal authorship, in which pages politicians, clergymen, and women have vied in strange tales and recriminations.

From this disencouraging tangle the following may be extracted.

In the Eikon's birth year the King's authorship was questioned by Goodwin n *Obstructions of Liberty* and Milton in his *Eikonoklastes,* but more especially by an anonymous writer in a treatise with the following title: *Eikon Alethine, the Pourtraiture of Truths most sacred Majesty truly suffering, though not solely, Wherein the false colours are washed off, wherwith the Painter-steiner had bedawbed Truth, the late King and the Parliament, in his counterfeit Piece entituled* Εικων Βασιλικη, *Published to undeceive the World.* Here it is proved that a clergyman, not the King, must be the author of the Eikon. The royal authorship was instantly vindicated in *The Princely Pelican,* Εικων η Πιστη and Εικων Αχλαστος, but then the discussion grew sporadic and occasional for some thirty years.

The starting-point for the hottest controversy is the year 1686. In this year an auctioner, Mr. Millington, declared he had found at a sale the following memorandum in a copy of the Eikon: "King Charles the Second, and the Duke of York, did both (in the last Session of Parliament 1675, when I shew'd them, in the Lords House, the written Copy of this Book, wherin are some Corrections, written with the late King Charles the First's own Hand) assure me, that this was none of the said King's compiling, but made by Dr. Gauden, Bishop of Exeter; which I here insert for the undeceiving others in this Point, by attesting so much under my Hand,

Anglesey."

As Gauden was dead, several persons turned to his curate, Anthony Walker, for information, and he confirmed the statement of the memorandum. This evoked a volume of vituperation on Walker from a brother-clergyman (*Defence of King Charles* etc. by Richard Hollingworth), in consequence of which he published a full account of the birth of the book. Hollingworth then bestowed some more volumes of a similar character on Walker, from the perusal of which the latter was saved by death. With H. sided other divines, Long, Wagstaffe, etc., while the opposite opinion was defended by Ludlow and Toland with equal passion and prejudice.

contained comments upon the last nine years of his reign. Thoughts, sentiments, and language were so well adapted to time and circumstances that the effect on the readers was very great. The many accusations against the King were now forgotten and people who

---

In the 18th century we need only mention Birch, who gives an impartial account of the matter in the appendix to his Milton edition, in 1738.

It might seem to anyone that the discovery of Gauden's correspondence with Clarendon, where, after the Restoration, Gauden somewhat insolently claims preferment on account of the great service done by him to the royalist cause through his writing the Eikon, — it might seem that this discovery would dispose of the King's authorship.

In the first half of the 19th cent., however, the Rev. Christopher Wordsworth wrote some 700 pp. in favour of Charles's claims. Todd, Broughton, Hallam, and, later on, Masson found for Gauden.

In 1883, finally, Mr. Doble published the full internal evidence founded on an investigation of style (The Academy, May 12th ff.). The Eikon is by Gauden because of 1) the alliteration characteristic of Gauden (piety and policy etc.); 2) the plays upon words characteristic of Gauden (mend me . . . end me, errors . . . terrors); 3) the vocabulary characteristic of Gauden; 4) the rhetorical expressions characteristic of Gauden; 5) the Biblical quotations characteristic of Gauden; 6) the faulty historical details in the book as to the events in which the King was the principal agent.

Impossible as it would seem, even after this the King has found a champion. In 1896, Mr. Almack proved, as he thought, the royal authorship in the following manner: he produced this Affidavit of Dugard's:

"Wm. Dugard printed

1. The King's incomparable Eikon Basilike, which he received from Mr. Simmons, his Majesty's chaplain.

2. Elenchus Motuum Nuperorum in Anglia.

3. Salmasii Defensio Regia: for which he was cast into Newgate, his wife and six children turned out of doors, and had been tried for his life by an High Court of Injustice,[1] had not Sir James Harrington saved him from that danger, and procured his release; and therefore in point of civility he thought he might entertain him for lodging in his house, being by the Act of Indemnity pardoned, as to life, and ready to render himself to his Majesty's pleasure whensoever his Majesty should so require it.

Ità testor,
Guil. Du Gard.

April 28, 1649. I received a letter from Sir Edward Nicholas from the Hague, with approbation of my service for his Majesty in that condition and withal a book to print entitled Στρατοστηλιτευτικοι, which afterwards was printed, though I could not do it then, in the time of my troubles."

A following document shows that this was written by Dugard in 1661 when imprisoned for having concealed Sir James Harrington in his house. Mr. Almack's conclusions from these documents are unexpected: — 1) Harrington had probably seen the King write the Eikon; 2) Dugard and Harrington would not have taken such strong measures if the book had not been the King's; 3) had the book not been the King's, Dugard would have procured his release by promising to keep the secret. (Almack, Bibliography, pp. 5, 6, 10). There is no arguing against pure belief.

Cf. further Ranke, Englische Geschichte III³, p. 316 f.; Hallam, Constitutional History of England I, p. 640, 4th ed.; Cambridge History of English Literature VII, pp. 161—2; Hume, History of England VII, Dublin 1780, pp. 152—4; Guizot, Histoire de la revolution d'Angleterre III, Paris 1864, pp. 28—30, and his collection of memoirs; Gardiner, History of the Great Civil War III, p. 599 f.

---

[1] Almack seems to think that "Court of Injustice" was Dugard's invention. Of course, it was a common joke at the time. See e. g. Evelyn's Diary, vol. II, p. 2, Lond. 1879 (or Everyman, vol. I, p. 245).

had lately proclaimed him a traitor now set him up for a saint
and martyr. The leaders of the revolution, who had sentenced
the King and put him to death, saw the danger arising from the
circulation of this book but in the beginning were at a loss what
to do. It was only when, in March, Milton became attached to
the new government as Latin secretary that the expedient was
thought upon of publicly answering the *King's Book*. Milton had on
the 13ᵗʰ of February brought forth his Tenure of Kings and Magistrates with its passionate attacks on Charles and monarchy, and
so appeared able to perform the task of exposing the dead King.
Milton's book was published late in the year, on the sixth of October. The title ran: Εικονοκλαστης *in Answer to a book intitl'd*
Εικων Βασιλικη, *The Portrature of his Sacred Majesty in his
Solitudes and Sufferings. The Author I. M.*

This book was on the whole a failure. One thing, however,
proved awkward to the royal cause. Milton accused the King of
having taken one of the prayers in Εἰκὼν Βασιλική from Sidney's
Arcadia. The passage is as follows: "In Praying therefore, and
in the outward work of Devotion, this King, wee see, hath not at
all exceeded the worst of Kings before him. But herein the worst
of Kings, professing Christianism have by farr exceeded him. They,
for ought we know, have still pray'd thir own, or at least borrowd
from fitt Authors. But this King, not content with that which,
although in a thing holy, is no holy theft, to attribute to his own
making other mens whole Prayers, hath as it were unhallow'd,
and unchrist'nd the very duty of Prayer it self, by borrowing to a
Christian use Prayers offerd to a Heathen God. Who would have
imagin'd so little feare in him of the true all-seeing Deitie, so little
reverence of the Holy Ghost, whose office is to dictat and present
our Christian Prayers, so little care of truth in his last words, or
honour to himself, or to his Friends, or sense of his afflictions, or
of that sad hower which was upon him, as immediatly before his
death to popp into the hand of that grave Bishop who attended
him, as a special Relique of his Saintly exercises, a Prayer stol'n
word for word from the mouth of a Heathen Woman praying to
a Heathen God; and that in no serious Book, but in the <u>vaine
amatorious Poem</u> of Sir Philip Sidneys Arcadia; a Book in that
kinde full of worth and witt, but among religious thoughts, and
duties not worthy to be nam'd; nor to be read at any time without good caution; much less in time of trouble and affliction to
be a Christian's Prayer-Book. It hardly can be thought upon without som laughter, that he who had acted over us so stately and
so Tragically, should leave the World at last with such a ridiculous
exit, as to bequeathe among his deifying friends that stood about
him, such a peece of mockery to be publisht by them, as must
needs cover both his and their heads with shame and confusion.
And sure it was the hand of God that lett them fall & be tak'n
in such a foolish Trapp, as hath expos'd them to all derision, if

for nothing els, to throw contempt and disgrace in the sight of all Men upon this his Idoliz'd Book, and the whole rosarie of his Prayers; thereby testifying how little he accepted them from those who thought no better of the living God, then of a Buzzard Idol, that would be serv'd and worshippt with the polluted trash of Romances and Arcadias, without discerning the affront so irreligiously and so boldly offerd him to his face." (pp. 11—13).

I here give Pamela's prayer from "The Countesse of Pembrokes Arcadia, Written by Sir Philip Sidney, 9th ed., London 1638": "O All-seeing Light, and eternall Life of all things, to whom nothing is either so great, that it may resist; or so small that it is contemned; looke upon my misery with thine eye of mercy, and let thine infinite power vouchsafe to limit out some proportion of deliverance unto me, as to thee shall seeme most convenient. Let not injurie, O Lord, triumph over me, and let my faults by thy hand be corrected, and make not mine unjuste enemy the minister of thy Justice. But yet my God, if in thy wisdome this be the aptest chastizement for my inexcusable folly; if this low bondage be fittest for my over-high desires; if the pride of my not enough humble heart be thus to be broken, O Lord, I yeeld unto thy will, and joyfully embrace what sorrow thou wilt have me suffer. Onely thus much let me crave of thee (let my craving, O Lord, be accepted of thee, since even that proceeds from thee), let me crave, even by the noblest title, which in my greatest affliction I may give myselfe) that I am thy creature, and by thy goodnesse (which is thyselfe) that thou wilt suffer some beame of thy Majestie so to shine into my minde, that it may still depend confidently on thee. Let calamity be the exercise, but not the ouerthrow of my vertue: Let their power prevaile, but prevaile not to destruction: let my greatnesse be their prey: let my paine be the sweetnesse of their revenge: let them (if so seeme good unto thee) vex me with more and more punishment. But, O Lord, let never their wickednesse have such a hand, but that I may carry a pure minde in a pure body. (And pausing a while) And O most gracious Lord, said she, What ever become of me, preserve the vertuous Musidorus."

The Eikon Basilike prayer I quote from Thomason's copy of the prayers, dated April 16th, 1649: "O Powerfull and Eternall God! to whom nothing is so great that it may resist; or so small, that it is contemned; look upon My misery with thine eye of Mercy, & let thy infinite power vouch safe to limit out some proportion of deliverance unto Me, as to thee shall seeme most convenient; let not injurie O Lord, triumph over Me; and let My faults by thy hand be corrected; and make not My unjust Enemies be Ministers of thy Justice: But yet My God, if in thy wisdome, this be the aptest chastisement for My unexcusable transgressions; if this ingratfull bondage be fittest for My over-high desires; if the pride of My (not enough humbled) heart be thus to be broken,

O Lord, I yield unto Thy will, and cheerfully imbrace what sorrow thou wilt have Me suffer. Onely thus much let Me crave of Thee (let My craving O Lord, be accepted of since it even proceeds from Thee) that, by Thy goodnesse which is Thyselfe; Thou wilt suffer some beame of Thy Majesty so to shine in My minde, that I, who in my greatest afflictions acknowledge it My Noblest Title to be thy Creature, may still depend confidently on Thee. Let Calamity be the exercise, but not the overthrow, of My vertue. O let not their prevailing power be to my destruction. And if it be Thy will that they more and more vex Me with punishment, yet, O Lord, never let their wickednesse have such a hand, but that I may still carry a pure mind and stedfast resolution ever to serve Thee, without feare or presumption, yet with that humble confidence which may but please Thee; so that at the last I may come to Thy Eternall Kingdome, through the Merits of Thy Son our alone Saviour Jesus Christ. Amen."

While the refutations of the Eikonoklastes were rather coolly received, the idea that the King should have committed the action imputed was very trying to the Cavaliers. Before long, however, suspicions arose as to another being the author of the prayer interpolation. In a pamphlet, Εικων Αχλαστος, of the year 1651, there is the following passage: "His (Milton's) meaning is, as followes afterward, that the King vsed a prayer taken out of S. Philip Sydnies Arcadia. After the first Edition of his Majest: booke, the Printers finding the greate vent of them, in the following Editions Printed prayers, and other things in the Kings name, not belonging to the booke. Among these prayers, there is a prayer taken out of the Arcadia. That prayer is neither made by a heathen woman, nor to a heathen God, but is composed by the Author a Christian without reference to any heathen Deitie, and the Author is not thought to unchristen prayer by it, the libeller himselfe saying the booke in its kinde is full of worth, and wit, but as his outcry hath noe cause from the matter, so heere is no evidence of the fact, that his Majest: made use of that prayer, or popt into the Bishopps hands as a relique of his exercise, though he might warrantably have vsed it and professed it" (p. 82).

The newspapers of the time contain nothing on the matter. Milton does not appear there save in some stray remark about "Mr Mylton (who houlds forth the Doctrine of Divorce, and like a State Champion, sham'd himselfe with handling his penne to oppose those Divine Meditations of our late King of happy memory)," (Mercurius Pragmaticus, Tuesday, January 22 to Tuesday, January 29, 1649).

If we may believe Milton, however, the matter caused much sensation in some way or other. When editing for the second time the Eikonoklastes, in 1650, he enlarges on the prayer-adaptation in words to this effect: "They who are yet incredulous of what I tell them for a truth, that this Philippic Prayer is no part of the

4

King's goods, may satisfie thir own eyes at leasure in the 3d. Book of Sir Philips Arcadia p. 248. comparing Pammela's Prayer with the first Prayer of his Majestie, delivered to Dr. Juxon immediatly before his death, and Entitl'd A Prayer in time of Captivity Printed in all the best Editions of his Book. *And since there be a crew of lurking raylers, who in thir Libels, and thir fitts of rayling up and down, as I hear from others, take it so currishly that I should dare to tell abroad the secrets of thir Ægyptian Apis,* to gratify thir gall in som measure yet more, which to them will be a kind of almes (for it is the weekly vomit of thir gall which to most of them is the sole meanes of thir feeding) that they may not starve from me, I shall gorge them once more with this digrestion somwhat larger then before: nothing troubl'd or offended at the working upward of thir Sale-venom thereupon, though it happ'n to asperse me; beeing, it seemes, thir best livelyhood and the only use or good digestion that thir sick and perishing mindes can make of truth charitably told them. However, to the benefit of others much more worth the gaining, I shall proceed in my assertion; that if only but to tast wittingly of meat and drink offerd to an Idol, be in the doctrin of St. Paul judg'd a pollution, much more must be his sin who takes a prayer, so dedicated, into his mouth, and offers it to God. Yet hardly it can be thought upon (though how sad a thing) without som kind of laughter at the manner, and solemn transaction of so gross a cousenage: that he who had trampl'd over us so stately and so tragically should leave the world at last so ridiculously in his exit, as to bequeath among his Deifying friends that stood about him such a pretious peece of mockery to be publisht by them, as must needs cover both his and their heads wth shame, if they have any left. Certainly they that will, may now see at length how much they were deceiv'd in him, and were ever like to be hereafter, who car'd not, so neer the minute of his death, to deceive his best and deerest freinds with the trumpery of such a prayer, not more secretly then shamefully purloind; yet giv'n them as the royall issue of his own proper Zeal. And sure it was the hand of God to let them fal & be tak'n in such a foolish trapp, as hath exposd them to all derision; if for nothing els, to throw contempt and disgrace in the sight of all men upon this his Idoliz'd Book, and the whole rosarie of his Prayers; thereby testifying how little he accepted them from those who thought no better of the living God then of a buzzard Idol, fitt to be so servd and worshipt in reversion, with the polluted orts and refuse of Arcadia's and Romances, without being able to discern the affront rather then the worship of such an ethnic Prayer. But leaving what might justly be offensive to God, it was a trespass also more then usual against human right, which commands that every Author should have the property of his own work reservd to him after death as well as living. Many Princes have bin rigorous in laying taxes on thir

subjects by the head, but of any King heertofore that made a
levy upon thir witt, and seisd it as his own legitimat, I have not
whom beside to instance. True it is I lookt rather to have found
him gleaning out of Books writt'n purposely to help Devotion. And
if in likelyhood he have borrowd much more out of Prayerbooks
then out of Pastorals, then are these painted Feathers, that set
him off so gay among the people, to be thought few or none of
them his own. But if from his Divines he have borrow'd nothing,
nothing out of all the Magazin, and the rheume of thir Mellifluous
prayers and meditations, let them who now mourn for him as for
Tamuz, them who howle in thir Pulpits, and by thir howling
declare themselvs right Wolves, remember and consider in the
midst of thir hideous faces, when they doe onely not cutt thir
flesh for him like those ruefull preists whom Eliah mock'd,
that he who was once thir Ahab, now thir Josiah, though faining
outwardly to reverence Churchmen, yet heer hath so extremely
set at nought both them and thir praying faculty, that being at
a loss himself what to pray in Captivity, he consulted neither with
the Liturgie, nor with the Directory, but neglecting the huge
fardell of all thir honycomb devotions, went directly where he
doubted not to find better praying, to his mind with Pammela
in the Countesses Arcadia. What greater argument of disgrace &
ignominy could have bin thrown with cunning upon the whole
Clergy, then that the King among all his Preistery, and all those
numberless volumes of thir theological distillations, not meeting
with one man or book of that coate that could befreind him with
a prayer in Captivity, was forc'd to robb Sr. Philip and his Captive
Shepherdess of thir Heathen orisons, to supply in any fashion his
miserable indigence, not of bread, but of a single prayer to God.
I say therfore not of bread, for that want may befall a good man,
and yet not make him totally miserable: but he who wants a
prayer to beseech God in his necessity, tis unexpressible how
poor he is; farr poorer within himself then all his enemies can make
him. And the unfitness, the undecency of that pittifull supply
which he sought, expresses yet furder the deepness of his poverty.

Thus much be said in generall to his prayers, and in speciall
to that Arcadian prayer us'd in his Captivity, anough to undeceave
us what esteeme wee are to set upon the rest. For he certainly
whose mind could serve him to seek a Christian prayer out of a
Pagan Legend, and assume it for his own, might gather up the
rest God knows from whence; one perhaps out of the French
Astræa, another out of the Spanish Diana; Amadis and Palmerin
could hardly scape him. Such a person we may be sure had it
not in him to make a prayer of his own, or at least would excuse
himself the paines and cost of his invention, so long as such
sweet rhapsodies of Heathenism and Knighterrantry could yeild him
prayers. How dishonourable then, and how unworthy of a Christian
King were these ignoble shifts to seem holy and to get a Saintship

among the ignorant and wretched people; to draw them by this deception, worse then all his former injuries, to go a whooring after him. And how unhappy, how forsook of grace, and unbelovd of God that people who resolv to know no more of piety or of goodnes then to account him thir cheif Saint and Martyr, whose bankrupt devotion came not honestly by his very prayers; but having sharkd them from the mouth of a Heathen worshipper, detestable to teach him prayers, sould them to those that stood and honourd him next to the Messiah, as his own heav'nly compositions in adversity, for hopes no less vain and presumptuous (and death at that time so imminent upon him) then by these goodly reliques to be held a Saint and Martyr in opinion with the cheated People." (pp. 12—16).

It does not appear in the whole passage that any accusation had been made against Milton by this time, however eagerly the matter was discussed.

CHAPTER III.

The History of the Case.

Milton accusers and Milton apologists. Anglesey's memorandum. Ludlow contra Hollingworth and Long. Wagstaffe accuses Milton. Hills's testimonies. Toland's refutation. Birch. Lauder. Later authorities.

During the latter half of the 17th century we now and then hear of the Eikonoklastes, mostly from clerical authors of the royalist party. The reader may be referred to Du Moulin's Regii Sanguinis Clamor ad Coelum adversus Paricidas Anglicanos, The Hague, 1652; L'Estrange's (?) No Blind Guides, London, 1660; Bates's Elenchus Motuum Nuperorum, London, 1660; Robert South's Sermons; Skinner's Motus Compositi, London, 1676; Winstanley's Lives of the English Poets, London, 1687; Hacket's Life of Archbishop Williams, London, 1693, etc. None of these, however, mentions the prayer question. This subject was once more touched upon when Lord Anglesey's well-known memorandum opened the celebrated discussion as to whether the King or bishop Gauden was the author of the Eikon Basilike. Then there was published "A Letter from Major General Ludlow to Sir Edward Seymour comparing the tyranny of the first four years of King Charles the Martyr, with the tyranny of the four years reign of the late abdicated king, Amsterdam, 1691." As a postscript are here given Pamela's prayer and the Eikon Basilike prayer in parallel columns, with a sneer that Charles did not want to govern by precedent but would not pray without it. "Restitution to the Royal Author or a Vindication of King Charles the Martyr's most Excellent Book Intituled Eikon Basilike, May 1691, London, Printed for S. Keble at the Great Turks Head in Fleet str., 8 pp.", was a contribution to the question about the authorship but mentioned our case to the effect that the prayer was grave, pious, and unexceptionable, not made by a heathen woman to a heathen god but by a Christian, and not printed in two or three of the first impressions of the Eikon but inserted later on by the printer for his advantage.

A second and third letter then followed from Ludlow, as he was attacked by the champion for the royal authorship, Richard Hollingworth. In the third letter, "Ludlow No Lyar or a Detection of Dr. Hollingworth's Disingenuety in his Second Defence of King Charles I., Amsterdam, 1692", we now hear the old railings against Charles for using the Pamela Prayer (Preface, pp. XVII, XX). Curiously enough, the author has inserted in his text Milton's own words for half a page without warning the reader. Hollingworth replied with "The Character of King Charles I . . . with a further Defence of the King's Holy Book. To which is Annex'd Some Short Remarks upon a Vile Book call'd Ludlow no Lyar." There we find on pp. 11—12: "Good Reader, there is one thing more to take Notice of, which had almost slipt my Memory, and that is this bold mans triumphing over King Charles I, upon the score of a Prayer taken out of Sir Philip Sidney's Arcadia, made to a Heathen God; and as he impudently assert, made use of by him in the time of his Captivity. Now I must desire thee to observe, the Spight as well as Falsity of this Reflection; for if Dr. Gauden made this whole Book, as Dr. Walker asserts, and the Copy he sent to the King was never returned, nor made use of in any of the Impressions, then the Prayer was put in by Dr. Gauden, and the King noways concerned in it, and consequently it is a Scandal founded in the greatest Malice and ill Will to the Reputation and Vertue of this Great Man; but as I deny, and have fully proved that Dr. Gauden was not the Author of this Book, so I must acquaint thee, that this Prayer, which this man makes himself and his Party so prophanely merry withal, was not printed in the first Edition, by that Copy sent by Mr. Simmonds to the Press, but was foisted in afterwards by some crafty and designing Person, on purpose to expose the Book, and to lessen that deserved Credit and Influence that they found it had amongst, and upon all the wise and considering men of the Kingdom, and therefore I expect to hear no more of this base Story for the time to come, or if they will take the boldness to raise it again, I hope Reader, I have furnished thee with a sufficient Answer to it."

Next year we hear more of this in "Dr. Walker's True, Modest, and Faithful Account of the Author of Eikon Basilike, strictly examined, and Demonstrated to be False, Impudent, and Deceitful," by the Rev. Thomas Long. The author terms Milton "a Compendium of all the Villanies and Impieties of the Age, who had been a profest Enemy to Monarchy, a Pleader . . . against Tithes and the Clergy" (p. 2), "Sacrilegious Milton," "venemous Spider" (p. 3) etc. But the passage which concerns us is found on pp. 59—63 (pagination faulty): "I am loath to defile my hands again by medling with Milton, but I must to stop the foul Mouths of some People whom he hath taught to object, that his Majesty made use of a Prayer made by a Heathen to a false God or Goddess in time of Captivity. To which I answer, 1st, . . ." and then follow reasons to the effect that the prayer was very fit to be used by Christians. "Lastly, This Prayer was not heard of until a considerable time after the King's Death: I have seen his Majesty's Book printed and reprinted, one of which I can produce where there is no Footstep of this Prayer, it might perhaps be found among some other loose Papers of his Majesty, which the Printer for his Benefit, finding how great Esteem the People had of his Majesty's Devotions, clapt in with his Book, as we are wont to bind up the Apocripha with the Canonical Scriptures. This therefore is the Malice of a Rebel, and the Scoff of an Atheist, of one that exceeds the Grand Regicide Bradshaw, who when Mr. Royston told him on his Oath, That he knew no other but that it was the King's Book; Askt him, How he could believe that so ill a Man could make so good a Book?" etc.

Ludlow replied in 1693. "Truth brought to Light: or the Gross Forgeries of Dr. Hollingworth" etc. reads as follows on pp. 7—8: "I grant that the Prayer to Pamela was not in the first Edition of that Book, called The Portraiture of the King, and give you Thanks for your Information; for by it you have removed all the Scruples any one could have of Dr. Gauden's being the Author of it; because the Doctor being as able in Praying as Preaching, an Argument might have been raised, that he needed not to make use of a Prayer to a Heathen Deity; and therefore he could not be thought the Author of that Book; but that Objection is now clearly out of doors. And if this Prayer be found in K. Charles's Works, it will clear those you call his Enemies from being guilty of foisting it in, as you lay it to their Charge: for that Book being printed at so great an Expence, as to make the Price near 3 l. (for I never thought it worth my buying) it cannot be supposed that his Enemies, but his greatest Friends were the Printers of it, and perhaps such as knew the King made use of this Prayer in his private Devotions."

A more interesting passage is found on p. 31: "Now you shall see that I am the bold Man that will raise this Story again about the Arcadian Prayer, and maintain it also, against your impertinent Answer. I agree this Prayer was not in the first Edition of Icon Basilice, but I affirm it was in the second, which Mr. Royston printed; this is a truth which Mr. Milbourn who help'd to print the Book, hath lately owned upon the sight of one of the second Impressions; but that it was foisted in to expose the Book and lessen its credit, is as rashly as confidently asserted; for I will shew you an invincible Evidence of its being used by the King. I have look'd into both the Impressions of the Book called the Works of King Charles the First, in Folio, and find this very Prayer, intituled, a Prayer in time of Captivity, in the 197th Page of the Edition printed Anno 1662, and in the 93d Page of the second Edition. It is the fourth amongst seven Prayers, which have this general Title standing above them, Prayers used by his Majesty in the time of his Troubles and Restraints. To this I add, that Mr. Milton was the first that discover'd and charg'd the Prayer to be stolen, and it was never contradicted till now by you (Doctor) who talk at random, little regarding what you say . . . . and that he (Charles) may appear devout (as Cromwell), he pirates upon Pembroks Arcadia, and steals thence Pamela's Prayer."

Next comes Wagstaffe's "Vindication of King Charles I.", in 1693, 1ˢᵗ edition:

"I know but of one Objection more, and that respects a Prayer added to some Editions of the King's Book, as used by the King, and said to be taken out of a Romance, etc. Now, altho I know no manner of harm in this, and the Objection is plainly peevish and querulous; for why may not a Man use good Expressions in his Prayers, let them be borrowed from whom they will, as well as a good Sentence out of a Heathen Writer, and which was never any Blemish, tho on the most pious Occasions, yet there is great reason to believe, that the King did never make use of it, for that it is not found in the First, nor in several other the most early Editions of this Book. And for the Readers satisfaction in this Point, I have here subjoin'd a Catalogue of the several Editions of it, both without & with the Prayers, Collected with great Care and Industry, by Mr. Keeble at the Turks-Head in Fleet-street; & for preventing any Mistake, he hath with great Exactness given the Size of each Volume, the Time of Printing, the Number of the Pages that Contents consist of, the Number of the Pages of the Book it self, when there were any such. And in which it is observable, that there are no less than Twenty six Editions without the Prayers, and Sixteen of them Printed 1648" (p. 44).

In 1697 the 2ⁿᵈed. added: "But since the first edition of this Vindication, I have receiv'd full and convincing Information concerning the Mystery of this Prayer that it was an Artifice of Bradshaw, or Milton or Both, and by them surreptitiously thrust into the King's Works, to discredit the whole. This Information comes originally from Mr. Hill the Printer, but convey'd by two very worthy Gentlemen, and against whom there can be no possible Exception; Dr. Gill and Dr. Bernard, who both were Phisitians to him, and very intimate with him and because their Testimony is so very important the Reader shall have it in their own words, from a Letter of Dr. Gill to the Honorable Charles Hatton Esq.; at the End of which is added, the testimony of Dr. Bernard, and which I have now in my Custody. And is as follows verbatim:

May 1ˢᵗ 1694.

Sir,

I most readily comply with your Request in informing you from whom I heard what I was saying (the last time I had the honour to be in your Company). That I was told Pamela's Prayer, was transferr'd out of Sir Philip Sidney's Arcadia into Ἐικὼν Βασιλική by a contrivance of Bradshaw's and Milton's. Sir I make no secret of it, and I frankly tell you my Author, who was Mr. Henry Hill Oliver's Printer, and the occasion, as he many years

ago told me, was this, Mr. Dugard, who was Milton's intimate
Friend, happen'd to be taken printing an Edition of the King's
Book; Milton used his interest to bring him off, which he effected
by the means of Bradshaw, but upon this Condition that Dugard
should add Pamela's Prayer to the aforesaid Books he was printing,
as an attonement for his fault, they designing thereby to bring a
scandall upon the Book, and blast the Reputation of its Author,
pursuant to which design they industriously took care afterwards
as soon as published to have it taken notice off. Mr. Hill hath
affirm'd this to me several times of his own knowledge, and I
need not tell you how easy it was for him to know it, who being
a forward, and confiding man was in most of the intrigues of that
time, and intrusted with business of the greatest privacy by the
then governing Partys, and no man, that I have met with was
better vers't in the Secret History of that time than himself, as I
have found by the often discourse I had with him, for being his
Phisitian for several years, I had many opportunities to talk with
him about those affairs, from whom I have received a different
account of the transactions of those times, than what was commonly known or made Publick, and many passages that I was a
stranger to before. Thus Sir I have given you my Authority, for
what I said, which if you please, you may communicate to the
Rest of our Friends and beleive me alwaies

Your most humble Servant
Tho. Gill

I do remember very well that Mr. Henry Hills the Printer
told me that he had heard Bradshaw and Milton laugh at their
inserting a Prayer out of Sir Philip Sidney's Arcadia at the end
of King Charles's his book and then Milton had jeer'd it in his
answer, adding withall that they were men would stick at nothing
that might gain their point and this I testifie.

May 10th 1694.

Francis Bernard" (pp. 50—51).

In reply to this statement Mr. Toland, though merely repeating
Milton's charge when writing the Life of Milton prefixed to the edition
of his Prose Works in 1698 (cf. vol. I, p. 27; and vol. II, p. 527,
where Pamela's prayer and the Eikon Basilike prayer are printed
in parallel columns; also an anonymous tract: "Defence of the
Parliament of 1640 and the People of England against King Charles I
and his Adherents," London, 1698, pp. 15—17), took up the
question in Amyntor, in 1699: "That nothing may be wanting I
shall in the last place consider what is objected to the Prayer us'd
by the King as his own in the time of his Captivity; but is, with
very small Variation, the same that is said by Pamela to a Heathen
Deity in Sir Philip Sydney's Arcadia. This Discovery, as we said
before, was first made by Milton in his Iconoclastes. But Dr. Gill

affirms, "That his Patient Henry Hill the Printer said it was put in by a Contrivance of Milton, who, catching his Friend Mr. Du Gard printing an Edition of Icon Basilike, got his Pardon by Bradshaw's Interest, on Condition he would insert Pamela's Prayer to bring Discredit on the Book and the Author of it. I wonder at the Easiness of Dr. Gill and Dr. Bernard to believe so gross a Fable, when it does not appear that Du Gard, who was Printer to the Parliament, ever printed this Book, and that the Prayer is in the second Edition publish'd by Mr. Royston, whose Evidence is alledg'd to prove the Genuinness of the Book. And if the King's Friends thought it not his own, what made them print it in the first Impression of his Works in Folio, by Royston in 62, when Milton could not tamper with the Press? Or why did they let it pass in the last Impression in Folio by Mr. Chiswel in the Year 86, when all the world knew that it was long before expos'd in Iconoclastes? After this I need not go about to shew that Dr. Gill had no Reason for the great Opinion he entertained of Henry Hill, and how little he consulted his own Reputation by asserting that no Man was better vers'd in the secret History of those times; that he was intrusted with Intrigues by the great ones of that Government, who, as all the World knows, manag'd their Affairs after another rate. Nor will I insist upon his turning Papist in King James's time to becom his Printer, as he was Oliver's before, or any other Circumstance to lessen his Credit, since it appears that what he averr'd is inconsistent with matter of Fact, Mr. Royston, and not Du Gard, having publish'd the Celebrated Prayer" (pp. 153—55).

The same year Wagstaffe answered Amyntor's reasonings. "A Defence of the Vindication of K. Charles the Martyr; etc., in Answer to A Late Pamphlet intituled Amyntor" reads as follows on pp. 93—94: "Lastly, our Author speaks to Pamela's Prayer, hath recited it at large, and takes abundance of pains to prove that it was really used by the King, which from him is the pleasantest thing in the world: He hath all along been indeavouring to prove the whole Book a forgery, and father'd upon the King, and why not the Prayer too? why is not the Prayer Dr. Gauden's, as well as the Book? And his reason for this makes it yet more pleasant, which is that Mr. Royston printed it: Why Mr. Royston printed the whole Book, and moreover affirms that it was brought to him from the King (which is more than ever was said of the Prayer) and if Mr. Royston's printing and attesting, are not sufficient to prove the Book genuine, how comes his bare printing without any farther circumstance, to be such an extraordinary proof for the use of the Prayer? This is very righteous dealing, and our Author shewes his justice, when any thing will pass to prove what he thinks reflects on the King's memory, and yet the very same proofs, and a hundred times more strong and pregnant, must be all insufficient to prove what makes for his Honour. And what-

ever our Author thinks, this is a very severe reflection on his
proceedings, and plainly shews that he disputes with a byass,
and there is corruption at the bottom; for there is nothing more
shameless and immodest, as well as irrational, to insist with assurance on those very proofs which he denies to his Adversaries.
In the mean time, that this Prayer was a forgery, and a forgery
of his friend Milton too, I had prov'd beyond exception, by a
testimony from Mr. Hill the Printer, "Who told Dr. Gill and
Dr. Bernard that it was inserted by the contrivance of Milton
and Bradshaw, to bring a scandal on the Book, and blast the
reputation of its Author; and the occasion was, that Mr. Dugard,
Milton's intimate Friend, being taken printing an Edition of the
King's Book, Milton got him off, by Bradshaw's interest, on
condition that he should add Pamela's Prayer to the Book."
This our Author calls a gross fable; and the reason is, when
it does not appear that Dugard, who was Printer to the Parliament, ever printed this Book. Does not appear, i. e. does not
appear to him; and it is very bold to call this a gross fable,
because he does not know whether Mr. Dugard printed the Book
or not. Does he think his ignorance of a matter is sufficient to
make it a gross fable? at this rate we are like to have a pure
History of the Canon, when every thing he is ignorant of, must
be a gross forgery; and we shall have spurious Authors enow, if
his ignorance be sufficient to give them that Title. However, whether our Author knows it or not, it is certain that Mr. Dugard printed
this Book, and was catch'd printing of it too; and I have now
before me an information of Mr. Hooker, given March 30. 91.
wherein he affirms that he (the said Mr. Hooker) was Corrector to
Mr. Dugard's Press in 48; that Icon Basilike was printed at that
Press, with the corrections of Mr. Hooker; that Mr. Dugard being
known, was thrown into prison, and turn'd out of his place of
Merchant Taylor's School, and that Mr. Hooker to save himself
went to travel for several years. And what now does he think of
his "does not appear?" if he did not know it before, I hope now
it appears sufficiently, not only that Mr. Dugard printed it, but
was like to be ruin'd for it; and Mr. Hill tells us how he escaped
the danger, and came into favour again, and was restor'd to the
School, even by performing an honest piece of work for Mr. Milton,
and claping in Pamela's Prayer into the King's Book, to discredit
the whole. And in the next Edition of John Milton's Life, our
Author, if he please, may add this as one of his Master-pieces."

No reply followed this time, probably owing more to the
political aspects of the period than to the acuteness of Milton's
accusers. A 3rd ed., however, of the Vindication was published by
Wagstaffe in 1711, the principal cause being a passage in the 2nd ed.
of Bayle's Dictionnaire historique et critique, 1702 (q. v. pp. 2116
—2118, and notes). Beyond the matter adduced in the previous
editions we note the following additions: a letter from Dr. Bernard

to Dr. Goodall: "Concerning the Prayer out of Sir Philip Sidney, (which Milton makes a great bustle about) I remember Henry Hills (who was Oliver's Printer, and my Patient) told me among other things, of the Artifice of that Party; that he had heard Bradshaw and Milton laugh how they had put the Cheat upon the World; and in order thereunto, had printed the whole Book anew, that they might add that Prayer thereunto; and that they were not more studious of any thing, than to rob that Good King of the Reputation of that Book. I doubt not, but Dr. Gill can remember something to this purpose from the same Hen. Hills. I am.

Your most assured humble Servant,
Francis Bernard.

March 13. 1693."

Further: "It does not anywhere appear, that Sir Philip Sidney's Arcadia was a Book that the King used to read, or delight in . . . (witness) Sir Thomas Herbert, who waited on the King from the time of his Imprisonment at Holdenby to his Death; who had the Charge of the King's Books, and gives a particular Account of what Books the King read, either in his Serious Studies, or for Divertisement, and alleviating his Spirits. And he mentions the Sacred Scriptures, Bishop Andrews's Sermons, Hooker's Ecclesiastical Polity, Dr. Hammond's Works, Villalpandus upon Ezekiel, Sandys's Paraphrase, Herbert's Poems; and among the less Serious, Godfrey of Bulloigne; Torquato Tasso, Englished by Mr. Fairfax; Ariosto, by Sir John Harrington; and Spencer's Fairy-Queen. And these are all he mentions, but not the least Syllable, nor Intimation of Pembroke's Arcadia, which Book had the King often used, or delighted much in the reading of it, to be sure he never would have omitted it; for it was as considerable in its kind, and deserv'd as much Commendation, as those other Facetious Authors, that he did mention; and his pretermitting it, is a good Argument that the King did not make use of it, and had it not by him to read, if he had been at any time so disposed. But on the other side, it is plain enough that Milton was very well acquainted with it, that he had spent much time in reading it, and that the Book was very familiar to him; and tho' he comes infinitely short of that Noble Author, in the cleanness and sprightliness of his Wit, and Expression, yet any Man, who is acquainted with both, will easily see, that he proposed to himself this very Book as a Pattern, to mend his Stile and Invention; But then he was of too foul, gross and sowr a Complexion; Sir Philip Sidney was the most accomplish'd Gentleman of his Age; and what came from his Pen was like himself, very fine, candid, generous, pleasant, and easy; but in Milton's Mouth, it is turn'd into Poison, and runs into fulsom, nasty, and opprobrious Language; he aims at the same Wit, but corrupts it, and it stinks of the Wessel. However, it is evident that he had read the Arcadia over and over; again if there was no other Reason, this before us is sufficient to shew how familiar he was with it, and how well vers'd in all Parts of it, he could it seems find out Pamela's Prayer immediately; it was no sooner printed, but he lays his Hands on it, hits the Blot presently, and falls a bawling as loud as he could, of stealing, forging, unhallowing, and unchristening; and I cannot tell what. But if it was in his Account, a thing so ungodly and wicked, only to use it; What must it be to invent it, to forge it, to steal it into the Kings Book, and then impudently to rail upon him, for that which was only the Work of Milton's own Hands? this is Iniquity multiplied, Lye upon Lye, Forgery upon Forgery, and one degree of Villany superadded to another, that it exceeds the Audaciousness ev'n of Hell it self . . . And it is not the least remarkable, that Milton must have compos'd his Scorn and Raillery upon this Prayer, even before any of the Prayers were Printed and Published. For Miltons Answer came out 1649, and I have now a Book by me of that Edition, on the Title-Page of which is this Manuscript Note (It came not out till this Nov. 7.) And what Milton saith about this Prayer, is in Chap. 1. of his Answer, and makes no small part of that Chapter; and then allowing a moderate time for his Composing the rest, and for the Printing and Publishing the whole; and it will appear pretty plain, that he must have finish'd all his invectives about this Prayer, some time before the Prayer itself was printed; for none of the Prayers were Printed in any of the seventeen first Impressions; and it was but 9 Months after the King's Murder that Milton's Book came out: And 'tis probable enough, that he caused the Prayers to be printed in the interim, and got them published, that they might be ready, and just fit for his Purpose, to play his Pranks upon. And to this I add: 2. It deserves Inquiry, Who it was that caused these Prayers to be printed, or, by whose hand they were conveyed to the Press? All the Prints that I have seen, which give any Account of them, only say, they were deliver'd by the King into the Hands of Dr. Juxon Bishop of London, at his Death; And this Milton himself confirms, As immediately (says he) before his Death, to popp into the Hand of that grave Bishop who attended him, as a special Relic of his Saintly Exercises, a Prayer stollen, word for word & c. Now from hence it will appear plainly and undeniably, that that Party, and they only, were the Persons who conveyed the Prayers to the Press, and caused them to be Printed; and for what purpose, let any Man judge: to be sure, not to do any Justice, or Honour to the King, or service to his Memory, but for their own villanous Designs. For what Papers soever the King might deliver to Bishop Juxon, it is most certain he could Print none of them, nor yet keep them to himself. For the Regicides immediatly laid Hands on him, and Imprison'd him, Examin'd him with all the Rigor and Severity imaginable. What the King said to him, and what was the meaning of the King's Words to him on the Scaffold: and not only so, but search'd him narrowly for all Papers that he might have from the King, and ev'n to Scraps and Parcels; and moreover rifled all the King's Cloaths, Scrutores, Cabinets and Boxes, and whatever they found, they kept in their own hands. But it is more proper to give Account of this in the Words of the Persons themselves, who have recorded it; which will both explain the Case, and confirm the Truth of it. (Follow citations from Regii Sanguinis Clamor, Sanderson's History, Bates's Elenchus, Perinchief's Life) ... Here is enough to satisfy any Man, that it was utterly impossible for Bishop Juxon, or any Person from him, or indeed any of the Royal Party, to transmit these Prayers to the Press; or any other Papers which the King deliver'd to Bishop Juxon, or left behind him in his Pockets, or any where else, within the compass of their Power. For they were all taken, and never, (like those at Naseby) restor'd again, but all was kept in their own custody. The Conclusion is this: That after that time whatever was printed, must come from themselves; and if any of the Papers that the King deliver'd to Bishop Juxon at his death, were made publick, they are the Persons who were the Publishers, and no others. Because no other Persons had them in their Power, but themselves. And there is no doubt, but that Milton himself first brought these Prayers, and got them printed at Dugard's Press, and from thence they were quickly translated to Mr. Royston's; for every little Addition having the King's Name to it, quickened the Sale, and made all Booksellers, so soon as they had notice of it, add the Prayers to their own Editions, supposing them all genuine, not being conscious of Milton's Forgery; but however, very instrumental, tho' innocently, to spread and propagate it. 'Tis very probable, that some of these Prayers were such as were used and penn'd by the King. For it had been ridiculous and impolitick, to have counterfeited four Prayers, when it was one only they had to play upon, and they suffer'd those that were genuine to pass, to give Countenance to the other: And Milton having them in his Hands, he added this of his own coining to the rest, to discredit the whole, and to supply himself with Matter to burlesque the Book, and to abuse the King. And I have a very good Evidence, that the King left but three Prayers behind him, and deliver'd to Bishop Juxon no more but Three Prayers, the Fourth, that is Pamela's was of their own framing. It is the Testimony of the same Gentlewoman, the Daughter of Sir Ralph Whitfield (whom I have mention'd before) in these Words: And farther she says, that within two Days after the King's Death, she saw in a Spanish-Leather-Case three of those Prayers that are printed in some, if not in all the Editions of that Book, which were said to be used by him in the time of his Restreint, and delivered to the Bishop of London at his Death; from whom they were taken away by the Officers of the Army; and it was from one of those Officers in whose custody they then were, that she had the Favour o see them; and that the Person who shew'd her those Prayers, shewed her also the George with the Queen's Picture in it, and wo Seals, which were the King's. This farther confirms the Truth, hat the Prayers were only in their Custody; and moreover, that he Number of those Prayers were but Three, the Fourth is their own; and Milton vouchsafed to Print the other three, for the sake of the fourth; and he was contented the World should see some of the King's Prayers; provided he might add one more, to disparage all the rest. And I believe any Man who will impartially consider and compare the Prayers, will find enough in the Prayers themselves to detect the Forgery. Let him in particular compare together the First and the last; the first is Pamela's Prayer, and by Milton called, A Prayer in time of Captivity; the last hath , Title, A Prayer in time of imminent Danger; let him, I say, compare both these together, and he will soon see that the sub-ect Matter, and Drift, and Intention of the Words is all the ame, but the latter is by many degrees more suitable to the King's Circumstances at that time, much more affecting his pre-ent State, representing his Condition in such pious and ardent Groans, as plainly arise from a Soul under the sense and feeling of those present Miseries which encompassed him round about. n short, there is nothing at all prayed or, petition'd for, in he Words of Pamela's Prayer, but what is also in the other; only in the latter the Expressions are more devout and ardent, nore accomodated to the King's Case, more express and parti-ular; more the Language of a devout and humble Heart, un-er the quick sense of a terrible and devouring Calamity; and n one word, by many degrees more adapted to the King's Use nd present Occasions; and I will leave it with any Man, whether e can think it probable, that the King could borrow Expressions rom a Romance, or from any other Book (besides the Scriptures) o cloath his Thoughts with; and for those very Things and Ends, or which he had already compos'd a Prayer, by many degrees, nd more particularly suited to his Necessities, and far more patheti-ally expressing the Sentiments of his Heart.

I have yet to add to this, that King Charles II. had so little Opinion of the Prayers added to this Book, that when Royston sked his Leave for the Reprinting it in 1680, he gave him leave, ut expressly order'd he should leave out those additional Prayers. And it is to be observed, that this was five Years after the pre-ended Memorandum. And it seems King Charles was then satisfied he Book was his Fathers, and he took so much Care of it, as to hrow out what he suspected might be supposititious. This I had rom Mr. Norton, who was Mr. Royston's Printer, and I have it et by me attested, under his Hand, Aug. 8. 1693, in these Words: find in my Book, March 15. 1680, I received from Mr. Royston parcel of Paper in order to Print the King's Meditations, about which time I had several conferences with him; he said he would not Print it, until he had the King's leave; some few Days after he had his Majesty's leave to print it, but without any Additions of Prayers; and which Mr. Royston liked very well, for he feared whilst he absconded, his Servants had some Tricks put upon them in the Additional Prayers, tho' he could not say certainly that he who brought it to his Servants, was sent by Mr. Milton, but he much suspected it. Mr. Norton adds, That Mrs Royston can tell, that her Husband, by the Men then in Power, had great Sums of Money offer'd him, if he would say that the King was not the Author of that Book, and that he himself (Mr. Norton) had often heard him say the same." (pp. 118—123.)

In this state the case was taken up by one of the ablest scholars of 18th century England. In his first edition of Milton's Prose Works, in 1738, Dr. Birch wrote an appendix to his Life of Milton, prefixed to this edition, the first part of which appendix was dedicated to an inquiry into the authorship of the Eikon Basilike and the prayer mystery. As the book, unlike those previously quoted, is accessible even out of England, full extracts are no longer needed. Birch first gives the two prayers in parallel columns, then Milton's words in his Eikonoklastes, 1st ed., further those of the Eikon Aklastos. Then follow Wagstaffe's account with the letters from Gill and Bernard, of May 1st, 1694, and March 13th, 1693; Hooker's story, Wagstaffe's reasonings as to the improbability of the King's favouring Arcadia, the necessity of the prayers being published by the regicides, Mrs. Fotherly's relation, and Mr. Norton's testimony. (A Complete Collection of the Historical, Political, and Miscellaneous Works of John Milton, vol. I, pp. LXXVIII—LXXXIII).

When re-editing Milton's Prose Works in 1753—54, Birch omitted the appendix and but briefly mentioned the prayer question in the "Life": "In the course of the controversy about the book, Milton's charge upon the King of borrowing the prayer of Pamela from Sir Philip Sidney's Arcadia, inserted in some editions of the Εικων, was retorted upon himself, as if this prayer had been added by his contrivance who, in conjunction with serjeant Bradshaw, had prevailed upon Du Gard to insert it, in order to cast a disgrace upon the King and blast the reputation of the Icon. This supposed fact was advanced chiefly upon the authority of Henry Hills the printer, who had frequently asserted it to Dr. Gill and Dr. Bernard, his physicians, as they testified. But Hills was not himself the printer who was dealt with in this manner; and consequently he could have the story only from hearsay; and though he was Cromwell's printer, yet afterwards he turned papist in the reign of James IId in order to be that king's printer; and it was at that time he used to relate this story. Besides which, it is highly improbable that Milton and Bradshaw should make him their confident unnecessarily in such an affair, and laugh in his presence at their imposing such a cheat upon the world; or that he should conceal it during the life of the former, who survived the restoration so many years".

This is somewhat surprising, as the appendix of the 1st ed. seemed to imply that the editor believed in Hills's words. Johnson thought so, at least. And, in fact, Birch's correspondence with Warburton is to this effect.

As Birch brought forth no additional proofs, I think the matter must be explained by the fact that Lauder's attack on Milton[1]) and the scandals connected with it determined Birch to have no more to do with any affairs of Milton's which were not finally proved, the more so as Birch himself was exposed to the fury of Lauder, who ended by accusing Milton on account of the present case. "King Charles I, Vindicated From the Charge of Plagiarism, Brought against him by Milton, and Milton himself convicted of Forgery and a gross Imposition on the Public", London, 1754, added nothing to Birch's appendix except opprobrious language.

The history of the case from this time down to the present day may be told in a few words. In addition to the matter given in this introduction, I shortly refer to Nichols's Literary Anecdotes I, p. 526; Todd's edition of Milton's Poetical Works, in 1801, vol. I, pp. LXXIV—LXXV, 273; Wordsworth's Letter to the Archbishop of Canterbury I, p. 139 n., and Stern's Milton und seine Zeit, all of them insignificant repetitions of previous relations.

---

[1]) Gentleman's Magazine 1747, pp. 24—7, 58, 67—8, 82—6, 189—91, 211 —2, 278—9, 285—6, 312—4, 322—4, 363—6, 423—4, 530—1; 1748, pp. 67—8, 114.

CHAPTER IV.

Early History of the Prayers.

Origin of the prayers. Charles and Juxon before the execution. The scaffold scene according to contemporary narratives. Juxon after the execution. The fate of the King's property. Thomlinson, the prayers, the seals, and the George. The sale. Charles II. and the George.

At the outset of the investigation naturally occurs the question whether the King really composed and left any prayers or not. Now, it was a common custom at the time to draw up forms of prayers on special occasions. Charles did so himself e. g. at the treaty of Newport, which prayer was printed by Royston in the autumn of 1648. Other prayers were made by him and printed after his victory over Essex in Cornwall and at the treaty of Uxbridge [1]). It was quite natural, then, that he should compose some prayers during his last days.

Another case in point is the following. The most popular devotional manual of the 17th century was the *Practise of Piety*. Entered on the Stationers' Registers Jan. 11th, 1612, the 3rd edition followed in 1613, the 6th in 1615, the 11th in 1619, the 20th in 1627, etc. Few books at the time could produce such an imposing number of editions. The author was Lewis Bayly (1565—1631), domestic chaplain to Henry, Prince of Wales, (who died in 1612) and afterwards preceptor to Charles, with whom we find him in correspondence as late as April 7th, 1630 [2]). It was quite natural that Charles should take his daily Morning and Evening Prayer out of this most popular work by his preceptor. In 1862, Mr. John Bruce, when summarizing the Domestic Correspondence of the years 1631—1633 in the Public Record Office, found a paper written in the hand of Charles I., endorsed by him, *A Prayer,* and, by another hand, *Lent Preachers, 1631,* as if it had been written upon the blank half-sheet of a list of Lent preachers at Court [3]). This was mainly a copy of the first daily Morning Prayer in the *Practise of Piety,* which in this way we

---

[1]) Published in Mercurius Rusticus.
[2]) The Bibliographer 1883, p. 63 ff.
[3]) Calendar of State Papers 1862; The Antiquary, May 1880.

know that the King favoured. Now, among the prayers said to have been delivered to Juxon the above daily one, evidentially used by Charles, is found, which speaks in favour of their really being left by him as commonly believed [1]).

Finally, two of the prayers contain apt allusions to Charles's personal affairs.

The King's leaving prayers granted, their history must be traced as far as possible. In order to get a positive result out of the tangle of partial and confused relations of the case it seems necessary to proceed as far as possible according to chronology. As the prayers were unanimously declared to be delivered by the King to Juxon either on the scaffold or else immediately before his death, attention must be paid to the then circumstances of both.

The opening session of the trial of Charles was on Jan. 20th. During the week of the proceedings he was lodged in the house of Sir Robert Cotton, in Old Palace Yard. Here he evidently asked for Juxon at once, as we read in the Commons' Journals: —

"Die Sabbati, 20° Januarii, 1648.

. . . Ordered, That Dr. Juxon have Leave to repair to the King, According to the King's Desire: And that the said Dr. Juxon do continue there so long as the King shall require him; but shall not be permitted to go to-and-fro, but continually to abide with the King."

In spite of this order the bishop was not yet admitted to Charles, whence a fresh permission was issued a week later which finally procured Juxon access on the above conditions that he was to remain confined with the prisoner [2]).

"Die Sabbati, 27° Januarii, 1648.

. . . Ordered, That Dr. Juxon have Leave to go to, and continue with, the King in private, under the same Restraint that the King is."

Sir Philip Warwick tells us that this order was not executed till Sunday evening. (Mem., London 1707, p. 340).

Some few visits were allowed, e. g. the Prince Elector's.

---

[1]) The identity of this prayer was naturally discovered at once on account of the popularity of the "Practise." As it had evidently become known in some quarters that Charles left three prayers only (see infra), and the interpolation of the Pamela Prayer was not as yet detected, someone, unconscious of the above proofs that Charles had written down the "Practise" prayer, caused the printer to put in the following note on the last page of the Eikon appendix, 6th impression: —

"The second of the foure Prayers under the Title of [Another Prayer] pag. 4 & 5 though it be here set down according to other printed Copies, was yet none of His Majesties, (but composed by some body out of the first Morning Prayer, and one other in the Practice of Piety) there being indeed but three left by His Majesty. Of which the Reader to prevent his mistake is desired to take notice."

[2]) Differently Herbert. His account of the trial may be seen in Guizot, Coll. IV, pp. 115—52. My narrative is based upon C. J., Whitelocke's Mem., Cobbett-Howell's State Trials, and contemporary tracts and broadsides.

"Die Sabbati, 20° Januarii, 1648.

. . . Ordered, That the Prince Elector shall have Liberty, in the Presence of the Guards, to go and visit the King."

Charles refused to see him, but a week later the King's children got similar permission.

"Die Sabbati, 27° Januarii, 1648.

. . . Ordered That the Duke of Gloucester, and the Lady Elizabeth, have Liberty to visit the King."

On the same day the death-sentence had been read to him, and he was removed to Whitehall, and thence to St. James's on Sunday evening, in order that he might not be disturbed by the men that were building his scaffold before Whitehall. Next day, Monday 29th, his children came to see him according to the above permission. For reasons that will appear later, Whitelocke's relation is preferred : —

"The King's children came from Sion-House to visit him at St. James's, he took the Princess in his Arms, and kissed her and gave her two Seals with Diamonds, and prayed for the Blessing of God upon her, and the rest of his Children and there was great weeping." (Memorials, London 1732, p. 374).

After his sentence the King was attended by Juxon, Herbert, and Colonel Thomlinson (who had had charge of the King by order of Parliament till the sentence, and now remained about him at Charles's special request, the King having learnt to estimate the Colonel's sympathetic character); and finally Colonel Hacker, who was to execute the death warrant. Together with these the King walked from St. James's to Whitehall on Tuesday, the 30th January, about ten o'clock in the morning. When he arrived there, the carpenters were not yet ready. In the mean time he retired into the Banqueting House, whence he stepped out on the scaffold about two o'clock. As the following scene bears intimately upon our subject it has been thought necessary to give several representative, contemporary relations. First one that appeared in the King's Collected Works after his death : —

"Because we have no other Relation of what His Majesty then spoke, save what His Enemies have set forth, nor had his Majesty any Copy (being surprized and hastened by those that thirsted after His blood), save onely a few Heads in a little Scrip of Paper, which the Souldiers took from the Bishop of London, to whom He gave it; therefore the Reader must be content with this Copy which they have published (som few words being altered to make the sence perfect, which either wilfully, or by mistake of the Writer or Printer were perverted).

The King being come upon the Scaffold, and looking about him upon the people, who were kept off by Troops of Horse, so that they could not come near to hear Him, omitted what he had purposed to have spoken to them (as tis thought) and turning himself to the Souldiers and Officers (the Instruments of the Regicide) spoke to them to this effect."

(Follows the King's speech)

"Then the King, after some short and fervent ejaculations in private, with hand and eyes lift up to Heaven; immediately stooping down, laid His neck upon the Block: And then the Wretch appointed to give the fatal blow putting His hair under His Cap, the King said, Stay for the Signe.

And after a very little pause, stretching forth His hands, The Villain at one blow, severed His Head from His Body."

(Reliquiæ Sacræ Carolinæ, The Hague, 1650, Samuel Browne, pp. 340—45).

One of the followers of the Dutch ambassadors just arrived to prevent the execution had himself witnessed the scene and gives the following account: —

"De Coninck quam met sulcken couraghe op het Schavot, dat ick hem verscheyden mael hebbe sien lacchen: hy maeckte vele van sijne Cleederen selve los, en heeft zijn Hooft goetwilligh nedergeleyt op het Block, sprack niet tot het volck, maer alleene tot die geene die by hem stonden op het Schavot, waer van de exempelen nu opgedragen sullen werden. Sijn Majesteyt gaf sijn St. George, die hy om den hals hadde, met sijn Hantschoenen, Hoet en Stockjen dat hy inde hant hadde, aen Docter Juxter, Bisschop van Londen, die de Nacht over by de Coninck geweest is, en hem het Sacrament hadde toegedeylt. En dewijle men vermoet dat den gemelden Bisschop veel secrete dingen vanden Coninc int heymelic verstaen heeft, so west dien ouden Man met Soldaten bewaert, dat hy by geen menschen mach komen om yets te ontdekken . . ."

(Copye van eenen Brieff verhalende ghetrouwelijck het gene in het Ombrengen van den Groot-Machtigen Coninck van Groot-Brittannien Charles Stuwaert gepassert is Geschreven wt het Huys van de Heeren Nederlandsche Ambassadeurs door een Persoon die de Executie heeft gesien).

Other foreign relations, which in these passionate days of national party conflict are often preferable to English ones, have mostly been rejected. The French, Italian, and German versions are rather fanciful and uncritical. In this case, as not seldom at the time, the Polish account offers special interest as well in respect of trustworthiness as of details. Only the part that approaches the present subject is given.

". . . and having taken off the cloak and removed the royal order of St. George from his neck, he handed them to Dr. Juxon saying [1]: — "Remember what I told you!" Then he took off the jacket and, remaining in his nether garments, he again donned his cloak. Looking at the block he asked the hangman if it stood firmly?

---

[1] A contemporary sketch of the scene represents Juxon holding these things.

He answered, "Firmly enough, Your Majesty." Again the King (said). "It ought to be higher [1])." The hangman: "For the present it cannot be higher." The King: "When I stretch out my hand dispatch what you must do." Standing, the King then pronounced two or three words in a low voice, and having raised hands and eyes towards heaven he bowed down his head, laying it on the block (and) said to the hangman: "Wait till I give you the sign." The hangman answered: "I will do so." Swiftly then the King stretched out his hand, and the hangman at a single stroke severed his neck and, lifting up the head, showed it to the people [2])."

Contemporary history is rather irrelevant to the present matter, contrary to expectation. Fuller's Works, however, offer an exception inasmuch as the deliverance of some papers is at least mentioned.

"His Majesty held in his hand a small piece of paper, some four inches square, containing heads whereon in his speech he intended to dilate; and a tall soldier, looking over the King's shoulders, read it as the King held it in his hand. As for the speech, which passeth in print for the king's though taken in shorthand by one eminent therein, it is done so defectively, it deserveth not to be accounted his speech by the testimony of such as heard it. His speech ended, he gave that small paper to the bishop of London. After his death, the officers demanded

---

[1]) The mention of this particular testifies to the fidelity of the account. We recall the recent controversy.

[2]) I here somewhat hesitatingly offer the Polish text. I have made no attempts at modernising forms, such as "potym", "szyie", adding diacritic marks, or altering spellings, as in "zdjąć", "oglądać", "prędko", "Krol", "bydź", "vczynię", "ći", "á", etc.

". . . y zdiawszy Płaszcz z siebie y od szyie noszenie Krolewskie Jerzego S. oddał Doktorowi Juxtonowi mowiac: Zátrzymaycie iakom wam rzekł. Potym Kabat z siebie zdiał à w spodniey sukni zostawszy Płaszcz z nowu ná się wźiał. Pniak ogladáiac spytał Kátá ieżli mocno stoi? Odpowiedźiał dosyć mocno Mśći. Jáśnieyszy Krolu. Znowu Krol: Zszedłby się wyższy. Kát: Ná ten czás wyższy bydź nie może. Krol: Kiedy rękę wyciagne odpraw co masz czynić. Stoiac zátym Krol, dwie álbo trzy słowá ćicho wyrzekł ręce y oczy ku Niebu podniozszy zchylił głowę ná pniak kładac do Kátá mowił: Poczekay áż ći znák dam. Odpowiedźiał Kát: Ták vczynię. Predko potym wyciagnał rękę Krol, á Kát iednym ćięćiem szyię mu vciał y głowę podniozszy pokazał Ludowi. (Opisanie Krotkie Niesłycháných Dźieiow w Angliey z Krolem Brytániey Wielkiey, Karolem I. Jáko od Woyská swego, y Párlámentu obwiniony, oskárżony, Sadzony, Dekretowany, y ná śmierć wskazány iest W Krakowie 1651).

the paper of the bishop; who, because of the depth of his pocket, smallness of that paper, and the mixture of others therewith, could not so soon produce it as was required. At last he brought it forth; but therewith the others were unsatisfied, (jealousy is quick of growth) as not the same which his Majesty delivered unto him; when presently the soldier, whose rudeness (the bad cause of a good effect) had formerly overinspected it in the King's hand, attested this the very same paper, and prevented further suspicions which might have terminated to the bishop's trouble." (Fuller, Church History III, 3rd ed., p. 501).

The result of these documents is negative in respect of our purpose. It seems most reasonable that the King delivered the prayers to Juxon along with other papers at Whitehall or St. James's on some of the previous days. In any case it becomes necessary to trace the steps of the bishop.

The day after the King's death he was released by order of Parliament.

"Die Mercurii, 31° Januarii, 1648.
. . . Ordered, That Dr. Juxon be discharged from any Restraint, by any former Order of this House."

Before his release, however, he was strictly examined and everything taken from him, as may be inferred from the above Dutch narrative and Perrinchief's Life: — "Besides this they take care to suppress all those more Lively figures of Him and most lasting Statues, His Writings, and therefore force from my Lord of London, whom they kept prisoner, all those Papers His Majesty had delivered to him, and make a most narrow search of his Cloathes and Cabinets, lest any of those Monuments of Piety and Wisdom should escape to the Benefit of Mankind," (Perrinchief, Life and Death of King Charles, 3rd ed., p. 225).

Further corroborative evidence of this we find in the Journals of the House of Commons on the day after the execution. There we gather that the Lady Elizabeth, too, had been searched and deprived of her two seals after her visit to the King as related by Whitelocke; and that the George, delivered to Juxon on the scaffold as we have witnessed, was in the hands of the revolutionaries, together with the *King's Papers*.

"Die Mercurii, 31° Januarii, 1648.
. . . Commissary General Ireton reports a Paper of divers Particulars touching the late King's Body, his George, his Diamond and Two Seals.

The Question being put, That the Diamond be sent to Charles Stuart, Son of the late King, commonly called Prince of Wales;
It passed with the Negative.
The Question being put, That the Garter be sent to him;
It passed with the Negative.

The Question being put, That the George be sent to him; It passed with the Negative.

The Question beeing put, That the seals be sent to him; It passed with the Negative.

Colonel Harrison, Sir John Danvers, Sir Michael Liversey, Mr. Scott, Lord Grey, Mr. Holland, Mr. Allen, Mr. Edwards, Mr. Oldesworth, Mr. Trenchard, Mr. Price, Mr. Love, Colonel Fleetwood, or any Three of them, are to consider of the Particulars presented, concerning the King's Body, and other Things contained in that Paper, presented by Commissionary General Ireton; and also to peruse the Papers of the late King, and make Report to this House, What they think fit to be done therein; And this Committee is to meet in the Queen's Court, Tomorrow at Two of the Clock in the Afternoon; and Mr Marten is to take care of it."

The question now arises who had taken the things from the Princess and from Juxon. If we turn to the previously cited account of Mrs. Fotherly, the details of which excellently tally with the preceding, we learn that it was an officer of the army.

"Mrs. Fotherly of Rickmansworth, daughter of Sir Ralph Whitfield, first Serjeant-at-law to Charles I. and grand-daughter to Sir Henry Spelman, declared to Mr. Wagstaffe that within two days of the King's death, she saw, in a Spanish leather case, three of these prayers said to be delivered to the Bishop of London at his death, from whom they were taken away by the officers of the Army; and it was from one of those officers, in whose custody they then were, that she had the favour to see them; and that the person who showed her those prayers, showed her also the "George", with the Queen's picture in it, and two seals which were the King's."

At first sight Mrs. Fotherly's testimony seems of doubtful value, as being elicited from her by a clergyman in support of a party cause. But on closer scrutiny it is possible to verify nearly every detail. In Whitelocke's Memorials and in the Commons' Journals we have learnt the existence of the two seals, a circumstance that appears little known to people in 1649 outside the set of the revolutionaries, as I have found it mentioned nowhere else [1]). Mrs. Fotherly is even ignorant of the fact that the King had given them to the Lady Elizabeth, as otherwise she would undoubtedly have said so.

And at Windsor there now exists a George remarkable among all others because its back has evidently once been adapted to contain a portrait, though this is lost at present and the stones removed. If this George is compared with the one that is visible on Charles's breast as he is pictured at his trial by a contemporary painter, they may with tolerable certainty be pronounced identical [2]).

---

[1]) Not even by Herbert.

[2]) For this information I am indebted to the book of Sir Ralph Payne-Gallway, excellent as regards heraldry and related matters, but hesitating in historical details.

But the George worn at the trial would naturally be the one worn some days later on the scaffold. Thus the George that Mrs. Fotherly saw really must have contained a portrait.

The statement that this George was actually in the custody of an officer of the army is verified by an entry in the "Sale Lists" of the King's property. (see infra).

Finally, that the King left but three prayers is asserted in a note in the Eikon appendix of the 6th edition (see above). And in the Reliquiæ Sacræ Carolinæ, the Hague 1649—50, p. 323, the King's prayers have the following heading: — "Divers of His Majesties Prayers: Whereof the *three* last, used by Him in the time of His Restraint, were delivered to the Bishop of London at His Death; From whom they were taken away by the Officers of the Army."

This extraordinary correctness of Mrs. Fotherly's allows us to infer that she had really seen the things as she told, and that they were together in the custody of the officer. It remains to find out the name of this man.

The choice seems to lie between Colonel Thomlinson and Colonel Hacker, the two officers who were about the King's person during his last days and were both present on the scaffold. Now, Colonel Hacker was a gruff and uncivil person whom the King disliked very much. The other was quite the contrary. Gentle and well-bred, he was most true to the Parliamentary cause, but had learnt to estimate and love Charles during his captivity and tried to render him every service concordant with his duty. These feelings were returned by the King to such a degree that, when Thomlinson had to hand his prisoner over to Hacker, Charles presented him with his gold toothpick-case and asked as a favour that Thomlinson would remain with him to the end.

It is more than probable, then, that when the Princess had to be searched and deprived of the two seals, Thomlinson did it himself in order to save her from the brutality of the other, and this would have been the case with Juxon too, when he was searched after the King's death. The conjecture becomes certainty in view of other information.

To raise money the revolutionaries determined to sell the King's goods and for several months there were repeated orders about it in the Commons' Journals.

"Die Martis, 20° Februarii. 1648.

. . . Ordered, That it be referred to the Committee of the Navy, to raise Money by Sale of the Crown Jewels, Hangings, and other Goods of the late King . . . and that the Committee that had the charge of the Crown and Jewels, & c. be joined to the Committee of the Navy as to this Purpose."

"Die Sabbati, 24° Februarii, 1648.

. . . Mr. Gordon, Mr. Weaver, Mr. Boone, Colonel Harrison, Colonel Venne, Mr. Blackestone, Lord Mounson, Colonel Marten,

Mr. Whittacre, Mr. Humprey Edwards, Mr.Scott, Mr. Seaman, Mr. Say, Colonel Jones, Mr.Robinson, Sir James Harrington, Mr. Aulaby, Sir John Bourchier [1]), Lieutenant General Cromwell, Commissary General Ireton [2]), Mr. Allen, Mr. Holland, Mr. Dove, Colonel Purefoy (are appointed as a committee); . . . Ordered, That it be referred to the same Committee, to bring in an Act to appoint Commissioners for the Preservation and Disposal of the Goods and personal Estate of the late King, and of the Queen and Prince."

"Die Lunæ, 5° Martii, 1648.

. . . Ordered . . . That the Committee for the Goods of the late King do, by sale thereof, or otherwise, take care to raise Monies. . . ."

"Die Veneris, 23° Martii, 1648.

Resolved, &c. That the personal Estate of the late King, Queen, and Prince, shall be inventoried, appraised, and sold; except such Parcels of them as shall be thought fit to be reserved for the Use of State."

"Die Martis, 26° Junii, 1649.

An act for Sale of the Goods of the late King, Queen, and Prince, was this Day read the Third time."

For this sale there were made out two duplicate lists (Harleian MSS. 4898, 7352) of the King's property at Whitehall, St. James's, Somerset House, Hampton Court, etc., with notes about reception, purchase, appraisement, and price, e. g. "408 Fifty and Six books of French and Lattin being papist and in a Trunk together . . . Sold Mr Clerk ye 22 of Nov. 1649 for Six pounds." "Severall Things receved from some Gents. in whose Custody they were and now remain in Sommersett house Closett in Mr. Henry Brown's Charge," etc.

Cromwell retained several pictures of naked boys, "ten pieces of Arras hangings of Abraham" etc. But for our purpose we may stop at the following note: —

"Recd. from   A Garter of blew vellvett sett with 412 small
Captain Preston   dyamonds valued at £ 160 Sold Mr. Ireton ye
                     3rd Jany. 1650, for £ 205."

This Preston was one of those to whom the King's body was handed over before burial. The Garter accordingly is the one Charles wore on the scaffold and which afterwards had to be taken off with his clothes.

The note on Preston tends to show that those who were about the King at his death took care of and kept his things, each according to his duty, in order finally to hand them over to the Committee appointed to dispose of the royal property.

---

[1]) Cromwell's father-in-law.
[2]) Cromwell's son-in-law.

We are next to consider this entry in the sale lists: —

"Recd from   A George of gold sett with dyamonds, valued
Coll. Thomlins   at £ 70 Sold Mr. W. Widmor ye 17 May
                1650 for £ 70."

In the sale lists the pictures which Mrs. Hutchinson in her memoirs reports as bought by her husband are sold to "Col. Hutchins." [1]) This abbreviation confirms the assumption that Thomlins stands for Thomlinson. The George, then, must be the one worn by Charles on the scaffold and handed to Juxon.

The leather case with the prayers and the two seals are impossible to trace in the lists, where only items of considerable value could be specified.

A survey of the ground covered may be useful at the present point.

The King gave the prayers to Juxon. The latter was guarded and could not take them along when released, but had instead to leave them as well as several other things with the officer in charge. This officer showed them to Mrs. Fotherly together with the Scaffold George and the two seals. Finally, this officer, who kept the George and consequently the other things too, was evidently Colonel Thomlinson.

We remember Colonel Thomlinson as a highly attractive person who had conceived a real affection for Charles I. during his captivity. He certainly found it barbarous not to hand over the few things left by Charles to his son, then residing at the Hague. Parliament had resolved, however, (see ante) that the Prince of Wales was *not* to have them. So that the only honourable course open to Thomlinson was to suffer a copy of the prayers to be made for the Prince, and to watch where the George and the two seals went at the sale in order to buy them back if necessary and send them to the Hague. The former conjecture will be looked into later on, the other at once.

The Council of State determined that out of the money raised by means of the sale of the King's property his debts should be paid. As creditors counted also the servants whose wages were unpaid. [2]) In the "Necessitous List of the late King's servants" appears the name of the above Mr. Widmor who got the George.

According to Lucy Hutchinson the servants were sometimes paid in kind, and so apparently was Mr. Widmor; or partly so at least, as is seen by several entries in the sale lists. In this way Widmor got the George and, perhaps, the seals. Behind him, however, was concealed Colonel Thomlinson, to whom a servant of the late King would prove the best means of recovering the things for the Prince of Wales. The final proof that Thomlinson restored the George and the two seals is found in a letter from Charles II. himself: —

---

[1]) Cf. Mem. p. 292.
[2]) Mem. of Col. Hutchinson, p. 292; valuable for practical details but somewhat biassed in judgment.

"Mris Twisden

Hauing assurance of your readines to performe what I desired of you by my Letter of the 7th of February from Jersey, according to your Brothers promise in order to the conveying to me the George and Seales left me by my blessed Father, I have againe imployed this bearer (in whom I haue very much confidence) to desire you to deliver the said George and Seales into his hand for me, assuring you, that as I shall haue great reason thereby to acknowledge your owne and your Brothers civilitys and good affections, in a particular soe deerly valued by me soe I will not be wanting, when by Gods blessing I shall be enabled, deseruedly to recompence you both for soe acceptable a service done to

Your loving friend,

St. Johnston, 2 8[ber] 1650.   Charles R.

(Diary of John Evelyn, vol. IV., p. 200, Lond. 1879).

This Mrs. Twisden was Jane Thomlinson, the Colonel's sister, who had married Mr. Twisden in 1639,[1]) and both her husband and her brother were certainly rewarded according to the promises in the letter. Both served the Commonwealth most faithfully: Thomlinson was a member of the Council of State, of Parliament, a commissioner for Ireland and was knighted by Henry Cromwell; Twisden was made a Serjeant-at-Law.[2]) Yet the Restoration did not bring arrest and misery to them as to the other revolutionaries. On the contrary, Mr. Twisden was made a Puisne Judge in the King's Bench, member of the Commission for the Trial of the Regicides, and Knight in 1660, and created a Baronet in 1666.[3]) Thomlinson, though indicated as present at the reading of the sentence on Charles I. in 1649, even if he had abstained from signing the death warrant, was not only included in the Indemnity Bill, but was also excepted from the bill rendering incapable of any office those who had given sentence of death in the "illegal" courts of the Commonwealth.

"Provided likewise that all those who, since the 5th of December, 1648, did give sentence of death upon any person or persons in any of the late illegal and tyrannical high courts of justice in England or Wales, or signed the warrant for the execution of any person there condemned (except Colonel Richard Ingoldsby and Colonel Matthew Thomlinson) shall be and are hereby, made incapable of bearing any office, ecclesiastical, civil, or military, within the kingdom of England or dominion of Wales, or of serving as a member of any Parliament after the 1st day of September, 1660." (C. J., Aug. 13th).

There can be no doubt, then, that the negotiations mentioned in the letter led to a satisfactory result.

---

[1]) Dict. Nat. Biogr.
[2]) Cal. State Papers, pass.
[3]) Cal. State Papers, pass.

CHAPTER V.

Printing History of the Eikon Basilike.

English printing in 1649. Description of the Eikon. Its origin. Charles and Gauden. Royston. Dugard. He prints the Eikon. Matthew Simmons prints the book.

Having traced the prayers so far, the next step is to examine the circumstances of their publication. As this publication is inseparably connected with the "King's Book", Eikon Basilike, very minute attention must be paid to the birth, form, and appearance of this book, which, in its turn, necessitates some preliminary notes on the making of books in England about 1649.

The general course was that when an author wanted to print a book of his, he went to a publisher and sold the manuscript to him. The publisher then had to get it licensed. A license had long been obtainable from the Master and Wardens of the Stationers' Company but in course of time successive ordinances named special licensers, e. g. the bishop of London, the Privy Council, etc. In 1643, the Lords and Commons resolved that "no order or declaration of either House be printed but by order of one or both Houses and that no other Book be printed, bound, stitched or put to sale unless first licensed and entered on the Register Book of the Stationers' Company." Licensers were at the same time expressly appointed by the House of Commons, some for books on religion, others for politics; plays had to be licensed by the Master of the Revels, etc.

If he could get a license, the publisher went to Stationers' Hall, the office of the City Corporation of Printers and Stationers, whose charter conferred on the members sole right of printing books in England and power to search for unlicensed or surreptitious prints, to arrest or mulct the offender, destroy the presses, and burn or damask the books. The Stationers' Company was governed by a Master, two Wardens or Keepers, and a Court of Assistance, and on its famous registers the publisher had to enter the book as his copy, under the hand of the Master or Wardens. This entry conferred the copyright upon the publisher, and anyone who wanted to print a book entered in due form at Stationers' Hall must buy the right to do so from the publisher and in his turn enter the book as his copy.

Next he would turn to a Printing House. By a decree of the Star Chamber in 1586 the number of Master Printers in London was fixed at about 25, with 53 presses. The reign of the Long Parliament, however, brought about a considerable increase in this number.

The printer might have many presses or one only, print the book alone or hire the presses of other printers too, cause the type to be set up in his shop or let the compositors do it at home and carry their work to him for printing. Woodcut initials and showy ornaments, emblems, and printer's marks abounded in the first half of the 17th century. The danger of these ornaments as helping to trace anonymous printers was finally recognized by the latter and it is curious to observe how, in a few years only [1]), books where the smallest space was occupied by an ornament were succeeded by totally naked ones.

During the course of printing the author, the printer, or a special corrector would at times peruse the sheets and rectify errors, sometimes more than once, so that in the same edition three, four, or more different sets of copies may exist side by side.

When printed and ready, the book was put on sale by the stationer.

It is necessary to keep in mind that these different trades could be united in the hands of one person but were not necessarily so.

We now turn to the form of the Eikon Basilike and the editions. First, a description of the ordinary appearance of the book will be useful. The size was quarto, octavo, duodecimo, or vigesimo quarto. In many copies a folding-plate was inserted between the fly-leaf and the title-page, representing the King kneeling with a wreath of thorns in his right hand, the left hand laid on his breast, his face in profile, turned upwards in prayer. Before him, on the table, is a prayer-book. To the left, outside the King's chamber, rages the sea with a rock in the middle, and on the beach is a palm-tree with two weights attached to it and the device: *Crescit sub pondere virtus.* Two stigmatizing rays descend from Heaven at an angle towards the King's head, right and left, inscribed *"coeli specto"* and *"clarior e tenebris"*. There are several other emblems and devices. The folding-plate contained small variations in some of the impressions and was often a later addition. The earliest editions had it not.

Then came the title-page: Εἰκὼν Βασιλική, *The Pourtraicture of His Sacred Maiestie in His Solitudes And Sufferings. Rom. 8. More then Conquerour, &c. Bona agere, & mala pati Regium est.* MDCXLVIII (or 49). No printer's name at first.

On the next leaf began the contents: —

1. Upon His Majestys calling this last Parliament.
2. Upon the Earle of Strafford's death.
3. Upon his Majesty's going to the House of Commons.

---

[1]) During the Commonwealth.

4. Upon the Insolency of the Tumults.

5. Upon His Majesty's passing the Bill for the Trienniall Parliaments: And after setling this, during the pleasure of the two Houses.

6. Upon His Majesty's retirement from Westminster.

7. Upon the Queens departure, and absence out of England.

8. Upon His Majestie's repulse at Hull, and the fates of the Hothams.

9. Upon the Listing, and raising Armies against the King.

10. Upon their seizing the King's Magazines, Forts, Navy, and Militia.

11. Upon the 19. Propositions first sent to the King; and more afterwards.

12. Upon the Rebellion, and troubles in Ireland.

13. Upon the Calling in of the Scots, and their Comming.

14. Upon the Covenant.

15. Upon the many Jealousies raised, and Scandals cast upon the King, to stirre up the People against him.

16. Upon the Ordinance against the Common-Prayer-Booke.

17. Of the differences between the King, and the 2 Houses, in point of Church-Government.

18. Upon Uxbridge-Treaty, and other Offers made by the King.

19. Upon the various events of the War; Victories, and Defeats.

20. Upon the Reformations of the Times.

21. Upon His Majesties Letters, taken, and divulged.

22. Upon His Majesties leaving Oxford, and going to the Scots.

23. Upon the Scots delivering the King to the English; and His Captivity at Holmeby.

24. Upon their denying His Majesty the attendance of His Chaplaines.

25. Penitentiall Meditations and Vowes in the King's solitude at Holmeby.

26. Upon the Armies Surprisall of the King at Holmeby, and the ensuing distractions in the two Houses, the Army, and the City.

27. To the Prince of Wales.

Meditations upon Death, after the Votes of Non-Addresses, and His Majesties closer Imprisonment in Carisbrooke Castle."

The several chapters contain the King's explanations of his own conduct in the various events shown by the headings, and every chapter ends with a prayer. After the prayer of the 28th (last) chapter there is a Latin motto: *Vota dabunt, quœ bella negârunt.*

The origin of the Eikon according to the royalists is that the King had begun to compose the book somewhere after 1640 and had brought down his notes to 1645 when he lost them in the battle at Naseby, together with his other papers. The Eikon alone, curiously enough, General Fairfax was prevailed upon to restore to the King by means of Major Huntingdon. Then the King continued his work when captured and imprisoned. The last chapter was written after the Votes of Non-Addresses. In the autumn of 1648 Charles handed the manuscript to one of his son's chaplains, the Rev. Edward Symmons, who brought it to the publisher, Richard Royston.

According to Gauden, his wife, and his curate, he (Gauden) had written the book with the knowledge and approval of Bishop Duppa and, perhaps, the King. Several persons, among them Gauden's curate and Prince Charles's chaplain, Symmons, had been employed to convey the manuscript to Royston as the King's. In support of this story Dugard's own "Affidavit" relates that Gauden's Στρατοστηλιτευτικοι was sent him to be printed from the Court of Charles II., apparently without information as to its author. It seems certain, anyway, that Royston got the manuscript. Naturally, he would take care not to apply for a license or enter the book on the Stationers' Registers. The licensers were the chaplains of the Council of State and the latter body now very closely watched all printing and publishing. Royston therefore secretly engaged William Dugard to print the Eikon. Some words about this man are necessary.

Possessed of some learning, he had become Master of Merchant Taylors' School, in 1644, and Milton's friend. He seems to have enjoyed a certain amount of fame as an editor of schoolbooks, and this may have been the cause of his acquaintance with Milton when the latter was himself engaged in teaching in the early forties. Apparently for financial reasons, Dugard managed "to be made free of" the Stationers' Company and to buy Young's press only a few years before 1649, as is shown by these entries: —

(Minute Book of the Stationers' Company, Feb. 10th, 1647.)

"This day an order of the Court of Aldermen for making Mr. William Dugard free of this company was read and upon debate hereof, it was thought fitt hee being a gentleman well deserving and may bee helpfull in the correction of the Companies Schoole Bookes to admit him into the freedome of this company. And whereas a fyne hath alwayes beene taken for admitting of a member in this nature, It was now ordered all fees to the house and offices shall bee freely remitted to him which said hee thankfully acknowledged and promised to doe his utmost in his way for correcting freely the companies school bookes, or any other service he may doe them, and hereupon the said Mr. Wm. Dugard was sworne a member of this company."

(June 8th, 1648).

"Mr Younges coppies. The Court hath appointed Mr. Lowndes, Mr. Flesher, Mr. Stephens, and Mr. Clarke to examine the coppies belonging to Mr. Younge before they bee entred to Mr. Dugard,

and upon their representacon to the Court thereof, the said coppies
are to bee entred to the said Mr. Dugard [1]).''

As mentioned, he was employed to print the Eikon, a signal
financial success, and a very great number of the editions betray
his types and presses. We know that he used singularly showy
ornaments, whence it was really to no purpose that he left out his
own name on the title-page. In fact, there is little doubt that
it was Dugard who was seized as Eikon printer, together with
his presses and copies, by order of Parliament on March 17th, 1649
(see ante). He was apparently released within a few hours, as
there is no further trace of the incident.

The next thing of interest in connection with Dugard is that,
in 1649, he bought "halfe" of Sir Philip Sidney's Arcadia, shortly
before acquired by Legat, according to two entries on the
Stationers' Registers.

"August 21, 1648

Mr. Legatt.   Assigned over unto him by virtue of a note under
              the hand & seale of Mr. John Waterson & subscribed
              by bothe the Wardens all the estate right title &
              interest which the said Mr. Waterson hath in these
              copies and parts of copies following
              1 Sydney's Arcadia. halfe'' etc.

"Oct. 20, 1649

Wm. Dugard.   Assigned over unto him by vertue of a note un-
              der the hand & seale of Mr. Legatt & with con-
              sent of Mr. Waterson all the estate right title &
              interest which, the said Mr. Legatt or the said
              Mr. Waterson gave or claimed in the book or
              copie called Sir Philip Sidneys or the Countesse
              of Pembrooks Arcadia.''

This book had counted a dozen editions since 1590 and
was worth much to a printer.

Next year Dugard tried to make money out of Salmasius'
Defensio Regia but was caught *in flagranti* and imprisoned. See
the following "Orders by the Council of State."

"Feb. 1, 1650

2. To write the Company of Merchant Tailors of London to elect
a schoolmaster, Mr. Dugard having shown himself an enemy to
the State by printing seditious and scandalous pamphlets, and
therefore unfit to have charge of the education of youths.

3. John Armstrong, corrector to Mr. Dugard's printing press, to
be apprehended and brought before the Council.

12. The letter to the Merchant Tailors Company approved."

"To Joseph Hunscott, officer of the Stationers' Company.

To seize the printing presses and stock of William Dugard,

---

[1]) Among the copies was "halfe" of the Arcadia which book Robert Young
shared, first with Simon Waterson and then with John W.

schoolmaster of Merchant Taylors school, for publishing certain scandalous and seditious books."

"Feb. 2, 1650
To Keeper of Newgate.
To receive William Dugard into his custody, for printing several scandalous books against the Commonwealth."

This time his life was endangered, but he was saved by Sir James Harrington (see "Affidavit") and released after a month on his promise of good behaviour.

"March 7, 1650
Council of State, Day's Proceedings.
1. Mr. Frost to take Mr. Dugard's subscription to the engagement, and his recognizance for his future good abbearance according to the sense of a paper sent by him to the Council."

"April 2, 1650
23. *Sir James Harrington,* Sir Wm. Masham, and Mr. Scott, to be a committee to consider what is to be paid by Mr. Dugard, upon restoring his press to him.
24. Mr. Dugard to have his press, upon entering into recognizance that he will not employ it to the prejudice of the Commonwealth, and paying those who were employed in the taking of it."

Dugard then became the printer to the Commonwealth and collaborated further with Milton.

"March 5, 1651
The Committee of Examinations to view Mr. Milton's book, and give order for reprinting it if they think fit, and examine the complaint made by him about Peter· Cole's printing a copy concerning the Ricketts, which Mr. Dugard alleges to be his."

"July 20, 1652
Note to send to Mr. Dugard to speak with Mr. Milton as to printing the declaration." (C. S. P.)

The rest of his life offers nothing of interest to us.

Dugard's was not the only printer's name connected with the Eikon editions. On the contrary, the book was pounced upon and reproduced by a whole crew of his fellow-printers, Bentley, Grismond, etc., and the editions swelled to about fifty within a year.

We pass by the other names, however, as of little importance for the present matter, and turn to Matthew Simmons. According to a most remarkable entry on the Stationers' Registers this printer intended to send forth an edition of the book which Parliament had ordered to be seized on the very day of this entry.

"March 16, 1649
Mr. Symmons

This is crossed by my owne hand Aug. 6. 1651 Mathew Symons At a Court held this day.	Entred for his copie under the hands of Mr. Caryl & Mr. Dawson warden a book called Εικων Βασιλικη. The pourtracture of his Sacred Ma:ty in his solitudes and sufferings."

It must be kept in mind what an entry on the Stationers' Registers really meant. It signified that the printer had bought or otherwise obtained the sole right of printing the book entered. If Simmons had wanted only to make money out of the Eikon, he would have printed it surreptitiously, like the others. It seems certain, then, that he had acquired the copyright. But he could not have done this by purchase, nor would he wish it, as to do so would not protect him against his rivals. We must suppose, then, that he was authorized by the government to print the very book which they wanted to suppress. This is further proved by the fact that the book is licensed by one of the Council of State's preachers, Mr. Caryl. And also by the circumstance that just in 1649 Simmons was one of the chief printers of the government. A month before he had printed Milton's Tenure.

There is yet another sign of the government's favour.

"An Act against unlicensed and scandalous books and pamphlets and for better regulating of printing", of Sept. 20th, 1649, contained the following paragraph: —

"Every Printer, or other Person, in London, being the Owner of Printing-Presses, Rolling-Presses, or other Instruments for Printing, shall, before the first Day of October, 1649, enter into Bond, with two Sureties, of 300 l. Penalty, to the Keepers of the Liberty of England, by Authority of Parliament, not to print, or cause or suffer to be printed, any seditious, scandalous, or treasonable Book, &c. dishonourable to, or against, the State and Government; nor any Book of News, &c. not enter'd and licensed as aforesaid [1]); and shall also, to every Book, &c. they shall imprint, prefix the Author's Name, with his Quality and Place of Residence, or at least, the Licenser's Name, where Licensers are required, and his own Name and Place ot Residence at Length, in the Title-Page, on Pain of forfeiting 10 l. for every wilful Failing, and to have all their Printing Materials defaced; and, for the second Offence, to be disabled from exercising his Trade of Printing."

Simmons was *not* requested to procure sureties or to enter into bond. At all events, his name is wanting in the list of recognisances as seen here.

"List of Recognisances to the Council of State, viz.

Oct.	9 Jas. Flesher, Little Brittain	printer
»	Rich. Coates, Aldersgate str.	»
»	Wm. Dugard, Merch. Taylors' School	»
Oct.	10 Bernard Alsop, Grub str.	»
»	Thos. Brudnell, Newgate Market	»
»	Rob. Austin, Addlehill	»
»	John Maycock, »	»
»	Jane Bell, Christchurch	»
»	Hen. Hills, Southwark	»

---

[1]) Entered at Stationer's Hall and licensed by the Council's licensers.

Oct. 10 Rob. Ibbitson, Smithfield   printer
  »   Roger Norton, Blackfriars   »
  »   Abraham Miller,   »   »
  »   Robert Leyborne, Mugwell str.   »
  »   Francis Neale, Aldersgate str.   »
  »   Thomas Newcombe, Near Barnard's Castle [1]   »
  »   Elizabeth Purslow, Little Old Bailey   »
  »   William Ellis, Thames str.   »
  »   Edward Griffith, Old Bailey   »
  »   William Hunt, Pie Corner   »
  »   James Moxon, Hounsditch   »
  »   Thomas Warren, Foster Lane   »
  »   John Clowes, Grub str.   »
Oct. 11 Gertrude Dawson, Aldersgate str.   »
  »   Richard Bishop, St. Peter's, Paul's Wharf   »
  »   William Bentley, Finsbury   »
  »   William Wilson, Little St. Bartholomew's   »
  »   Thomas Radcliffe and⎫   »
  »   Edw. Mottershead,   ⎬ Doctors' Commons   »
  »   Thomas Mabb and⎫   »
  »   Amos Coles,   ⎬ Ivy Lane   »
  »   Thomas Maxey, Bennet's [2]), Paul's Wharf   »
Oct. 15 Thomas Harper, Little Brittain   »
  » 16 Adam Hare, Red Cross str.   »
  » 19 John Grismond, Ivy Lane   »
  » 20 Rich. Constable, Smithfield   »
  »   John Field, Andrew Wardrope's [3]), stationer
  » 26 Thomas Broad, City of York   »
  »   Thomas Bucks, Cambridge   »
  » 27 John Buck,   »   »
  » 29 Leonard Lichfield, Oxford   »
  »   Henry Hall [4]),   »   ''   »

As we have no reason to suppose that *Simmons* was forgotten by the government, we may perhaps be right in inferring from this list that he was favoured by the rulers. And, in fact, when Milton's Eikonoklastes, the book ordered by the government, was published in October, 1649, it bore the name of this printer.

---

[1]) *Baynard* in Stow.
[2]) *S. Benet Hude* in Stow.
[3]) *S. Andrew in the wardrobe* in Stow.
[4]) This list may also be found in C. S. P.

CHAPTER VI.

Printing History of the Prayers.

Connection of the prayers with the Eikon. Description of the prayers. Reports about them supported by evidence. Dugard, the prayers, and Hills. Simmons, the prayers, and Hills. John Playford.

We now turn to the prayers connected with the Eikon.

The first Eikon editions contained that book only, such as it has been previously described. By and by, however, there were inserted several other things not belonging to the book but having some relation to the King. E. g. the Pamela Prayer, which was put together with some more prayers under the title: "His Majesties Prayers which He used in time of his Sufferings. Delivered To Doctor Juxon, Bishop of London, immediately before his Death"; "A Letter from the Prince to the King his Father"; "The King's Speech to the Lady Elizabeth the day before his death"; "An Epitaph upon King Charles"; "Apophthegmata Carolina", etc. Such additions were generally placed at the end of the Eikon, more seldom some of the shorter came before the first chapter.

The number of the prayers that alone or together with others of the papers here mentioned were bound up with the Eikon, and entitled: *Prayers used by his majesty in his sufferings and delivered to Juxon*, is nearly always four, very seldom seven, six, or three. These prayers were:

1. A Prayer used by his Majesty, at his entrance in state into the Cathedral Church of Exeter.

2. A Prayer drawn by his Majestie's special direction and dictates, for a blessing upon the Treaty at Uxbridge.

3. A Prayer drawn by his Majestie's special direction for a blessing upon the Treaty at Newport.

4. *A Prayer in time of Captivity.*

5. Another Prayer.

6. A Prayer and Confession in and for the times of Affliction.

7. A Prayer in times of imminent Danger.

Of these the first three had been already printed separately in or before 1648 and are only once or twice to be found in the Eikon appendix, but they are always included in the Reliquiæ Sacræ

Carolinæ, or the King's Collected Works. They were undoubtedly made by Charles on the occasions stated.

The Eikon appendix generally begins with the Captivity (Pamela) Prayer, and the other three follow as above. If there are only three prayers, either this or »Another Prayer» is wanting, never the two last.

The variously reported history of these prayers may be summed up in the following manner.

Given by Charles before his death to Juxon, they were taken from the latter by the officers of the army. There were only three then. Angry and disturbed at the great fame of the Eikon, Milton and Bradshaw promised to procure pardon for Dugard, who had just then offended the government, if he would print the prayers, with the one from Sidney's Arcadia added, in his Eikon.

This story receives support from the following three facts.

1) An Eikon printer was seized, together with presses and copies, on March 17th, 1649, brought before Parliament, but apparently released without punishment, — as there is no order of arrest for any printer just then (see ante). This person must have been Dugard, because he was the first and principal printer of the Eikon and the one most easily betrayed, on account of his singular book-ornaments. Cf. also the corroborative testimony of Henry Hills. In a letter from Dr. Gill to the Hon. Charles Hatton we have seen the following passage:

". . . I was told Pamela's Prayer, was transferr'd out of Sir Philip Sidney's Arcadia into Ἐικων Βασιλικη by a contrivance of Bradshaw's and Milton's. Sir I make no secret of it, and I frankly tell you my Author, who was Mr. Henry Hills Oliver's Printer, and the occasion, as he many years ago told me, was this, Mr. Dugard, who was Milton's intimate Friend, happened to be taken printing an Edition of the King's Book; Milton used his interest to bring him off, which he effected by the means of Bradshaw, but upon this Condition that Dugard should add Pamela's Prayer to the aforesaid Books he was printing. . . ."

2) There exist two Eikon editions which, as will be shown later, must have been printed by Dugard somewhere about *March 17th* and thus *dated 1648,* and which have an appendix with the prayers (the Pamela Prayer too) bound up at the end. The signatures betray that Eikon and appendix were printed independently of each other and the appendix has a separate title-page *dated 1649* (printed after March 25th, 1649). These may be the editions seized together with Dugard and then restored to him and furnished with the appendix, which probably could not be managed before March 25th, whence the appendix is dated 1649 instead of 1648 like the corresponding Eikons.

3) In 1648—9 Dugard bought the copyright of the very book from which the prayer is taken. It *may* have been Dugard's transactions in connection with this book that turned the attention

of his friend Milton to the Arcadia and suggested to him the interpolation [1]).

But the printing history of the prayers does not stop here. The reader must remember a testimony of Henry Hills as reported in a letter from Dr. Bernard to Dr. Goodall:

"Concerning the Prayer out of Sir Philip Sidney, (which Milton makes a great bustle about) I remember Henry Hills (who was Oliver's Printer, and my Patient) told me among other things, of the Artifice of that Party; that he had heard Bradshaw and Milton laugh how they had put the Cheat upon the World, and in order thereunto, *had printed the whole Book anew,* that they might add that Prayer thereunto;"

When Hills in the 17th cent. states not only *that* the revolutionaries had committed the action in point but also describes *the manner of execution,* and two hundred years later his words are verified by an old entry at Stationers' Hall, we are really inclined to think the case fairly well proved by this fact alone.

We know, I think, from the entry of Matthew Simmons that the revolutionaries *did* print the Eikon anew as stated by Hills. And we must infer that they would not print a book so dangerous to themselves if they could obtain no advantage by so doing. But the only possible advantage was the one mentioned by Hills, and this a very great one, as is aptly expressed by Stern: —

"Es ist indessen klar, wie verdächtig damit alles das gemacht wurde was aus der royalistischen Presse hervorgieng. Eine überraschende Entdeckung wie diese konnte wahrlich nicht vorteilhaft auf die Beurtheilung des "königlichen Bildes" zurückwirken. Was aber war besser geeignet, seinen Nimbus zu zerstören, als wenn es gelang wahrscheinlich zu machen, dass bei seiner Herstellung Betrug die Hand im Spiele gehabt habe [2])?" (Milton und seine Zeit III, pp. 46—47).

That the revolutionaries had used this means of annihilating the Eikon seems certain from another reason. In 1651, there were apparently some rumours abroad that might have led to an inquiry into the provenience of the prayer and its original connection with the Eikon (see Eikon Aklastos as quoted ante). In the same year, on Aug. 6th, Simmons went to Stationers' Hall and got leave to cross the entry (see ante). I have worked through the registers of 1640—70 and found no quite parallel case. If, after the entry, a printer was prevented from printing his book, there was no need to tamper with the registers. When Simmons after two years took the trouble to go and look up and delete the item in the registers, it seems obvious that he was actuated by fear of prying eyes [3]).

---

[1]) D. bought half of the Arcadia on June 8th, 1648, but Legat forestalled him as to the other half which he got on Oct. 20th, 1649, only (see ante). His editions appeared in 1655 and 1662.

[2]) The identical reasonings are very candidly exhibited by Milton himself (see ante, pp. 47—48).

[3]) These precautions of the revolutionaries against uncalled-for investigation

There is yet somebody who has a right to be mentioned in connection with the publication of the prayers. John Playford is well known to the readers of Pepy's Diary as a musician and printer of music, and his shop near the Temple Church is mentioned as the meeting-place of musical enthusiasts. This circumstance, as well as the fact that he was very intimate with Milton's old friend, Henry Lawes, — Lawes even stood godfather to Playford's son (D. N. B.) — whose music he printed, makes it more than likely that he was no stranger to the music-loving Milton. Playford prefixed Milton's sonnet on Lawe's airs when printing these latter.

This man seems also to have had some connection with the more moderate among the revolutionaries. The following broadsides are all of them published by Playford.

"A proclamation by his Excellency the Lord Generall, For the regulating of Souldiers in their march to Ireland, March 18, 1648."

"A Proclamation by His Excellency the Lord General, Forbidding all Souldiers to forbear to put their Horses into Mowing-Pastures, June 21, 1649."

"A Proclamation by His Excellency the Lord General, Feb. 13, 1648."

"A Proclamation by His Excellencie the Lord Generall, concerning Free-Quarter, Feb. 25, 1648."

"Petition of . . . Lord Fairfax . . . and his Council of Officers for the recalling of all Penal Laws etc., Aug. 18, 1649."

---

of their public records are seen in another instance that lends support to this explanation of Simmons's crossed entry: —

In 1649, the celebrated Salmasius launched a vituperative pamphlet against the revolutionaries on account of their execution of Charles I. Milton was ordered to answer and did so with equal vigour. Among other things, he — without cause — accused Salmasius of having received money from Charles II. for his service. Now, to Milton himself a sum was paid for *his* book, as is seen in the following entry: —

"That thanks be given to Mr. Milton, on behalf of the Commonwealth, for his good service done in writing an answer to the Book of Salmasius, written against the proceedings of the Commonwealth of Engl.: *And it is ordered that ye sum of . . . hundred pounds be given to him as reward from this Council for his . . . Salmasius.*" (Council Order Book, June 18th, 1651).

But as it would not do if it were generally known that Milton, while exposing Salmasius as a paid defender of Charles, was himself being paid for *his* defence, the above passage is cancelled and the lines so thoroughly deleted that a few words are really indecipherable. The whole is replaced by the following.

"The Council, taking notice of the many good services performed by Mr. John Milton, their Secretary for Foreign Languages, to this State and Commonwealth, particularly of his Book in vindication of the Parliament and People of England against the calumnies and invectives of Salmasius, have thought fit to declare their resentment and good acceptance of the same, and that the thanks of the Council be returned to Mr. Milton, and their sence represented in that behalf." It is evident that there was no need to *delete* that part of the former entry which mentioned the sum of money if there had been no fear of espionage. Cf. also the fact that, on the eve of the Restoration (in the spring of 1660), the Commons voted that several passages in their Journals of 1649 should be deleted and rendered illegible, as, in fact, they were (see C. J., 1649, 1660, pass.).

"Narrative being the last and final dayes Proceedings of the High Court of Justice ... Together with a Copy of the Sentence of Death.

Published by Authority. Printed for John Playford, Jan. 29, 1648."

During 1649 he also made money by picking up little odds and ends connected with the King's death etc. and printing them.

"Jan. 22, 1648
John Playford — Entred for his copy under the hand of Master Mabbot a pamphlett called, A perfect narrative of the whole proceedings of the High Co^{rt} of Justice in the tryall of the king &c."

"Feb. 22, 1648
Peter Cole,
Fran. Titon,
John Playford — Entred for their copy under the hand of Master Mabbot, King Charles his triall, or, a pfect narrative of the whole proceedings of the High Co^{rt} of Justice &c with a pfect Copie of the kings speech upon the scaffold &c."

"Feb. 27, 1648
Fran. Titon and
John Playford — Entred for their copy under the hand of Master Mabbot a pamphlett called, The Marquesse of Ormonds proclamation."

"March 17, 1648
Peter Cole,
Fran. Titon,
John Playford — Entred for their copy under the hand of Master Mabbot, The severall speeches & prayers of Duke Hamilton, the Earle of Holland, & the Lord Capell upon the scaffold imediatly before their execution the 9th March, 1648, Together with the severall prayers of Dr. Sibball & Mr. Boulton & the passages there that day."

"April 2, 1649
Fran. Titon,
John Playford — Entred for their copy under the hand of Master Mabbot a pamphlett called, A modest narrative of Intelligence fitted for the Republike of England & Ireland.

John Playford — Entred for his copy under the hand of Cranford (licensed by him the 23th of Febr. last) Four prayers used by his late Ma^{ty} in the tyme of his sufferings, also a copie of a letter of Prince Charles to his father." (Stat. Reg.)

Here are the celebrated prayers published separately. As seen above, Playford was connected in some way with the revolutionaries, and when the three prayers left among the King's papers were examined and found harmless, Playford may have got them from a friend to make something out of, by printing them as he had already printed other scraps of the same kind. It is not quite sure that they were removed by strictly honest means, as several possessions of the late King's seem to have vanished within the first weeks after his death.

"Die Jovis, 22° Februarii, 1648

Lieutenant General Crumwell reports from the Council of State, That divers Goods belonging to the State are in Danger to be imbeziled. . . .

Ordered, That the Care of the *publick Library* at St. James', and of the Statue and Pictures there, be committed, to the Council of State, to be preserved by them, And that the said Council of State be, and are hereby, impowered to dispose of such of them as are for the present Service of the State, as they shall think fit." (C. J.)

It is to be observed that though some of the prayers — probably those seen by Mrs. Fotherly — were licensed on Feb. 23rd (if this unusual note is right), they were not entered till April 2nd, which seems to be an unaccountable neglect of the monetary purpose. As Playford ought to have been to Stationers' Hall for entries on Feb. 22th, 27th, and March 17th, there may have been some intervening reason that delayed publication. The nature of this reason may be conjectured with sufficient certainty, as we have seen how the interpolation was apparently originated and executed during March.

CHAPTER VII.

The Bibliography of the Eikon. I.

Keble's list. Editions with and without prayers. Wagstaffe's amendments. Octavo or duodecimo first edition? Walker's testimony. Solly.

It next becomes our duty to examine the many Eikon editions with or without appendix. Because we want to know two things: — First, if — contrary to expectation at the present stage of the investigation — the Pamela Prayer was in the earliest editions the appearance of which took the revolutionaries unawares. In this case they could not have interpolated the prayer. Second, if there is anything in the editions that suggests that the Pamela Prayer is later than the accompanying prayers or else has a distinct position by itself.

The importance of examining and determining the editions of the Eikon was found out very early. Wagstaffe in his *Vindication,* in 1693, already gives a list of editions made by "Mr. Keeble at the Turks-Head in Fleet-Street."

The list divides the Eikons examined into two groups, without or with the prayer appendix at the end.

"An account of the several Impressions or Editions of King Charles the Martyr's most Excellent Book. Intituled Εἰκων Βασιλική, that were printed without the Prayers at the End.

The First impression in Octavo, Printed 1648, last Page 269, Contents Two Leaves.

The 2^d Imp. in 8° Prin. 1648. last pag. 268. Cont. 3 Leaves.

The 3^d Imp. in 8° Prin. 1648. last p. 268. Cont. 2 Leaves.

The 4th Imp. in 8° Prin. in R. M. 1648. last p. 268. Cont. 2 Leaves.

The 5th Imp. in 8° Prin. 1648. last p. 270. Cont. 2 Leaves.

The 6th Imp. in 8° Prin. 1648. with only the Lady Elizabeth's Relation.

The 7th Imp. in 8° Print. 1648. the last p. 242.

The 8th Imp. in 8° Print. 1648. last p. 302. Cont. 2 Leaves.

The 9th Imp. in Twelves. Print. 1648. last p. 187. Cont. the last Page.

The 10th Imp. in 12° Print. 1648. last p. 164. Cont. 1 Leaf.

The 11th Imp. in 12° Print. 1648. last p. 187. Cont. 1 Leaf.
The 12th Imp. in 12° Print. 1648. last p. 225. Cont. 1 Leaf.
The 13th Imp. in 12° Print. 1648. last p. 269. Cont. 3 Leaves.
The 14th Imp. in 12° Print. 1648. last p. 269. Cont. 1 Leaf.
The 15th Imp. in 24° Printed 1648. last p. 342. Cont. 2 Leaves.
The 16th Imp. in 24° Print. 1648. no Figures. Cont. 2 Leaves.
The 17th Imp. in 8° Print. 1649. last p. 204. Cont. 1 Leaf.
The 18th Imp. in 12° Print. 1649. last p. 264. with Epitaphs.
The 19th Imp. in 12° Print. 1649. last p. 195. Cont. 1 Leaf.
The 20th Imp. in 12° Print. in 1649. (in Latin) last p. 272. with Apothegms.
The 21st Imp. in 12° Print. 1649. (Latin) last p. 272. not the same.
The 22^d Imp. in 12° with the Works Print. 1649. last p. 182.
The 23^d Imp. in 12° Print. 1649. (Latin) last p. 272. not the same.
The 24th Imp. in 12° Printed (Latin) 1649. last p. 258.
The 25th Imp. in 24° Printed at the Hague by Sam. Brown, 1649. last p. 318. Cont. 4 Leaves.
The 26th Imp. in 8° Print. 1681. last page 256. Cont. 1 Leaf.

The same Book with the Prayers added at the latter End of the Book.
The first Impression in Octavo. Printed 1648. last Page 270. added the Prayers 1649.
The 2^d Imp. in 24° Print. 1648. last p. 354.
The 3^d Imp. in 8° Print. 1649. last p. 258.
The 4th Imp. in 8° Print. 1649. last p. 236. with Apothegms.
The 5th Imp. in 8° Printed 1649. last p. 247. Prayers added.
The 6th Imp. in 8° Print. 1649. last p. 269. Cont. 3 Leaves.
The 7th Imp. in 12° Print. 1649. with Apothegms.
The 8th Imp. in 12° Print. 1649. in Dutch.
The 9th Imp. in 12° Printed 1649. in French.
The 10th Imp. in 12° Print. 1649. a different Edition.
The 11th Imp. in 12° Print. 1649. last p. 230. Cont. 1 Leaf.
The 12th Imp. in 12° Print. 1649. last p. 260. Cont. 1 Leaf.
The 13th Imp. in 24° Print. 1649. last p. 266.
The 14th Imp. in 24° Print. 1649. last p. 175.
The 15th Imp. in 24° Printed in 1649. last p. 354.
The 16th Imp. in 8° with the Works. Print. 1657.
The 17th Impression in 24° with the Works. Print. 1651.
18 The King's Works in 8° Printed at the Hague, without Date, the last p. 119.
19 The King's Works in 2 Volumes in 8°. Printed 1659.
20 The King's Whole Works in Folio. Printed 1662.
21 The King's Whole Works in Folio, Printed 1686.
22 The Eikon Basilike in 8°. Printed 1685. last p. 272. per Royston".

In each of the two groups, such editions as were printed (roughly speaking) before March 25th, 1649, and are therefore dated 1648, are placed before those that appeared after that day, dated 1649 or later, but otherwise the editions seem to be arranged at haphazard.

When Wagstaffe published his Vindication a second time, in 1697, the list had suffered some apparently arbitrary changes. This new list follows, with indications within brackets by the present author as to the number in the former list.

"The First Impression in 12° Printed Anno Dom. 1648. last Page 187. Contents one Leaf at the end. (This seems to be the 9th imp. of the 1st list).

The 2d Imp. in 8° Prin. 1648. last page 269. Cont. 2 Leaves (1st imp.).

The 3d Imp. in 8° Prin. 1648. last pag. 269. Cont. 3 Leaves. (2d imp.?).

The 4th Imp. in 12° Prin. 1648. last p. 269. Cont. 3 Leaves (13th imp.).

The 5th Imp. in 12° Prin. 1648. last pag. 269. Cont 1 Leaf. (14th imp.)

The 6th Imp. in 8° Prin. 1648. last pag. 268. Cont. 2 Leaves (3d imp.)

The 7th Imp. in 8° Reprinted in R. M. 1648. last pag. 268. Contents two Leaves. (4th imp.?)

The 8th Imp. in 8° Prin. 1648. last pag. 270. Cont. 3 Leaves. (5th imp.?)

The 9th Imp. in 8° Prin 1648. with only the Lady Elizabeth's Relation last pag. 302. Contents two Leaves. (6th imp.)

The 10th Imp. in 8° Print. 1648. the last pag. 242. (7th imp.)

The 11th Imp. in 8° Print. 1648. last p. 302. Cont. 2 Leaves. (8th imp.)

The 12th Imp. in 8° Reprinted for James Young 1648. last pag. 268. Contents two Leaves. (Wanting)

The 13th Imp. in 12° Prin. 1648. last pag. 164. Cont. 1 Leaf. (10th imp.)

The 14th Imp. in 12° Prin. 1648. last p. 187. Cont. 1 Leaf. (11th imp.)

The 15th Imp. in 12° Print. 1648. last p. 225. Cont. 2 Leaves. (12th imp.?)

The 16th Imp. in 24° Print. 1648. last p. 342. Cont. 3 Leaves (15th imp.?)

The 17th Imp. in 24° Print. 1648. no Figures. Cont. 2 Leaves. (16th imp.)

The 18th Imp. in 8° Print. 1649. last p. 204. Cont. 1 Leaf. (17th imp.)

The 19th Imp. in 8° Print. at Paris (English) 1649. last pag. 196. Cont. 1 Leaf. (Wanting)

The 20th Imp. in 12° Print. 1649. last p. 264. with Epitaphs. (18th imp.)

The 21st Imp. in 12° Print. 1649. last p. 195. Cont. 1 Leaf. 19th imp.)

The 22^d Imp. in 12° Print. 1649. (in Latin) last p. 272. with Apothegms. (20th imp.)

The 23^d Imp. in 12° Print. at the Hague by Sam. Brown 1649. (in Latin) last pag. 272. Cont. 2 Leaves. (21st imp.?)

The 24th Imp. in 12° Print. 1649. at the Hague for Williams and Eglesfield. (Latin) last p. 272. Cont. two Leaves. (23^d imp.?)

The 25th Imp. in 12° Print. (in Latin) 1649. last p. 258. (24th imp.)

The 26th Imp. in 12° Print. with the Works 1649. last p. 182. (22^d imp.)

The 27th Imp. in 24° printed at the Hague by Sam. Brown. 1649. last p. 318. Cont. 4 Leaves. (25th imp.)

The 28th Imp. in 8° Print. for R. Royston 1681. last p. 256. Cont. 1 Leaf. (26th imp.?)."

Here is the group *with* prayer appendix: —
"1st Imp. (= 1st imp.)
2^d Imp. (= 2^d imp.)
The 3^d Imp. in 24° Print. 1649. last p. 436. Cont. 2 Leaves. with the Additions of the Prayers. (Wanting)
4th Imp. (= 3^d imp.)
The 5th Imp. in 8° very large. the best Printed 1649. the last p. 263. Cont. 2 Leaves. (Wanting).
6th Imp. (= 4th imp.)
7th Imp. (= 5th imp.)
8th Imp. (= 6th imp.)
9th Imp. (= 7th imp.)
10th Imp. (= 8th imp.)
11th Imp. (= 9th imp.)
12th Imp. (= 10th imp.)
13th Imp. (= 11th imp.)
14th Imp. (= 12th imp.)
15th Imp. last p. 226. (Misprint? = 13th imp.?)
16th Imp. (= 14th imp.)
17th Imp. (= 15th imp.)
The 18th Imp. in 8° Print. at the Hague by Sam. Browne. Reliquiæ Sacræ Carolinæ the Works of King Charles the I. without date. Last pag. 119. (= 18th imp.?)
The 19th Imp. in 8° Printed at the Hague by Sam. Browne 1651. last p. 324. (?)
The 20th Imp. in 8° of the King's Works in 2 Vol. Prin. 1659. (19th imp.)
The 21st Imp. in 24° Print. at the Hague by Sam. Browne. in 1657. the King's Works. (16th imp.?)
The 22^d Imp. in 24° Print. in 1651. with the King's Works. (17th imp.)

The 23^d Imp. in 24° Reprinted in 1649. Reg. M. last pag. 181. Contents two Leaves. (Wanting)

The 24th Imp. in 12° of the King's Works Print. in 1650. at the Hague by Sam. Browne, with divers of His Majesty's Prayers, whereof the three last used by him in the time of his Restraint, were delivered to the Bishop of London at his death, from whom they were taken away by the Officers of the Army: And amongst these six Prayers that entitled to be said in Time of Captivity, and taken out of Sir Philip Sidney's Arcadia is not one of them, however it came to be printed in some of them. (?)

The 25th Impression in Folio being the whole Works of King Charles the I.. and by Order of King Charles the II. Printed in 1662. for R. Royston. (20th imp.)

The 26th Imp. in 8° large. Printed in 1685. last pag. 272. for R. Royston. (22^d imp.?)

The 27th Imp. in Folio being the whole Works of King Charles I. and by Order of King James the II. Printed in 1686. (21st imp.)"

The Vindication was published a third time and once more the list of editions was changed. This time, however, Wagstaffe only added two editions which he inserted between the 27th and 28th impression of the first group as described in the second Vindication.

"The 28th Imp. in 12° printed 1649 at Cork by Peter de Pienne, last page 320. Contents 2 leaves.

The 29th Imp. in 12° (in Latin by Dr. Earle) print. 1649. at the Hague, by S. B. for Williams, last pag. 252. Cont. 1 leaf, together with an account of the King's Tryal, (Latin) dedicated to K. Charles II.

30th imp. (= 28 imp.)"

The most remarkable feature about these lists is that the second Vindication substitutes the duodecimo of 187 pp. as the first edition for the octavo of 269 pp. The reason cannot be a good one, perhaps it was only that the book was scarce and alone among all other editions had the contents at the end. In fact, Thomason's note (see infra) proves the priority of the octavo. But another testimony exists, hitherto overlooked.

The man who, in 1690, of all living persons best knew which was the first edition ought to have been Anthony Walker, who was the curate of Bishop Gauden and was conscious of the fact that his master had written the Eikon (see ante). Now, in his "True Account of the Author of a Book, entitled Εἰκὼν Βασιλική, or the Portraiture of his Sacred Majesty in his solitudes and sufferings, proved to be written by Dr. Gauden, late Bishop of Worcester", Walker says: —

"And I perfectly remember, that in the second chapter, which is of the death of the Earle of Strafford, there being these words, which now in the printed work, of the first edition, are page 8, line 18, 19, 20, 'He only hath been least vexed by them, who counselled me not to consent against the vote of my own conscience', he told me whom he meant by that passage, viz. — the then Bishop of London, Dr. Juxon, which, though most readers understand now, after it hath been so long spoken of, yet many then did not, of which number I was, my age rendering me less acquainted with the character of great men."

The words *are* in this place in the Thomason octavo but not in Wagstaffe's duodecimo.

That Walker *must* have known which was the first edition is evident from his statement that he was employed by Gauden as a means of conveying the manuscript to the printer, and that he received six copies from the latter in acknowledgment of his services.

"Dr. Gauden delivered to me with his own hand what was last sent up, after part was printed, (or at least in Mr. Royston's hand, to be printed), and after he had shewed it to me, and sealed it up, gave me strict caution with what wariness to carry and deliver it: and according to his direction, I delivered it, Saturday, December 23, 1648, in the evening, to one Peacock, (brother to Dr. Gauden's steward or bailiff, some time before deceased), who was instructed by what hands he should transmit it to Mr. Royston; and, in the same method, a few days after the impression was finished, I received six books, by the hand of Peacock, as an acknowledgement of that little I had contributed to that service, one of which I have still by me."

Further, Dugard's "Affidavit" evidently implies that he was the original printer of the Eikon (see ante), and the Thomason Eikon *is* printed by Dugard but not the duodecimo, as is evident from the ornaments and general get-up.

The Wagstaffe-Keeble list remained unchallenged for a long time. Another one, it is true, seems to have existed about the middle of the 18th century, but then vanished. (Almack, Bibliography, p. 117).

Edw. Solly, the Eikon collector and expert, made out a scheme towards a bibliography of the "King's Book" in the Bibliographer, Feb. 1883. Cf. also Transactions of the Bibliographical Society, vol. I. The same year Mr. Doble wrote some articles upon the Eikon in "The Academy" and at the same time gave some hints about the printers and publishers.

CHAPTER VIII.

The Bibliography of the Eikon. II.

Almack's bibliography. The scheme. Before and after March 25th, 1649. The seventy-six editions.

In 1896 was published the great bibliography by Mr. Edw. Almack, himself the owner of more than a hundred copies of the Eikon, and to these copies he added a great number lent him for the purpose by persons in England and abroad. Moreover he received many descriptions of Eikons which their owners did not dare or choose to lend.

His arrangement of the editions is the following. First come the English ones before 1660, Nos 1—50; then Latin, Nos 51—53; French, Nos 54—57; German, No 58; Dutch, Nos 59—60. Then English editions 1660—1880, Nos 61—76 (No 68 is German; No 71, Guizot's French one).

The impressions of most interest for the present purpose are Nos 1—50. These are divided by Almack into two groups: Nos 1—26, dated 1648 (before March 25th, 1649), and Nos 27—50, dated 1649 or later (after March 25th, 1649).

The two groups are again subdivided into sets consisting of impressions that betray intimate relations with each other, being of identical size, arrangement, number of pages, etc. Such sets are e. g. Nos 1—6, 7—9, 10—14, etc.

To permit a view of the field of investigation, I now give the necessary particulars from Almack's book, stating the date, measurement of text, size of type, signatures, and extent of text of each edition.

"In B. M." indicates that one or more copies of the edition thus marked are in the British Museum and have been examined there by the *present* author. The press marks are added in a few instances.

1. *Printed* 1648.
Measurement: — text 5 1/2 by 3.
Size of type: — 12 point.
Signatures: — A 4 leaves; B to S in eights.
Text: — pp. 1—269 (Eikon).
Has an errata-list. Sheet G is wrongly paged. (C. 58. b. 16 in B. M.)

2. The same edition with the errata-list. Sheet G correctly paged. To this edition belongs the Thomason copy in the British Museum with Thomason's [1]) MS. notes: "The first impression" and "Feb. 9th". (C. 59. a. 24 in B. M.)

3. The same edition with the errata-list, but partly set up again.
(Not in B. M.)

4. The same edition, but without errata-list. Small oblong block inserted on title-page. Partly set up again.
(In B. M.)

5. The same edition, but the last page is 270 instead of 269, as a portrait of the Prince of Wales is inserted in the text. After p. 270 there is bound up "The Papers which passed at Newcastle betwixt His Sacred Majestie and Mr. Alex. Henderson", and "A Perfect Copie of Prayers used by His Majesty In the time Of His Sufferings: Delivered to Doctor Juxon, Bishop of London, immediately before His Death." (In B. M.)

6. Imperfect copy of the preceding. Has an additional page, signed V and following T8, with a fresh errata-list and this note:
"The second of the foure Prayers under the Title of [Another Prayer], pag. 4. & 5. though it be here set down according to other printed Copies, was yet none of His Majesties, (but composed by some body out of the first Morning Prayer, and one other in the Practice of Piety) there being indeed but three left by His Majesty. Of which the Reader to prevent his mistake is desired to take notice."
(Not in B. M.)

7. *Printed* 1648.
Measurement: — text 4 $^3/_4$ by 2 $^5/_8$.
Size of type: — Long Primer.
Signatures: — A to H in twelves.
Text: — pp. 1—187 (Eikon).
Only edition with Contents at the end.
(In B. M.)

8. *Printed* 1648.
Measurement: — text 5 by 2 $^1/_2$.
Size of type: — Long Primer.
Signatures: — A to H in twelves.
Text: — pp. 1—187 (Eikon).
(In B. M.)

---

[1]) Thomason was a bookseller who about 1640—1660 made a point of collecting every book, pamphlet, and broadside published during that time, and with his own hand noted the exact date on the fly-leaf. "The Thomason Collection" in the British Museum amounts to some 30000 numbers.

9. *Printed* 1648.
As preceding, but set up again. (In B. M.)

10. *Printed* 1648.
Measurement: — text 4 $^3/_4$ by 2 $^5/_8$.
Size of type: — Pica.
Signatures: — A 4 leaves; B to M in twelves; N 4 leaves.
Text: — pp. 1—269 (Eikon).
(In B. M.)

11. *Printed* 1648.
As preceding, but partly set up again.
(In B. M.)

12. *Printed* 1648.
Measurement: — text 4 $^{13}/_{16}$ by 2 $^{11}/_{16}$.
Size of type: — Pica.
Signatures: — Contents signed N2; B to M in twelves;
            N 4 leaves.
Text: — pp. 1—269 (Eikon).
(In B. M.)

13. *Printed* 1648.
Measurement: — text 4 $^3/_4$ by 2 $^5/_8$. (var.)
Size of type: — Pica.
Signatures: — * 2 leaves; B to M in twelves; N 3 leaves.
Text: — pp. 1—269 (Eikon).
(In B. M.)

14. *Printed* 1648.
Measureuent: — text 4 $^7/_8$ by 2 $^3/_4$. (var.)
Size of type: — Pica.
Signatures: — * 2 leaves; B to M in twelves; N 3 leaves.
Text: — pp. 1—269 (Eikon).
(In B. M.)

15. *Printed* 1648.
Measurement: — text 5 by 2 $^3/_4$. (var.)
Size of type: — 12 point.
Signatures: — A to V in eights; a 4 leaves (!).
Text: — pp. 1—302 (Eikon); four unpaged leaves (Four
            Prayers).
            Contents of appendix (often absent) varying.
(In B. M.)

16. *Printed* 1648.
Measurement: — text 3 $^3/_4$ by 1 $^1/_2$.
Size of type: — Long Primer.
Signatures: — A to Q in twelves; R 11 leaves.
Text: — pp. 1—393 (Eikon).
            The whole book unpaged.

Some copies contain the four prayers etc. bound up at the end.
(Not in B. M.)

17. *Printed* 1648.
Measurement: — text 3 ³/₄ by 1 ³/₄.
Size of type: — Long Primer.
Signatures: — A 4 leaves; B to P in twelves; Q 8 leaves.
Text: — pp. 1—342 (Eikon); pp. 343—54 (Four Prayers, Letter, Relations, Epitaph).
The prayers are mentioned on title-page and in Contents.
(Not in B. M.)

18. *Printed* 1648.
"An edition from which No. 17 probably was composed. The Titlepage is like No. 17, but without mention of Prayers. The list of Contents also only includes the Eikon." (Almack)
(In B. M.)

19. (This edition of the Eikon is included in "Reliquiæ Sacræ Carolinæ The Workes of that Great Monarch and Glorious Martyr King Charles the 1ˢᵗ both Civil and Sacred, the Hague, Printed by Sam. Browne")
Printed 1648.
Measurement: — text 5 ¹/₈ by 3 ¹/₄. (var.)
Size of type: — Pica and 12 point.
Signatures; — A 3 leaves; B to R1 in eights; S to Z, Aa to Bb in eights; Cc 2 leaves; R 4 leaves, etc.
Text: — pp. 1—242 (Eikon); pp. 245—374 (Newcastle papers, Prayer in Captivity); pp. 9—15 (Six additional Prayers), etc.
(In B. M.)

20. The preceding, but not accompanied by the Reliquiæ.
(Not in B. M.)

21. (In the Reliquiæ) Only slightly different from No. 19.
(Not in B. M.)

22. (In the Reliquiæ, the Hague, Printed by Samuell Browne. 1651).
Printed 1648.
Measurement: — text 5 ¹/₂ by 3.
Size of type: — Pica and 12 point.
Signatures: — A to R in eights; S 6 leaves; S to Ee in eights.
Text: — pp. 1—268 (Eikon); pp. 1—10 (Four Prayers etc.); pp. 149—324 (Newcastle papers etc.).
(In B. M.)

23. Eikon and Prayers as preceding.
(Not in B. M.)

24. *Printed* 1648.
Measurement: — text 5 ^{3}/$_8$ by 2 ^{1}/$_4$.
Size of type: — 12 point.
Signatures: — A 4 leaves; B to R in eights; S 7 leaves.
Text: — pp. 1—269 (Eikon).
(Not in B. M.)

25. *Printed* 1648.
Measurement: — text 4 ^{7}/$_8$ by 2 ^{3}/$_4$.
Size of type: — Pica.
Signatures: — A 6 leaves; B to K in twelves.
Text: — pp. 1—225 (Eikon); pp. 1—6 (Four Prayers, printed
      1649, etc.). Prayers not mentioned on title-page nor
      in Contents.
(Not in B. M.)

26. *Printed* 1648. (Hage, Samuell Broun)
Measurement: — text 3 ^{1}/$_4$ by 1 ^{5}/$_8$.
Size of type: — Brevier.
Signatures: — A 7 leaves; B to V in eights; X 7 leaves.
Text: — pp. 1—318 (Eikon).
(In B. M.)

27. *Printed* 1649.
Measurement: — text 4 ^{3}/$_4$ by 2 ^{5}/$_8$.
Size of type: — Long Primer.
Signatures: — A 2 leaves; B to I in twelves; K 2 leaves;
      L 4 leaves.
Text: — pp. 1—195 (Eikon); four unpaged leaves (Four
      Prayers, Letter, printed 1649). Title-page and Con-
      tents include Eikon only.
(Not in B. M.)

28. *Printed* 1649 ('At Paris').
Measurement: — text 5 ^{1}/$_2$ by 3 ^{1}/$_4$.
Size of type: — Pica.
Signatures: — A to C in eights; D to V in fours; X 4 leaves;
      Y 2 leaves; A 8 leaves.
Text: — pp. 1—196 (Eikon); pp. 1—15 (Declaration, Pray-
      ers, etc.).
      Number of prayers 4. Prayers not mentioned on
      title-page nor in Contents.
(Not in B. M.)

29. *Printed* 1649.
Measurement: — text 5 ^{1}/$_2$ by 3.
Size of type: — Pica.
Signatures: — A to O in eights.

Text: — pp. 1—204 (Eikon); pp. 205—16 (Four Prayers, Letter). Title-page and Contents only include the Eikon.

(Not in B. M.)

30. *Printed* 1649 (Hage, Samuel Broun).
Measurement: — text 4 $^1/_4$ by 2 $^1/_4$.
Size of type: — Long Primer.
Signatures: — A 6 leaves; B to O in twelves.
Text: — pp. 1—294 (Eikon); pp. 297—312 (Declaration, Four Prayers, etc.). Prayers mentioned in Contents but not on title-page.

(Not in B. M.)

31. (In Reliquiæ Sacræ Carolinæ, the Hague, Printed by Samuel Browne. 1650).
Printed 1649.
Measurement: — text 4 $^7/_8$ by 2 $^5/_8$.
Size of type: — Long Primer.
Signatures: — Π 8 leaves; A to Dd in twelves; Ee 4 leaves (the whole).
Text: — pp. 1—182 (Eikon); pp. 185—361 (Newcastle papers, Six Prayers, Quæries, etc.).

(In. B. M.)

32. *Printed* 1649.
Measurement: — text 4 $^7/_8$ by 2 $^3/_4$.
Size of type: — Pica.
Signatures: — A to I in twelves; K 10 leaves; L 4 leaves.
Text: — pp. 1—230 (Eikon); pp. 1—7 (Three Prayers, Relations, etc). Prayers mentioned on title-page but not in Contents.

(Not in B. M.)

33. *Printed* 1649.
Measurement: — text 4 $^1/_2$ by 2 $^1/_2$.
Size of type: — Long Primer.
Signatures: — *2 leaves; B to M10 in twelves.
Text: — pp. 1—246 (Eikon); pp. 247—60 (Three Prayers, viz. Captivity, Affliction, Danger; etc.). Prayers mentioned on title-page and in Contents.

(Not in B. M.)

34. *Printed* 1649.
Measurement: — text 4 $^3/_4$ by 2 $^3/_4$.
Size of type: — Pica.
Signatures: — A 2 leaves; B to M in twelves; N 1 leaf.
Text: — pp. 1—268 (Eikon); pp. 269—88 (Prayers, Speeches, Reasons, etc.). Prayers mentioned on title-page and in Contents.

(Not in B. M.)

35. *Printed* 1649 ("at London").
Measurement: — text 4 3/4 by 2 3/4.
Size of type: — Pica.
Signatures: — B to N in twelves.
Text: — pp. 1—269 (Eikon); pp. 273—88 (Prayers (four),
Reasons, etc.). Prayers mentioned on title-page and
in Contents.
(Not in B. M.)

36. *Printed* 1649.
Measurement: — text 3 3/8 by 1 5/8.
Size of type: — Long Primer.
Signatures: — A 4 leaves; B to T in twelves; V 2 leaves.
Text: — pp. 1—412 (Eikon); pp. 413—36 (Three Prayers,
viz. Captivity, Affliction, Danger; etc.). Prayers
mentioned on title-page and in Contents.
(In B. M.)

37. *Printed* 1649.
Measurement: — text 3 1/2 by 1 5/8.
Size of type: — Nonpareil.
Signatures: — A to H in twelves; Π 12 leaves; ΙΙΠ 11
leaves.
Text: — pp. 1—175 (Eikon); five unpaged leaves (Three
Prayers, Reasons etc.); pp. 1—42 (Newcastle papers).
Prayers mentioned on title-page and in Contents.
(In B. M.)

38. This edition differs but slightly from the preceding.
(In B. M.)

39. *Printed* 1649.
Measurement: — text 3 1/2 by 1 9/16.
Size of type: — Nonpareil.
Signatures: — a 4 leaves; A to D in twelves; e 2 leaves;
E to H in twelves.
Text: — pp. 1—175 (Eikon); nine unpaged leaves (Three
Prayers, Reasons, etc.). Prayers mentioned on title-
page and in Contents.
(In B. M.)

40. *Printed* 1649.
Measurement: — text 3 3/5 by 1 1/2.
Size of type: — Nonpareil.
Signatures: — A 4 leaves; B to L8 in twelves.
Text: — pp. 1—185 (Eikon); pp. 186—226 (Newcastle
papers); three unpaged leaves (Three Prayers, Rela-
tions, etc.). Prayers mentioned on title-page and in
Contents.
(In B. M.)

41. *Printed* 1649.
Measurement: — text 4 ¹/₈ by 2 ¹/₈.
Size of type: — Brevier.
Signatures: — A 4 leaves; B to L in twelves; M 2 leaves.
Text: — pp. 1—182 (Eikon); pp. 1—12 (Four Prayers etc.);
　　　　pp. 1—48 (Apophthegmata Aurea Regia Carolina,
　　　　Printed 1649.). Prayers mentioned on title-page and
　　　　in Contents.
(In B. M.)

42. *Printed* 1649.
Measurement: — 6 ¹/₂ by 3 ⁷/₈.
Size of type: — 16 point.
Signatures: — A 4 leaves; B to R in eights; S 4 leaves.
Text: — pp. 1—251 (Eikon); pp. 253—63 (Four Prayers,
　　　　Letter, etc.). Prayers mentioned on title-page and in
　　　　Contents.
(Not in B. M.)

43. *Printed* 1649.
Measurement: — text 6 ¹/₂ by 3⁷/₈.
Size of type: — 16 point.
Signatures: — A 4 leaves; B to R in eights; S 4 leaves.
Text: — pp. 1—251 (Eikon); pp. 253—63 (Four Prayers etc.).
　　　　Prayers mentioned on title-page and in Contents.
(In B. M.)

44. *Printed* 1649.
Measurement: — text 6 ¹/₂ by 3 ⁷/₈.
Size of type: — 16 point.
Signatures: — A 4 leaves; B to R in eights; S 4 leaves.
Text: — pp. 1—251 (Eikon); pp. 253—63 (Four Prayers etc.).
　　　　Prayers mentioned on title-page and in Contents.
(In B. M.)

45. (In Reliquiæ Sacræ Carolinæ, the Hague, Printed by
Sam: Browne).
Printed 1649 (by W. D. in R. M.).
Measurement: — text 5 ⁵/₈ by 3 ¹/₄.
Size of type: — Pica and 12 point.
Signatures: — A 5 leaves; B to Q6 in eights; S to Bb in
　　　　eights, etc.
Text: — pp. 1—236 (Eikon); pp. 245—370 (Newport papers);
　　　　pp. 9—15 (Six Prayers etc.). In the Contents of the
　　　　Eikon the Four Prayers are erroneously mentioned
　　　　as coming in after p. 236. In the general Contents
　　　　the Captivity Prayer occupies pp. 373—74.
(Not in B. M.)

46. *Printed* 1649.
Measurement: — text 5 ³/₈ by 3 ¹/₈.
Size of type: — 12 point.
Signatures: — A 4 leaves; B to S in eights; T 4 leaves;
    ₊₊ 2 leaves.
Text: — pp. 1—269 (Eikon); pp. 270—78 (Three Prayers,
    Letter, etc.). Prayers mentioned on title-page and
    in Contents. Pagination of the last leaves faulty.
(Not in B. M.)

47. *Printed* 1649.
Measurement: — text 5 ⁵/₈ by 2 ³/₈.
Size of type: — 12 point.
Signatures: — A 2 leaves; S 6 leaves; B to Q in eights;
    R 4 leaves; T 2 leaves; S to Ee in eights.
Text: — Five unpaged leaves (Prayers (four), etc); pp. 1—247
    (Eikon); pp. 149—324 (Newcastle papers, Diverse
    Prayers, etc.). Prayers mentioned on title-page but
    not in Contents.
(Not in B. M.)

48. Same as preceding, with insignificant changes in the
get-up.
(Not in B. M.)

49. (In Reliquiæ Sacræ Carolinæ, the Hague, Samuell Browne
1651). Same as the two preceding.
(Not in B. M.)

50. The same edition, with a slight variation in the title-page.
(Not in B. M.)

51. *Printed* 1649 (Hagæ-Comitis).
Measurement: — text 4 ¹/₈ by 2 ¹/₄.
Size of type: — Long Primer.
Signatures: — A to L in twelves; Π 3 leaves; A4 to A12
    9 leaves.
Text: — pp. 1—252 (Eikon); pp. 253—58 (Explications);
    pp. 1—22 (Proceedings of the High Court, Speech,
    etc.). This edition is in Latin and does not contain
    the prayers.
(In B. M.)

52. *Printed* 1649 (Hagæ-Comitis Ex Officina Samuelis
    Broun).
Measurement: — text 4 ¹/₄ by 2 ¹/₄.
Size of type: — Long Primer.
Signatures: — A 6 leaves; B to M in twelves; N 4 leaves.
Text: — pp. 1—263 (Eikon); pp. 265—72 (Explications). In
    Latin. No prayers.
(In B. M.)

53. *Printed* 1649 (Hagæ-Comitis).
Measurement: — text 4 ¹/₄ by 2 ¹/₄.
Size of type: — Long Primer.
Signatures: — A 8 leaves; B to M in twelves; N 4 leaves.
Text: — pp. 1—263 (Eikon); pp. 265—72 (Explications). In
   Latin. No prayers.
(In B. M.)

54. *Printed* 1649 (A Rouen).
Measurement: — text 3 ⁷/₈ by 2.
Size of type: — Pica.
Signatures: — ā 6 leaves; 3 sheets in sixes; ū 2 leaves;
   A to Kk in sixes; Ll 2 leaves.
Text: — pp. 1—398 (Eikon). In French.
(In B. M.)

55. *Printed* 1649 (A Rouen).
Measurement: — text 6 ⁷/₈ by 4 ³/₈.
Size of type: — 16 point.
Signatures: — ĕ, ĭ, ŏ, ŭ, ăă in fours; ĕĕ 2 leaves; A to Z
   in fours; Aa to Vv in fours; Xx 4 leaves.
Text: — pp. 1—318 (Eikon); pp. 321—52 (Declaration,
   Raisons, Prières, etc.). In French. Prayers mentioned
   in Contents. Their number is four.
(Not in B. M.)

56. *Printed* 1649 (A Paris).
Measurement: — text 7 ¹/₁₆ by 4 ¹/₄.
Size of type: — Pica.
Signatures: — ā, ē in fours; A to S2 in fours.
Text: — pp. 1—139 (Eikon). In French, edited by the Roman
   Catholics in opposition to the preceding edition.
(Not in B. M.)

57. *Printed* 1649 (A la Hay).
Measurement: — text 4 ¹³/₁₆ by 2 ⁷/₁₆.
Size of type: — Long Primer.
Signatures: — A 6 leaves; * 2 leaves; a 6 leaves; b 2 leaves;
   B to Bb in sixes; a to g4 in sixes.
Text: — pp. 1—269 (Eikon); pp. 1—79 (Prières, Propos à
   la Princesse Elizabeth, etc). The number of prayers
   is four.
(In B. M.)

58. *Printed* 1649.
Measurement: —? text 6 ³/₅ by 4 ⁷/₈.
Size of type: — 10 point.
Signatures: —? 6 leaves; A to X3 in fours.
Text: — Not paged (Eikon and *Erklärung*). In German.
(In B. M.)

59. *Printed* 1649 (Tot Rotterdam).
Measurement: — text 4 $^1/_2$ by 2 $^1/_4$.
Size of type: — Long Primer.
Signatures: — * 5 leaves; A 11 leaves; B to O in twelves;
P 9 leaves.
Text: — pp. 1—350 (Eikon). In Dutch.
(In B. M.)

60. *Printed* 1649 (t' Amstelredam).
Measurement: — text 4 $^1/_4$ by 2 $^5/_8$.
Size of type: — Long Primer.
Signatures: — A to O in twelves.
Text: — pp. 5—332 (Eikon). In Dutch.
(Not in B. M.)

61. (In Basilika, the Works of King Charles the Martyr,
Printed 1662).
Printed 1662.
Measurement: — 10 $^1/_4$ by 5 $^7/_8$.
Size of type: — 16 point.
Signatures: — B to N in sixes; O 4 leaves.
Text: — pp. 1—151 (Eikon); pp. 155—98 (Newcastle papers,
7 Prayers).
(In B. M.)

62. *Printed* 1681 (London).
Measurement: — text 5 $^7/_8$ by 3 $^1/_4$.
Size of type; — 12 point.
Signatures: — A2 to A8 7 leaves; B to R in eights.
Text: — pp. 1—256 (Eikon).
(In B. M.)

63. *Printed* 1685 (London).
Measurement: — text 5 $^7/_8$ by 3 $^1/_8$.
Size of type: — 12 point.
Signatures: — A to S in eights.
Text: — pp. 1—256 (Eikon); pp. 259—72 (Four Prayers, etc).
Prayers mentioned in Contents. (In B. M.)

64. *Printed* 1687 (In Basilika).
Measurement: — text 11 $^3/_8$ by 6 $^1/_8$.
Size of type: — 12 point.
Signatures: — Nnnn 4 leaves; Oooo to Zzzz in fours.
Text: — pp. 93—95 (Seven Prayers); pp. 647—720 (Eikon).
(In B. M.)

65. *Printed* 1706 (Dublin).
Measurement: — text 5 $^1/_4$ by 2 $^7/_8$.
Size of type: — Long Primer.
Signatures: — A 4 leaves; B to N in eights.
Text: — pp. 1—172 (Eikon); pp. 173—88 (Four Prayers, etc.).
(In B. M.)

66. *Printed* 1727.
Measurement: — text 6 1/4 by 3 5/16.
Size of type: — Pica.
Signatures: — a 4 leaves; b 2 leaves; B to Gg6 in eights.
Text: — pp. 1—207 (Eikon); pp 211—24 (Four Prayers etc.).
        Contents include the prayers.
(In B. M.)

67. *Printed* 1735 (In the works of Charles I.).
(In B. M.)

68. *Printed* 1747 (Dresden und Leipzig). In German.
(In B. M.)

69. *Printed* 1766 (Aberdeen).
(In B. M.)

70. *Printed* 1824 (London).
(In B. M.)

71. *Printed* 1827 (Paris).
(In B. M.)

72. *Printed* 1876 (London, D. Stewart).
(In B. M.)

73. *Printed* 1879 (London, D. Stewart).
(In B. M.)

74. *Printed* 1869 (London, James Parker).
(In B. M.)

75. *Printed* 1879 (London, James Parker).
(In B. M.)

76. *Printed* 1880 (London, Elliot Stock).
(In B. M.)

Almack disclaims completeness and any systematic treatment
and, in fact, his book lacks pertinent matter to such a degree as to
prevent us from deriving any considerable advantage (beyond the
one stated) from it. Besides the above list it contains mostly ramblings
in regions connected with the authorship of the Eikon. Even the
list of editions is arranged somewhat at haphazard, with full notes
as to who possessed where and when, but very scanty information
about matters that might be useful for determining printers, relation
of editions, typography, etc. All examining, collation, and the like had
therefore to be done by myself, and the result of this will, as far as
necessary, be put down in the following chapters. I am sorry that
I must often be content with offering hints only, where a photo-
graphic reproduction would have been more to the purpose.

CHAPTER IX.

The Evidence of the Eikons.

The six early Dugard editions. Armstrong copy and Thomason copy. Nos 5 and 6. The collaboration copies. Simmons's edition? The errata-list.

The first six editions were undoubtedly printed by Dugard. The big woodcut initial on the first page, the border of which is damaged in a peculiar way, occurs in many books which according to their title-pages are printed by Dugard. These editions are all but identical in get-up. Some types aud ornaments are changed, fluctuation of orthography appears, sometimes one or more pages are re-set, a parenthesis disappears, etc., as is seen by a collation of the first pages in Nos 1, 2, 4, and 5.

Comparative table showing typographical peculiarities in the first pages of Nos 1 and 2.

No 1	No 2
Title-page = No 2.	= No 1.
Contents = No 2.	= No 1.
Contents faultily signed A 2, A 4 = No 2.	= No 1.
Errata-list = No 2.	= No 1.
Headpiece = Nos 2, 4.	= Nos 1, 4.
Εικὼν = Nos 2, 5.	= Nos 1, 5.
P. 1. and = No 2.	= No 1.
( ) = No 2.	= No 1.
P. 2. = No 2.	= No 1.
Lawes = No 2.	= No 1.
Zeale = No 2.	= No 1.
regulations = No 2.	= No 1.
My owne Judgement = No 2.	= No 1.
P. 4. ὁ Lord = No 2.	= No 1.
ὁ Lord = No 2.	= No 1.
M (angular) = No 2.	= No 1.
P. 5. = No 2.	= No 1.

Comparative table of the corresponding typographical peculiarities in the first pages of Nos 4 and 5.

No 4	No 5
Title-page = No 5.	= No 4.
Contents: Angular and rounded capitals interchanging; signed A 2, A 3.	Cont.: Capitals interchanging, but differently from No 4; signed as No 4.
Catchword, "Εικών".	No catchword.
No errata-list.	No errata-list.
Headpiece = Nos 1, 2.	A different headpiece.
Εικών different.	Εικών = Nos 1, 2.
P. 1. as No parenthesis.	— as No parenthesis.
P. 2. = No 5.	= No 4.
P. 3. different from Nos 1, 2, 5. Lavves Zeal regulations My own Judgement	— different from Nos 1, 2, 4. Laws zeale Regulations my own judgement
P. 4. O Lord ô Lord M (rounded)	= No 4. (O Lord) = No 4
P. 5. different from Nos 1, 2, 5.	— different from Nos 1, 2, 4.

No 1 differs from No 2 in having sheet G wrongly paged. An interesting copy of this edition exists which has "Guil. Armstrong" in pencil and "London, Printed for R. Royston in Ivie-lane" in print on the title-page. This book may have been in the possession of Armstrong, the corrector to Dugard's press [1]). The lines betraying the publisher were naturally removed before the whole edition was printed.

No 2 is Thomason's first impression.

Nos 1—4 contain the Eikon only, Nos 5 and 6 have the appendix, too, with the prayers. On examination, however, Eikon and appendix turn out to be printed independently of each other, as they have separate signatures. The Eikons are dated 1648, the appendixes 1649. As these Eikons are apparently later than the other four editions, the first of which was out in the beginning of Feb., Nos 5 and 6 were probably ready but shortly before March 25th. The appendix was evidently printed immediately after March 25th and just for these Eikons, because, if the latter were finished in the middle of March and the appendices were an afterthought, say, in May, June, or later, most, if not all, of these

---

[1]) Suggested by Almack, Bibl.

Eikon copies would have been sold without appendix whereas now all of them seem to have it. This fact fits in very well with the Parliament's seizure of Dugard and his copies on March 17th and the tradition of his release on Milton's intervention, (who two days before had become Latin secretary to the revolutionaries), and on his promise to add the Pamela Prayer to the Eikon.

I here subjoin details of signatures and extent of text in the British Museum copy of No 5 and in the Guildhall copy of the same edition.

Signatures: A 4 leaves; B to S in eights; A to D in eights; T eight leaves (B. M. copy).

A 4 leaves; B—S in eights; S eight leaves; T two leaves; A—D in eights: A—B in eights; C 6 leaves (Guildhall copy).

Text: — pp. 1—270 (Eikon); pp. 1—58 (Papers which passed at Newcastle Betwixt His Sacred Majestie and Mr. Alex Henderson concerning the Change of Church-Government. Anno Dom. 1646. London. Printed for R. Royston, **1649**); pp. 3—16 (A perfect copie of Prayers used by His Majesty In the time of His Sufferings: Delivered to Doctor Juxon, Bishop of London, immediately before His Death; Also a Copie of a Letter from the Prince; His Majesties Reasons against the pretended Jurisdiction of the High Court of Justice; Three Relations of the Lady Elizabeth; Epitaph, Printed in **1649** (B. M. copy).

— pp. 1—270 (Eikon). Then follow Prayers, Letter, Relations, Epitaph, Reasons, Printed 1649; and Newcastle papers, Printed 1649 (Guildhall copy) [1]).

Nos 7—9 are another set apparently issued by one single printer in rapid succession. They offer nothing of special interest save that No 7 was indicated by Wagstaffe as the first edition (see ante). The prayers are absent.

Nos 10—14 are extremely remarkable; they betray the haste and secrecy of their publication inasmuch as the printing is unusually bad, types are turned topsy-turvy, leaping up over and tumbling down beneath the lines, and these are crooked and broken themselves; in running head-lines and pagination letters and figures are often missing; the pages are but indifferently leaded and spaced, etc. The wretched headpieces in these Eikons betray Grismond. They consist of a row of small lighted lamps or candlesticks appearing in G.'s earlier prints, but then evidently rejected.

Different copies of one single edition are often of very unequal value. The character of these editions may be illustrated by a comparison of one copy of No 11 and two of No 12.

---

[1]) These six ed. are apparently successive, all of them exhibiting Dugard's well-known 12 point. On other occasions he would employ another printer to collaborate in order to procure a fair-sized edition on short notice. Cf. the two sets of Milton's Defence in 1650, both marked *Typis Dugardianis*.

Comparative table of typographical peculiarities in the first pages of Nos 11 and 12 a.

No 11	No 12a
Title-page different from Nos 12 a and b.	Title-page as No 12 b.
Contents different from Nos 12 a and b.	Contents as No 12 b.
P. 1. in the most minute details identical with No 12.	P. 1. as Nos 11 and 12 b.
P. 2. Childreus	P. 2. Childrens
P. 3. offences	P. 3. offences
exceeding	exceeding
advantages	advantages
practicebut supply	practicebut supply
P. 4. is identical with No 12 b.	P. 4. different from Nos 11 and 12 b.
P. 5. identical with Nos 12 a and b.	P. 5. as Nos 11 and 12 b.
P. 6. identical with Nos 12 a and b.	P. 6. as Nos 11 and 12 b.
envions (for envious)	envions
P. 7. nnfortunate	P. 7. nnfortunate
mans	mans
P. 8. Not paged.	P. 8. Paged.
un ust (for unjust).	un ust
P. 9. as Nos 12 a and b.	P. 9. as Nos 11 and 12 b.
P. 10. would	P. 10. would
terrifi'd	terrifi'd
do	doe
future	future
and	and
should	should
bearing	bearing
P. 11. as Nos 12 a and b.	P. 11. as Nos 11 and 12 b.
Pp. 12—17. as Nos 12 a and b.	Pp. 12—17. as Nos 11 and 12 b.
P. 18. must	P. 18. must
cōmand	cōmand
obstructions	obstructions
P. 19. of	P. 19. of
owne	owne
P. 34. by Sea to a storm	P. 34. by Sea to a storm
P. 49. (sign. D.). Types changed from preceding.	P. 49. (sign. D). Types changed from preceding.

Table of corresponding typographical peculiarities in the first pages of No 12b.

No 12b	No 12b
Title-page as No 12a.	beering
Contents as No 12a.	P. 11. as Nos 11 and 12a.
P. 1. as Nos 11 and 12a.	Pp. 12—17. as Nos 11 and 12a.
P. 2. Childreus	P. 18. mnst
P. 3. offeuces	cōmand
ezceeding	obwructions
aduantages	P. 19. o⌒⊣
practice, but upply	o⋏⋏ne
P. 4. as No 11.	Pages 18 and 19 transposed.
P. 5. as Nos 11 and 12a.	P. 34. by Sea to a storm
P. 6. as Nos 11 and 12a.	P. 49. (sign. D). Types chan-
envions	ged from preceding.
P. 7. nnfortunate	
Man$_s$	
P. 8. Not paged.	
un ust	
P. 9. as Nos 11 and 12a.	
P. 10. woule	
terrifid	
do	
futnre	
aud	
shonld	

It is evident that sheets B and C of No 12b are earlier than the corresponding sheets of the others. "Practice, but upply", in No 12b has been rectified in the others by removing the space between "practice" and "but". Next comes No 11 where the erratum "Childreus" remains. The last sheets of a bad edition, however, may be decidedly superior to those of a better one [1]), types used in one edition suddenly disappear and turn up again in another. As will be seen presently, the Contents of the bad No 12b is superior to that of No 12a, and its D-sheet to that of Nos 10 and 11.

Here follow tables of some remarkable differences or coincidences in Nos 10, 11, 12a and b, 13, and 14. = indicates close affinity either in get-up or correctness. (E. g. the A-sheets of Nos 12a, 13, 14 are related as to correctness, but No 13 is different in get-up.).

---

[1]) Such interchange of the sheets has been more fully explained in a forthcoming article in E. St.

Table of Nos 10 and 11.

No 10	No 11
Sheet A different from the other ed.	Sheet A = No 12b.
Sheet B different from the other ed.	Sheet B == No 12b.
Sheet C = Nos 11, 12a and b.	Sheet C = Nos 10, 12a and b.
Sheet D = Nos 11, 12a and b.	Sheet D = Nos 10, 12a and b.
Sheet E, p. 73. an my side	Sheet E, p. 73. an my side
P. 74. strength	P. 74. rength
Pp. 76—7. Change in types, as in Nos 11, 12a and b, to those till now used in No 14.	Pp. 76—7. Change in types, as in No 10 etc.
Pp. 78—9. Types of p. 75, as in Nos 11, 12a and b.	Pp. 78—9. as in No 10.
Pp. 80—1. Types of p. 76 (and No 14).	Pp. 80—1. as in No 10.
Pp. 82—3. Types of p. 75.	Pp. 82—96. as in No 10.
P. 84. Types of p. 76.	Sheet F as in No 10.
Pp. 85—91. Types of p. 75.	Sheet G as in No 10 etc.
Pp. 92—3. Types of p. 76.	Last words on p. 135.
Pp. 94—6. Types of p. 75.	be able
Sheet F has throughout the types of p. 76 (and No 14).	shi
Sheet G = Nos 11, 12a and b.	Sheet H = Nos 12b, 14.
Last words on p. 135.	Sheet I = Nos 10, 12a and b, 14.
be able	Sheet K = Nos 12a and b.‧
Sheet H == Nos 12a, 13.	Sheet L = Nos 10 and 12b.
Sheet I = Nos 11, 12a and b, 14.	Sheet M = No 10.
Sheet K different from other ed.	Sheet N = No 10.
Sheet L = Nos 11, 12b.	
Sheet M = No 11.	
Sheet N = No 11.	

Table of Nos 12a and b.

No 12a	No 12b
Sheet A = No 14.	Sheet A = No 11.
Sheet B = No 14.	Sheet B = No 11.
Sheet C = Nos 10, 11, and 12b.	Sheet C = Nos 10, 11, etc.
Sheet D = Nos 10, 11, and 12b.	Sheet D = Nos 10, 11, etc.
Sheet E, p. 73. an my side	Sheet E, p. 73. an my side

No 12a	No 12b
P. 74. rength	P. 74. rength
Pp. 76—7. Change in types, as in No 10 etc., but re-set.	Pp. 76—7. Change in types, as in No 10 etc.
Pp. 78—9. as in No 10.	Pp. 78—9. as in No 10.
Pp. 80—1. as in No 10.	Pp. 80—1. as in No 10.
Pp. 82—3. as in No 10.	Pp. 82—3. as in No 10.
P. 84. as in No 10.	P. 84. as in No 10.
Pp. 85—91. as in No 10.	Pp. 85—91. as in No 10.
Pp. 92—3. as in No 10.	Pp. 92—3. as in No 10.
Pp. 98—9. as in No 12b, viz. a change in types not to be found in Nos 10 and 11.	Pp. 94—6. as in No 10.
	Pp. 98—9. as in No 12a.
P. 100 ff. Change in types every two pages as before.	Pp. 100—1. as in No 10.
	Pp. 102—3. as is No 12a.
Sheet G = Nos 10, 11, and 12b.	Pp. 104—5. as in No 10.
Last words on p. 135.	Pp. 106—7. as in No 12a.
be able	Pp. 108—9. as in No 10.
to	Pp. 110—1. as in No 12a.
Sheet H = Nos 10, 13.	P. 112 ff. Change in types every two pages as before [1]).
Sheet I = Nos 10, 11, 12b, 14.	Sheet G = Nos 10, 11, and 12a.
Sheet K = Nos 11, 12b.	Last words on p. 135.
Sheet L different from other ed.	be able
Sheet M different from other ed.	shi
Sheet N = No 12b.	Sheet H = Nos 11, 14.
	Sheet I = Nos 10, 11, 12a, and 14.
	Sheet K = Nos 11, 12a.
	Sheet L = Nos 10, 11.
	Sheet M = No 14.
	Sheet N = No 12a.

[1]) The regular change in type may appear puzzling at first sight but is easily explained. The extreme hurry of the printers to satisfy the demand for the book, unprecedented in the trade, made them employ every means of hastening the publication. The printer or printers of Nos 10—14 apparently unfolded the sheets of an Eikon to be pirated and placed them so that the recto of each unfolded sheet could be seen and composed by one or more compositors at the same time as the verso by other compositors. For some reason, want of type or the borrowing of type from another printer, the recto compositor(s) after a while had recourse to types as closely as possible resembling the original ones. Then the 1st, 4th, 5th, 8th, 9th, 12th, 13th, 16th, 17th, 20th, 21st, and 24th page of each sheet should offer the one type; the 2nd, 3rd, 6th, 7th, 10th, 11th, 14th, 15th, 18th, 19th, 22nd, and 23rd, the other. And so they do with great regularity, the exceptional pages being very few.

Table of Nos 13 and 14.

No 13	No 14
Sheet A different from other ed.	Sheet A = No 12a.
Sheet B different from other ed.	Sheet B = No 12a.
Sheet C different from other editions.	Sheet C different from other ed.
	Sheet D different from other ed.
Sheet D different from other ed.	Sheet E, p. 73. on my side
Sheet E different from other ed.	P. 74. strength
Sheet F different from other ed.	P. 76 ff. No change in types.
Sheet G = No 14.	Sheet F different from other ed.
Last words on p. 135.	Sheet G = No 13.
be able to hide the	Last words on p. 135.
shining	be able to hide
Sheet H = Nos 10, 12a.	the
Sheet I different from the other ed.	shining
	Sheet H = Nos 11, 12b.
Sheet K different from the other ed.	Sheet I = Nos 10, 11, 12a, 12b.
	Sheet K different from the other ed.
Sheet L different from the other ed.	Sheet L different from the other ed.
Sheet M different from the other ed.	Sheet M = No 12b.
Sheet N = No 14.	Sheet N = No 13 [1]).

It cannot be doubted that these editions are the result of a collaboration of different printers. The first page in No 10 is so minutely identical with the corresponding ones in Nos 11, 12a, b, and 14 that they must have been printed by the same press without the slightest alteration. The last sheets, on the contrary, go together in pairs.

An examination of printer's errors shows that the value of the sheets is interchanging. Some instances are offered.

Order of Contents in these editions according to correctness: — 14, 13, 12a, 12b, 11, 10 (best).

Order of sheet B: — 12b, 11, 14, 12a, 10, 13 (best).
Order of sheet C: — 12b, 11, 12a, 10, 14, 13 (best).
Order of sheet D: — 10, 11, 12b, 12a, 14, 13 (best), etc.

No 15 sometimes has the prayers at the end, of course a later addition.

No 17 is the only edition dated 1648 that has the four prayers as an integral part of the book. They are also mentioned in the Contents and on the title-page. This may be the edition printed by Simmons, because the following one, No 18, which has *not* the prayers nor any mention of them, is so similar to No 17 that Mr. Almack, who has been fortunate enough to see

---

[1]) The inconsistencies in the form of the tables will help in checking the contents.

some copies, thinks this edition composed from No 18. The edition is singularly naked and difficult to trace to any special printer.

No 22 was printed by Dugard. An oblong showy ornament inscribed *"cor unum vita una"* immediately betrays that printer. Type and get-up are the same as in Nos 1—6.

No 26 was printed at the Hague by Samuel Brown, an English printer who at the crisis in England left his country and brought along some of his printing materials. At the Hague he became the royalist printer, was protected by Charles II. (then residing in this city), and got an exclusive printing license for the Eikon from the States General. The prayers are wanting here, but Brown added them (four!) to the second Hague edition (No 30 in Almack) which was presumably printed in April, as the accompanying printer's license is dated April 2nd, 1649.

Nos 37—39 were evidently printed by William Bentley. Observe the mark with the device *"Deus est nobis sol et scutum* [1]*)"*.

Nos 43—44 came from Cambridge. The curious initial letter, a little damaged, on p. 1 in No 44, is found in a pamphlet "Of Religious Assemblies, 1642" printed by Roger Daniel, printer to the University, Cambridge.

To find out the possibility of eliciting the chronological order of the editions the errata-list given in the undoubtedly earliest edition has been followed up through the others. The editions are numbered as in Almack's Bibliography, copies of the same edition in some instances being distinguished by a and b.

The copies compared are those of Nos 1—44 which are found in the British Museum. Save in the case of the first one, the number of the edition is indicated at the head of each column, in some cases the press mark too, within brackets. "Grenville" belongs to the collection thus named in the British Museum. The figures before each erratum mean the page. If an erratum is without figures, it is on the same page as the preceding one, if a whole column, its pagination is identical with that of the preceding edition.

Table showing the correspondence of Nos 1, 2, 4, 5, to original errata-list.

(C. 58. b. 16; C. 59. a. 24)	4	5
12. of make me and Joy	O make Me of Joy	O make me of joy
14. attended	attended	attended
21. for any man	for any man	in any man
28. Men of Honors	men of Honour	men of Honour
33. by My sins	by my sins	for My sins
34. by Sea to a storm	by Sea to a storm	to Sea by a storm
37. detrusions	obtrusions	obtrusions

[1]) Cf. Doble in the Academy, 1883.

(C. 58. b. 16, C. 59. a. 24)	4	5
51. preparations	preparations	perpetrations
52. for his death	as his death	for as his death
58. as the Bill	was the Bill	was the Bill
61. know	knew	knew
68. power, or	power, or	power, so
87. through thy	through the	through the
112. popularity	populacy	populacy
114. crosse not though	crosse not the	crosse not their
131. No even	No Men	No men
142. it expected	it be expected	it be expected
186. every will	ever will	ever will
205. Saviour	Saviours	Saviours
233. le Bow [1])	le Bon	le Bon

Table showing the correspondence of Nos 7—9
to original errata-list.

7	8	9
8. O make me and joy	O make me of Joy	O make me of Joy
10. attended me	attended Me	attended me
15. in any man	in any man	in any man
19. men or honour	Men of Honor	Men of Honour
23. by my sins	for My sins	for My sins
25. by sea to a storm obtrusions	to Se by a storm detrusions	to Sea by a storm detrusions
35. perpetrations for as his death	perpetrations for as his death	perpetrations for as his death
40. was the Bill	was the Bill	was the Bill
42. knew	knew	knew
47. power, so	46. power, so	46. Power, so
60. through the	60. through the	60. through the
77. popularity	popularity	populacy
79. { cause not their though chiefe design	{ cross not their, though chief, Design	{ crosse not their, though chief, Design
91. No men	No men	No men
99. be expected	be expected	be expected
130. ever will	ever will	ever will
143. Saviours	Saviour s	Saviours
162. le Bon	le Bon	le Bon

[1]) The correct readings are seen e. g. in No 39a.

Table showing the correspondence of Nos 10—12 a
to original errata-list.

10	11	12 a
12. O make me	O make me	O make me
of Joy	of Joy	of Joy
14. attended Me	attended Me	attended Me
21. in any man	in any man	in any man
28. Men of Honour	Men of Honour	Men of Honour
33. by My sins	by My sins	by My sins
34. by Sea to a storm	by Sea to a storm	by Sea to a storm
37. obtrusions	obtrusions	obtrusions
51. perpetrations	perpetrations	perpetrations
52. for as his death	for as his death	for as his death
58. was the Bill	was the Bill	was the Bill
61. knew	knew	knew
68. power, so	power, so	power, so
87. through the	through the	through the
112. populacy	populacy	populacy
114. { crosse not their	{ crosse not their	{ crosse not their
{ chief Design	{ chief Design	{ chief Design
131. No men	No men	No men
142. be expected	be expected	be expected
186. ever will	will ever	will ever
205. Saviours	Saviours	Saviours
233. le Bon	le Bon	le Bon

Table showing the correspondence of Nos 12 b—14
to original errata-list.

12 b	13	14
O make me	O make me	O make me
of Joy	of Joy	of Joy
attended Me	attended Me	attended Me
in any man	in any man	in any man
Men of Honour	men of Honour	men of Honour
by My sins	for my sins	for My sins
by Sea to a Storm	to Sea by a Storm	to Sea by a Storm
obtrusions	obtrusions	obtrusions
perpetrations	expectations (!)	expectations
for as his death	for as his death	for as his death
was the Bill	was the Bill	as the Bill
knew	knew	knew

12 b	13	14
power, so	power, so	power, so
through the	through the	through the
populacy	populacy	populacy
{crosse not their chief { Design	{crosse not their {chiefe Designe	{crosse not their {chief Design
No men	No men	No men
be expected	be expected	be expected
ever will	ever will	will ever
Saviours	Saviour	Saviours
le Bon	le Bon	le Bon

Table showing the correspondence of Nos 15, 18, 22
to original errata-list.

15	18	22
13. O make Me of Joy	15. O make me and Joy	12. O make Me of Joie
16. attended Me	17. attended	14. attended
24. in any man	26. for any man	21. for anie man
32. men of Honor for My sins	34. Men of Honours 40. for My sins	27. men of Honor 32. for My sins
38. to Sea by a storm	41. to Sea by a storm	33. to Sea by a storm
42. obtrusions	45. obtrusions	36. obtrusions
59. perpetrations for as his death	63. perpetrations 64. for as his death	51. perpetrations as his death
67. was the Bill	72. was the Bill	58. was the Bill
70. knew	76. knew	61. (transposed to 71) knew
78. power, so	84. power, so	68. power, or
101. through Thy	109. through the	87. through the
131. (numb. 135) po- pulary (!)	140. populacy	112. populacie
134. {crosse not though {chiefe Designe	144. {crosse not their {chief Design	114. {cross not the {Chief Design
145. No men	165. No men	145. (pag. faulty) No Men
159. be expected	179. be expected	142. bee expected
210. ever will	236. ever will	186. ever will
230. Saviours	260. Saviours	205. Saviour's
262. le Bon	295. le Bon	233. le Bon

Table showing the correspondence of Nos 26, 36, 37
to original errata-list.

26	36	37
14. oh make me of joy	18. O make Me of Joy	8. O make me of Joy
16. attended me	20. attended	9. attended me
25. in any man	32. for any man	14. in any man
32. men of Honour	41. Men of Honour	18. Men of Honour
38. for My sins	49. by My sinnes	22. for my sins
39. by a storm to Sea	50. by Sea to a storm	to Sea by a storm
43. obtrusions	55. obtrusions	24. obtrusions
59. perpetrations	77. preparations	33. perpetrations
60. for as his death	78. for as his death	for as his death
68. was the Bill	88. was the Bill	38. was the Bill
71. knew	92. knew	40. knew
79. power, so	103. power, or	44. power, or
103. through the	133. through the	57. through the
131. populacy	170. populacy	73. populacy
134. {crosse not the chiefe	174. {crosse not the Chiefe	74. {crosse not the chief
154. None ever(!)	200. No Men	85. No men
167. be expected	218. be expected	93. be expected
221. ever will	286. ever will	121. ever will
243. Saviours	315. saviours	134. Saviours
276. le Bon	358. le Bon	154. le Bon

Table showing the correspondence of Nos 38 a, b, 39 a
to original errata-list.

38 a (Grenville 11665)	38 b (808. a. 8)	39 a (292. a. 45)
8. O make me of Joy	= =	O make Me =
9. attended me	=	10. =
14. in any man	=	=
18. Men of Honour	=	19. =
22. for my sins to Sea by a storm	= =	22. for My sins 23. =
24. obtrusions	=	25. =
33. perpetrations for as his death	= =	34. = 35. =
38. was the Bill	=	39. =

38 a (Grenville 11665)	38 b (808. a. 8)	39 a (292. a. 45)
40. knew	=	41. =
44. power, so	=	46. =
57. through the	=	59. =
73. populacie	=	75. populacy

74. {crosse not the
    chief
	=	77. {crosse not their
		    chief

85. No men	=	89. =
93. be expected	=	96. =
121. ever will	=	126. ever wil
134. Saviours	=	137. =
152. le Bon	=	157. =

Table showing the correspondence of Nos 39 b, 40, 41
to original errata-list.

39 b (Grenville 11666)	40	41

9. O make me
    of Joy
	8. O make Me
	    and Joy
		8. O make Mee
		    of Joie

10. attended me	10. attended	10. attended
15. in any man	15. for any man	15. for anie man
20. Men of Honour	19. Men of Honor	men of Honor
23. for my sins	23. by My sins	22. for My sins
24. to Sea by a storm	25. by Sea to a storm	23. to Sea by a storm
26. obtrusions	obtrusions	25. obtrusions

37. perpetrations
    for as his death
	35. perpetrations
	    for as his death
		35. perpetrations
		    for as his death

42. was the Bill	40. was the Bill	39. was the Bill.
44. knew	42. knew	41. knew
49. power, so	47. power, so	46. power, so
63. through the	60. through thy	59. through the
82. populacy	77. populacy	75. Populacie

84. {crosse not the
    chief
	78. {cross not their
	    chief
		77. {cross not the
		    chief

97. No men	90. No men	88. No Men
93. (pag. faulty) be expected	98. be expected	96. bee expected
121. ever will	128. ever will	126. ever will
134. Saviours	141. Saviors	139. Saviour's
152. le Bon	160. le Bon	158. le Bon

Table showing the correspondence of Nos 43, 44 to original errata-list.

(599. e. 15; Grenville 1764; 599. e. 11.) 43	(C. 69. e. 7; 294. k. 25; 8122. bb. 14.) 44
11. O make me of Joy	11. O make me of Joy
13. attended Me	13. attended Me
20. in any man	20. in any man
26. Men of Honours	26. men of Honour
31. for My sins to Sea by a storm	31. for My sins to Sea by a storm
34. obtrusions	34. obtrusions
47. perpetrations	47. perpetrations
48. for as his death	48. for as his death
54. was the Bill	54. was the Bill
57. knew	57. knew
63. power, so	63. power, so
81. through the	81. through the
104. populacie	104. populacie [1]
107. crosse not the chief	107. crosse not the chief
123. No men	123. No men
133. be expected	133. be expected
175. ever will	175. ever will
192. Saviours	192. Saviours
218. le boon	218. le boon

It is evident that, helpful as these tables are in determining the relation of groups of ed., it is impossible to get at the strict chronology of all editions by this means. And the reason is obvious. While one set of editions was printing in one place, other printers sent forth rival ones from their presses in rapid succession. Beyond what has been obtained already, however, the knowledge of the exact chronological order may be dispensed with, owing to another circumstance enabling us to judge of the chronology of the Pamela Prayer and its singular position.

---

[1] Doble commits the error common to writers upon the printing of the period, assigning the spellings to authors and printers only, while very often due to the compositors. The spellings of Dugard's No 22 are not identical with those of his Nos 1—6.

CHAPTER X.

The Reliquiæ Sacræ Carolinæ.

Brown and the Court at the Hague. The three editions of the King's Collected Works. Their progressive growth. The original three prayers of the King's. The coming of the Pamela Prayer. Inadvertency of "1651" and correction of "No date." Summary.

Immediately on the death of Charles I. the idea seems to have been conceived at the Hague, where Charles II. then was, to gather every scrap of the dead King's writings as soon as possible into a complete edition. It would be a political stroke of no small significance as was seen from the immense effect of the first Eikons. And the printer was not unwilling because it meant profit to him. The work was to consist of two parts, the first comprising Charles's speeches, letters, etc, up to his death under the title *"Matters Civil"*, the second, Eikon Basilike and other things relating to the King's death, *"Matters Sacred."* The latter part was evidently easier to compile and seems to have been finished early in the spring of 1649, the former being achieved in time to bring out the whole volume next year, in 1650. The printer was Samuel Brown and the edition found so many purchasers that a new one was required very soon. Some additional matter that had turned up in the meanwhile was hurried in and the following year this impression was out too. Finally, a third edition, undated but bearing Brown's name, was printed. The title of these editions was *"Reliquiæ Sacræ Carolinæ* [1]*."*

A collation of the three editions elicits some very interesting facts. For convenience they may be denoted as "1650", "1651", and "No date." The last is preceded by a "Life of Charles I." and has a contents-list (including the whole volume) at the end of the second part; in the other two editions this list opens the

---

[1] That the first Reliquiæ edition was printed by Brown at the Hague is evident from the typographical appearance, and natural from the consideration that only the Court at the Hague could furnish such contents as the letters to Rupert, Charles II., Henrietta Maria, Ormond, etc. Some of the many subsequent editions, however, were apparently printed in London though retaining the name of Brown as the printer and the Hague as the place of printing. Of course, this does not affect the result of my collation of the editions.

volume. In order to show the relationship of the impressions to each other, the contents-lists will be given here, save for those heads of the first part that are absolutely identical in the three.

Comparative table showing the gradual increase of matter in the three successive editions of the Reliquiæ Sacræ Carolinæ; or pecularities in their relations.

1650	1651	No date
I.	I.	I.
Several speeches...	Several speeches...	Several speeches...
16. At Newmarket, to the Earls of Holland, Pembroke, & the rest of the Committee, &c. March 9. 1641.	16. At Newmarket, to the Earls of Holland, Pembroke, & the rest of the Committee, &c. March 9. 1641.	16. At Newmarket, to the Earls of Holland, Pembroke, and the rest of the Committee, &c. march 9. 1641
p. 22	p. 21	p. 21
	With some Passages that hapned between his Majesty and the said Committee,	Some passages as happened the ninth of march, &c.
	p. 23	p. 23
		With his Majesties Answ.
		Ibid.
17. To the Sheriff, Ministers, Gentry, &c. of Yorkshire, When they presented, &c. April 5. 1642	17. To the Sheriff, Ministers, Gentry, &, &c. of Yorkshire, when they presented, &c. April 5. 1642	17. To the Sheriff, Ministers, Gentry, &c. of Yorkshire, when they presented, &c. April. 5. 1642
p. 25	p. 24	p. 25
II.	II.	II.
His Majesties Messages for Peace...	His Majesties Messages for Peace...	His Majesties Messages for Peace...
26. The Message of Aug. 10....	26. The Message of Aug. 10....	26. The Message of Aug. 10....
*This Message is the same with the former, which by a mistake of the date in some printed copies, was taken for a different Message.	*This Message is the same with the former, which by a mistake of the date in some printed copies, was taken for a different Message.	This message is the same with the former, which by a mistake of the date in some printed copies, was taken for a different Message.

1650	1651	No date
27. The Message of Dec. 20 . . .	27. The Message of Dec. 20 . . .	27. The message of dec. 20 . . .
2. His Majesties Declar. concerning the Treaty, and dislike of the Armies proceedings, delivered by his Majesty to one of his servants, &c. from the Isle of Wight, &c. Anno 1648	2. His Majesties Declar. concerning the Treaty, and dislike of the Armies proceedings, delivered by his Majesty to one of his Servants at his departure from the Isle of Wight, &c anno 1648	2. His majesties Declar. concerning the Treaty, and dislike of the Armies proceedings, delivered by his Majesty to one of his Servants, &c. from the Isle of Wight &c. Anno 1648
III. Letters written by His Majesty . . .	III. Letters written by His Majesty . . .	III. Letters written by His Majesty . . .
23. To Prince Rupert after the losse of Bristol, Aug. 3. 1645 from Cardiffe p. 210	23. To Prince Rupert after the losse of Bristoll, Aug. 3. 1645 from Cardiffe p. 200	23. To Prince Rupert after the losse of Bristol, Aug. 3. 1645 from Cardiffe p. 217
24. To the M. of Ormond, June 11, 1646, Newcast. p. 212	24. To the M. of Ormond, June 11, 1646. from Newcastle p. 202	24. To the M. of Ormond, April 3. 1646 Newcast. p. 219
25. To the Governour of his Majesties Garrisons, June 10, 1646. from Newcastle, p. 213	25. To the Governours of his Majesties Garrisons, June 10, 1646. from Newcastle p. 203	25. To the Governour of his Majesties Garrisons, June 10, 1646 from Newcastle. p. 221
26. To the D. of York, July 4. 1647. Cawsham, p. 214	26. To the D. of York, July 4. 1647. Cawsham, p. 203	26. To the D. of York, July 4. 1647. Cawsham. p. 223
27. To the M. of Ormond, April 3. 1646, Oxf. p. 215	27. To the M. of Ormond, Apr. 3. 1646, Oxf. p. 204	27. To the M. of Ormond, June 11, 1649 Oxf. p. 222
This Letter and the next, should have come in after the 23. as appears by their Dates	*This Letter and the next should have come in after the 23. as appears by their Dates	

1650	1651	No date
28. To the P. of Wales, June 2. 1646. Newcastle, p. 217 His Majesties own Answer to a Pamphlet, intituled, A Declaration of the Commons of England, &c. expressing their Reasons for no further addresse, &c. p. 1	28. To the P. of Wales, June 2. 1646 Newcastle p. 206 His Majesties own Answer to a Pamphlet, intituled, A Declaration of the Commons of Engl. &c. expressing their Reasons for no further address, &c. p. 264	28. To the P. of Wales, June 2. 1646. Newcast. p. 221 His majesties own Answer to a Pamphlet, intituled, A Declaration of the Commons of England, &c. expressing their Reasons for no further addresse, &c. p. 293 The Papers which passed betwixt his majestie and Mr. Alexander Henderson, at Newcastle, concerning the change of Church-Government.
The Second part of His Majesties Works concerning Matters Sacred, Eikon Basilike. Or his Majesties Meditations	The Second part of His Majesties Works concerning Matters Sacred : Eikon Basilike, Or his Majesties Meditations	The second part of his majesties works concerning matters sacred. Eikon Basilike, The Pourtraicture of his sacred majesty in his solitudes and sufferings.
1. Upon his Majesties calling this Parl. p. 1	1. Vpon his Majesties calling this Parl. p. 1	(No contents-list of the Eikon here as in the other editions. S. B. L.)
28. Meditations upon Death, after the Votes of Non Addresse, and His Majesties closer imprison. &c. p. 171	28. Meditations upon Death, after the Votes of Non Addresse, and His Majesties closer imprisonment &c. p. 232 (No mention of the four prayers here, though they are inserted in the corresponding place in the text. S. B. L.)	

1650	1651	No date
II.	II.	II. The papers which passed between his majesty and Mr. Marshall, Mr. Vines, Mr. Caril, and Mr. Seaman, Ministers attending the Commissioners of Parliament at the Treaty at Newport in the Isle of Wight, concerning Church-Government and Episcopacy.
His Majesties Papers about Church-Government.	His Majesties Papers about Church-Government.	His majesties Papers concerning Church-Government.
1. Those that passed between his Majesty & Mr. Henderson, at Newcastle, 1646,	1. Those that passed between his Majesty & Mr. Henderson at Newcastle	1. Those that passed between his majesty and Mr. Henderson, at Newcastle, 1646
p. 182		p. 1
		(The ensuing pagination refers to the item of the first part as above in the index. S. B. L.)
		His Majesties first paper, May 29. 1646
		p. 309
		. . . fifth paper, July 16, 1646
		p. 353
		The papers which passed between his Majesty and the Ministers at Newport in the Isle of Wight, 1648
		(Now the pagination refers to the second part. S. B. L.)

1650	1651	No date
His Majesties final Answer <div align="right">p. 289</div>A Quære about Easter, . . .	His Majesties final Answer <div align="right">p. 251</div>A Quære about Easter, . . .	His majesties final Answer <div align="right">p. 324</div> His majesties letter to the Prince from Newport.
III. His Majesties Prayers with other things relating to His Majesties Death.	III. His Majesties Prayers with other things relating to His Majesties Death.	I. Prayers used by his majesty in the time of his sufferings, delivered to Dr. Juxton Bishop of London, immediately before his death. 2. A Prayer in time of Captivity. <div align="right">p. 371</div>
1. A Prayer used by his Majesty, at his entrance in state into the Cathedral Church of Exeter; &c. <div align="right">p. 323</div>2. A Prayer drawn by his Majesties special direction and dictates, for a blessing upon the Treaty at Uxbridge, <div align="right">p. 324</div>3. A Prayer drawn by his Majesties special directions for a blessing upon the Treaty at Newport, &c.<div align="right">p. 324</div>4. A Prayer for pardon of sin <div align="right">p. 325</div>5. A Prayer and Confession in and for	A Prayer used by his Majesty, at his entrance in state into the Cathedral Church of Exeter; &c. <div align="right">p. 287</div>2. A Prayer drawn by his Majesties special direction and dictates, for a blessing upon the Treaty at Uxbridge, <div align="right">ibid.</div>3. A Prayer drawn by his Majesties special directions for a blessing upon the Treaty at Newport, &c.<div align="right">p. 288</div>4. A Prayer for pardon of sin <div align="right">p. 289</div>5. A Prayer and Confession in and for	3. A Prayer used by his Majesties &c. <div align="right">p. 9</div>4. A prayer drawn by his Majesty, &c. <div align="right">p. 10</div>5. A prayer drawn by his Majesties <div align="right">p. 10</div>7. A prayer and confession in & for

1650	1651	No date
the times of Afflic-tion. p. 326 6. A Prayer in times of imminent danger p. 327 Several things relating to His Majesties Death 1. Three Quæres propounded by his Majesty, when the Armies Remonstrance was read unto him at Newport, concern. their intended trial of his Majesty, p. 328 2. His Majesties reasons against the pretended Jurisdiction of the High Court of Injustice, &c. p. 329 3. The names of those persons, who by a pretended Commis-sion from a few Mem-bers of the late House of Commons (acted by the Councel of War) &c. p. 333 The names of those persons, who at seve-ral times appeared, and sat actually as Judges upon the King, whereof about 73 did passe sentence of death upon him. With the names of the	the times of Afflic-tion p. 290 6. A Prayer in times of imminent danger p. 291 Several things relating to His Majesties Death 1. Four Quæres propounded by his Majesty, when the Armies Remonstrance was read unto him at Newport, concern. their intended trial of his Majesty p. 292 2. His Majesties reasons against the pretended jurisdiction of the High Court of Injustice, &c. p. 293 3. The names of those persons, who by a pretended Commis-sion from a few Mem-bers of the late House of Commons (acted by the Councel of War) &c. p. 296 The names of those persons, who at seve-ral times appeared, and sat actually as Judges upon the King, whereof about 73 did passe sentence of death upon him. With the names of the Councel	the times of afflic-tion. p. 13 8. A prayer in time of imminent danger p. 14 The tryall of Char-les the I. King of England in the great Hall at Westminster. 1. Three Quæres propounded by his maj. &c. p. 246 2. His maj. reasons &c. p. 245 3. The names of those persons, &c p. 25 4. The manner of the tryall of Charles King of Engl. &c

1650	1651	No date
Councel and Officers that attended them, p. 335	and Officers that attended them,	p. 27
5. A true Relation of the Kings Speech to the Lady Elizabeth and the Duke of Gloucester, the day before his Death. p. 337	5. A true Relation of the Kings Speech to the Lady Elizabeth and the Duke of Gloucester, the day before his Death. p. 300	5. The charge of the commons of England, &c. p. 30
6. Another Relation from the Lady Elizabeths own hand p. 338	6. Another Relation from the Lady Elizabeths own hand p. 301	6. At the High Court of Justice, &c. p. 40
7. Another Relation, from the Lady Elizabeth, p. 339	7. Another Relation from the Lady Eliz. p. 302	7. At the High Court of Justice, &c. p. 47
8. A Copy of a Letter sent from the Prince to the King, dated from the Hague, Jan. 23. 1648 p. 339	8. A Copy of a Letter sent from the Prince, to the King, dated from the Hague, Jan. 23. 1648 p. 303	8. Wednesday, Jan. 24. 1648 p. 54
9. His Majesties last Speech on the Scaffold at his Martyrdom, Jan. 30. 1648 p. 340	9. His Majesties last Speech on the Scaffold at his Martyrdom, Jan. 30. 1648 p. 304	9. The proceedings of the High Court of Justice, &c ib.
10. The names of the Mayor and Aldermen of London, that proclaimed the Act against Monarchy, p. 346	10. The Names of the Mayor and Aldermen of London, that proclaimed the Act against Monarchy, p. 309	10. Resolutions of the Court, &c p. 83
11. A Speech made in Latine by Dr. Lotius, to King Charles the second, in the name of the Consistory of Hague, and in the presence of the rest of the Ministers of that Church, upon	11. A Speech made in Latine, by Dr. Lotius, to King Charles the Second, in the name of the Consistory of Hague, and in the presence of the rest of the Ministers of that Church upon	11. Severall Elegies upon the Death of King Charles

1650	1651	No date
the death of K. Charles the first, 7. Calend. Martii, 1749 (sic!) <div align="right">p. 347</div> 12. The same in English, <div align="right">p. 349</div> Several Verses made by divers persons upon His Majesties death 1. An Epitaph upon K. Charls by I. H. <div align="right">p. 352</div> 2. Another <div align="right">p. 353</div> 3. Another by A. B. <div align="right">p. 353</div> 4. Upon the picture of his Majesty sitting in his chair before the High Court of Injustice, <div align="right">p. 354</div> 5. Upon the picture of his Majesty in his blue Wastcoat, <div align="right">p. 354</div> 6. An Elegy by the M. of Montrosse <div align="right">p. 355</div> 7. A Deep Groan at the Funeral of that incomparable and Glorious Monarch Charls the first, by D. H. K. <div align="right">p. 355</div>	the death of King Charles the First, 7 Calend. Martii, 1649. <div align="right">p. 309</div> 12. The same in English, <div align="right">p. 312</div> Several Verses made by divers persons upon His Majesties death 1. An Epitaph upon K. Charls by I. H. <div align="right">p. 314</div> 2. Another <div align="right">p. 315</div> 3. Another by A B. <div align="right">p. 315</div> 4. Upon the Picture of his Majesty sitting in his Chair before the High Court of Injustice <div align="right">p. 316</div> 5. Upon the Picture of his Majesty in His Blew Wastcoat <div align="right">ïbid.</div> 6. An Elegy by the M. of Montrosse <div align="right">p. ibid.</div> 7. A Deep Groan at the Funerall of that incomparable and Glorious Monarch Charls the First, by D. H. K. <div align="right">p. 317</div>	<div align="right">p. 119</div>

It is evident that each edition is enlarged beyond the preceding. In "1651" the speech at Newmarket has additions not found in "1650". "No date" offers the identical additions of "1651" + some of its own, which makes it probable that this text does not go back immediately to "1650" but was founded on "1651" as well. That the latter and "No date" are dependent on "1650" is evident from e. g. the note to the 26th message for peace. The Declaration from Wight shows the close connection of "No date" and "1650".

Letters 23—28 are interesting. In "1650" the chronology is Aug. 3rd, 1645; June 11th, 1646; June 10th, 1646; July 4th, 1647; April 3rd, 1646; June 2nd, 1646. "1651" slavishly reproduces this faulty order and the note on it. "No date" makes a clumsy attempt at correcting the fault and leaves out the note. The result, however, is very bad: Aug. 3rd, 1645; April 3rd, 1646; June 10th, 1646; July 4th, 1647; *June 11th, 1649(!); June 2nd, 1646*. It was only when making up the contents-list from the one in "1650" or "1651", however, that the printer of "No date" got confused. As will be seen on p. 137, he was more successful in arranging the letters in their actual place in the text.

"No date" has made one more step in the direction of exact chronology. Charles' papers to Henderson were dated earlier than the Eikon. Whereas "1650" and "1651" had placed these papers in the second part of the Reliquiæ, after the Eikon, "No date" transferred them to the first part, thereby causing some disorder in the arrangement.

The contents-list of the Eikon is wanting in the latter volume, and the items relating to the King's death are not so fully specified as in the other editions, though having increased considerably in numbers.

Next occur some very interesting things. "1650", as might be expected, reproduces the first Eikon that appeared in London, the one without appendix but with errata-list. For, if we follow up this list, it turns out that "1650" faithfully reflects the errors of Dugard's first impression (save the glaring "of make" and "and joy") down to p. 88, when the printer has apparently become aware of the errata-list and as faithfully corrects the rest accordingly. Among the Eikon editions compared above none answers exactly to "1650" in this respect. "No date" here only repeats "1650", "1651" on the contrary has corrected the errata throughout.

Table showing the correspondence of "1650", "1651", "No date"
to the original errata-list of Dugard.

1650	1651	No date
P. 8 and(!) make me	P. 11 O make me	P. 11 and(!) make me
8 of Joy	11 of ioy	11 of Joy
9 attended	13 attended Me	12 attended
14 for any Man	19 in any man	19 for any man
19 Honours	25 Honour	25 Honors
22 by my sins	30 for my sins	29 by my sins
22 by Sea to a storm	30 to Sea by a storm	29 by Sea to a storm
25 detrusions	33 obtrusions	33 detrusions
34 preparations	46 perpetrations	45 preparations
34 for his death	46 for as his death	45 for his death
39 as the Bill	52 was the Bill	51 as the Bill
41 know	55 knew	54 know
45 power, or	61 power, so	60 power, or
58 through thy	79 through the	78 through thy
51 popularity	101 populacy	100 popularity
77 the(!) chief	103 their chief	102 the chief
88 No men(!)	118 No men	117 No men
96 be(!) expected	128 be expected	127 be expected
126 ever(!) will	169 ever will	168 ever will
139 Saviours(!)	187 Saviours	185 Saviours
158 le Bon	214 Le Bon	210 le Bon

Not only these facts but several other things too point to the conclusion that the compiler of "1650" made his collections for the second part immediately on the King's death. The description of the execution, the speech on the scaffold, etc. are corrected and enlarged for each of the subsequent editions from their crude form in "1650". Hence it is quite natural that the "Four Prayers" should be wanting after the Eikon in "1650". As seen above, the fourth was apparently added about the middle of March, and they were printed only once before March 25th (even this case is suspected), but by the dozen after that date, so that the compiler of "1650" could not possibly have come across them in February or thereabouts. But such as they were left by the King, that is, the three prayers without the one from the Arcadia — he evidently got them, for after the Henderson papers in "1650" follow six prayers, the three first made by the King in 1648 or earlier, the others, however, being Nos 2—4 of the later "Four Prayers". If we turn to p. 323

in "1650", where the six prayers are to be found, we find that their heading runs as follows:

"Divers of His Majesties Prayers: Whereof the three last, used by Him in the time of His Restraint, were delivered to the Bishop of London at His Death; From whom they were taken away by the Officers of the Army."

As I think it fairly well proved in Chapter IV. that the King left three prayers, viz. Another Prayer, A Prayer in times of Affliction, A Prayer in times of imminent Danger; that these three prayers were in the hands of Col. Thomlinson; and that the latter, as far as possible, restored to Charles II. the things left in his custody at the execution, we may be allowed to infer that one of the civilities for which Charles II. thanked Col. Thomlinson in his letter (see ante) was the delivery of a copy of the prayers and other papers of interest to one of those agents from the Court at the Hague that were sent to London, first to prevent the execution (Gardiner, Hist. Civ. War III, p. 589) and then secretly to keep up communications with the English capital.

We are confirmed in this opinion by the following circumstances.

The title of the prayers in the numerous London Eikons regularly stated that the prayers were (made and) used by Charles before his death and, in his last moments, were by him handed to Juxon. When the prayers were published at the Hague, where we should expect the particulars of their origin to be less known, the title tells the above *and adds that they were taken away by the officers of the army*. The coupling together of these facts brings home to the reader two things: that the original publication of the prayers *in London* was due to the revolutionaries, who would naturally take care not to tell that the officers of the army had taken away the prayers, because then people must understand that the revolutionaries had published them; and that the secret agents of Charles II. really had got their copies from Thomlinson, because in that case it is very natural that they should know and reveal that the prayers were taken away by the officers of the army and that they should get only three of them so that the spurious prayer had to creep in afterwards inadvertently, as will be seen presently.

"1651" repeats the item of six prayers from "1650" in its due place, after the Henderson papers. But, as more of the King's writings were being hunted for in the meantime, the compiler had come across later Eikon editions with the *four* prayers, and without closer examination inserted the latter immediately after the Eikon in "1651", quite unaware of the fact that three of them were among the *six* prayers printed after the Henderson papers in the same volume.

This mistake has been noted by the printer of "No date" and corrected after his own clumsy fashion.

On page 373 is the title: "Prayers Used by His Majesty in the time of His Sufferings. Delivered to Dr. Juxon Bishop of London, immediately before His Death. Also a Letter from the Prince.

A Prayer in time of Captivity".

Follows the prayer occupying most of this leaf. Then comes a fresh heading on the next page (page 9!).

"Additionall Prayers used by His Majesty in the time of his Sufferings and Restraint."

And then follow the *six prayers* of "1650" and "1651", regardless of the fact that Nos 1—3 of these were not used by Charles in his "sufferings and restraint".

The evidence as to the relation of these editions to each others is corroborated by an examination of misprints, orthography, arrangement, etc.

Table showing some peculiarities of typography and arrangement in "1650", "1651", and "No date".

1650	1651	No date
P. 2. moneths (for months)	P. 2. moneths	P. 2. moneths
6. shewen	6. shewen	6. shewn
7. Kingdom I will moneth	7. Kingdom I will moneth	7. Kingdom, I will moneth
14. moneyes an other	13. monies an other	13. monies another
15. hapned	15. happened	15. happened
16. lesned	16. lessned	16. lessened
24. asklng askt Kinh	23. asking 24. askt King	23. asking 24. askt King
30. leavie	30. leavy	30. levy
34. Retinew	34. Retinew	34. Retinew
36. my L. of Cumberland	36. my L. of Cumberland	36. my Lord of Cumberland
42. Ile promise	42. Ile promise	42. ile promise
43. whilest	42. whilest	42. whilst
50. the eight day	50. the 8 day	50. the 8 day
51. Munday	50. Monday	50. Monday

1650	1651	No date
P.52. in this Kingdom	P.51. in the Kingdom	P.51. in this Kingdom
52. suspition	52. suspicion	52. suspition
59. entormed	57. informed	61. informed
which. He	which He	which, He
65. enformed	62. informed	68. informed
67. suspitions	65. suspicions	71. suspicions
210. 23 To Prince Rupert . . . August. 3, 1645	200. 23 To Prince Rupert	217. 23 To Prince Rupert . . . .
212. 25 To the Marquess of Ormond, June 11. 1646 From Newcastle	202. 25 To the Marquesse of Ormond, June 11. 1646 From Newcastle	219. 24 To the Marquess of Ormond, Aprill 3. 1646, From Oxford
213. 26 To the Governours of His Majesties Garrisons, June 10. 1646. From Newcastle.	203. 26 To the Governours of His Majesties Garrisons, June 10, 1646, From Newcastle	221. 25 To the Prince of Wales, June 2. 1646. From Newcastle
214. 26 To the Duke of York, July 4. 1647. From Cawsham	203. 26 To the Duke of York, July 4. 1647 From Cawsham	222. 26 To the Marquesse of Ormond, June 11. 1646 from Newcastle
113. 27 To the Marquesse of Ormond, April 3. 1646. From Oxford	204. 27 To the Marquesse of Ormond, Aprill 3. 1646. From Oxford	223. 27 To the Governours of His Majesties Garrisons, June 10. 1646. From Newcastle
217. 28 To the Prince of Wales, June 2. 1646. From Newcastle Minister papers	206. 28 To the Prince of Wales, June 2, 1646. From Newcastle. =	223. 28 To the Duke of York, July 4. 1647. From Cawsham =
228. commited	191. committed	245. committed
230. paces	192. places	246. places

Finally, a summary of the real contents of "1650", "1651", and "No date" will be given here for convenient collation.

Table showing the real contents of the three volumes
"1650", "1651", "No date".

1650	1651	No date

Contents
    Sign. Π2—8
	Contents
	    Sign. A2—8
		Life of King Charles
		I. by Perrinchief
		    Sign. A3—G2

The King's Speeches
    Sign. A—C4
	The King's Speeches
	    Sign. B—E3
		The King's Speeches
		    Sign. B2—E5

The King's Messages
for Peace
    Sign. C4—J9
	The King's Messages
	for Peace
	    Sign. E4—L5
		The King's Messages
		for Peace
		    Sign. E6—M4

The King's Letters
    Sign. G10—M8
	The King's Letters
	    Sign. L6—S4
		The King's Letters
		    Sign. M5—V4

The King's Answer
to No Adress
    Sign. M8—N2
	The King's Answer
	to No Adress
	    Sign. S 5—T2
		The King's Answer
		to No Adress
		    Sign. V5—X3

		The Papers which passed betwixt his majestie and Mr. Henderson . . . Sign. X4—Aa4
Signatures Π2 — N2 = 280 + 12 pp.	Signatures A2—T2 = 276 pp.	Signatures A3—Aa4 = 96 + 355 pp.

(Second Part) Eikon
    Sign. N4—V11
	(Second Part) Eikon
	    Sign. B—R4
		(Second Part) Eikon
		    Sign. B—R

	Four Prayers, Letter, Three relations, Epitaph, His Maje- sties Reasons Sign. S1—T2 (The Prayers etc. not included in the table of contents. S. B. L.)	

The Papers that passed
betwixt the King
and Mr. Henderson
    Sign. V12—Y10
	The Papers that passed
	betwixt the King
	and Mr. Henderson
	    Sign. S—U5	

The Papers between
the King and the
Ministers at New-
port
    Sign. Y11—Cc8
	The Papers between
	the King and the
	Ministers at New-
	port
	    Sign. U6—Cc5
		The Papers between
		the King and the
		Ministers at New-
		port
		    Sign. S—Cc

1650	1651	No date

Six Prayers
    Sign. Cc9—Cc11
	Six Prayers
	    Sign. Cc6—Cc8
		Seven Prayers
		    Sign. Cc2, T (on R), R2, T3, R4

Several things relating to His Majesties death
    Sign. Cc12—Ee4
	Several things relating to His Majesties death
	    Sign. Dd—Ee8
		Several things relating to His Majesties death
		    Sign. T5—Bb8
		Contents
		    Sign. Cc—Cc4

If we sum up the facts collected directly or indirectly from reliable documents, they amount to this.

The King left three prayers to Juxon, viz. "Another Prayer", "A Prayer in times of Affliction", and "A Prayer in times of imminent Danger". Before Juxon's release they were taken from him by Col. Thomlinson. The latter showed them to Mrs. Fotherly. As the Eikon was dangerous to their cause the revolutionaries authorized their own printer to edit the book with the Pamela Prayer added, as asserted by Hills, Cromwell's printer, and tried to suppress the original editions by the seizure of Dugard and his copies, releasing him, however, on his promise to insert the prayer, as is also asserted by Hills. The gradual mixing up of the spurious prayer with the original ones is seen in the different editions of the "Reliquiæ Sacræ Carolinæ."

Thus much granted it would seem impossible to suppose that Milton, the government's special agent in this matter and the identifier of the prayer, was unconscious of the interpolation. It is evident to anyone who cares to work through some volumes of the Calendar of State Papers of those years that the isolated and momentarily precarious position of the revolutionaries surrounded by the cowed mass of the people of England, Scotland, and Ireland, consolidated them almost into a fraternity as regards their outward actions. What one of them knew in this respect the others knew too.

But a special chapter may deal with this question.

CHAPTER XI.

The Eikonoklastes.

Psychology of the case. Milton's absolute and relative ethics. The secretaryship. The "Tenure". Milton and the crisis of 1649. The appointment. The order to answer. The Eikonoklastes. Puzzles of the preface. Hills's testimonies. Conclusion.

In order finally to fix Milton's position in the case we must begin with an inquiry into the psychological qualifications which condition the action.

In another place it is urged that, taken absolutely, Milton's ethical position is ultimately subjective, as was quite natural in the England of the Great Revolution, heir and receptacle of the extreme Reformation subjectivism of Zwickau and Munster. He does not accept any wholesale system of the period, but makes a selection suited to his own inclinations. His austerity, his ambition, and high self-esteem as the dominant elements actually remove the Christian ethics — we recall his repeated conflicts with this system — and make Roman Stoicism the chief foundation of his modes of thought and action. And not only directly, through his daily intimacy with Latin authors, but also indirectly, as the Roman ethics of will and ethics of power were transmitted, specifically coloured, by Macchiavelli (see Introduction).

The latter circumstance leads on to Milton's position, ethically, vis-à-vis the people. We have seen that, like the Italian, he found it wise in a ruler to impose on his subjects in order to be able safely to rule over them. We may then be allowed to infer that so much the less would Milton hesitate to commit an action of the present kind in order to restrain the mass of the English people in 1649 — a people which he, according to his own writings, considered insane and wicked because of their aversion to the tenets of his own party, and whose "folly" in adhering to Charles Milton thought it his very duty — for the people's own sake — to eradicate.

Add to this the more or less successfully willed belief of the Puritan's that the prospering of an action which would otherwise have made his conscience uneasy showed God's approval of that action; roughly speaking, that if e. g. he succeeded in misleading an enemy, the success was God's manifestation of the fact that He wished that enemy to be deceived. We remember that when Cromwell had massacred and burned alive the defenders and inhabitants of Drogheda he wrote to Lenthall: — *"I am persuaded that this is a righteous judgment of God upon these barbarous wretches,* who have imbrued their hands in so much innocent blood; and that it will tend to prevent the effusion of blood for the future. *Which are the satisfactory grounds to such actions, which otherwise cannot but work remorse and regret."*

Compare with this passage Milton's words when he accused the King of the "prayer-theft": — "It can hardly be thought upon without som laughter, that he who had acted over us so stately and so Tragically, should leave the World at last with such a ridiculous exit, as to bequeathe among his deifying friends that stood about him, such a peece of mockery to be publisht by them, as must needs cover both his and their heads with shame and confusion. *And sure it was the hand of God that lett them fall & be tak'n in such a foolish Trapp, as hath expos'd them to all derision, if for nothing els, to throw contempt and disgrace in the sight of all Men upon this his Idoliz'd Book."* It is evident that this passage, which is hardly to the point under the assumption that the King left the Pamela Prayer, as *he* cannot have wanted to set a trap for his friends, — that this passage becomes strikingly significant in the light of the revolutionaries' playing this trick upon the royalists, managing to publish and mix up the prayer with the King's own writings unobserved by the other party whom God had stricken with blindness.

But as *Milton* here, as in many other respects, went beyond the Puritan stage of development, God to him gradually becoming something of a mere formula while his real foundation was Roman Stoicism, he writes down a very curious passage in the last chapter of the Eikonoklastes, falling under this head; where he, putting matters on a footing wholly intra-terrestrial, states that, "in the affaires of mankind", [1]) justice is and ought to be stronger than truth, and that to deceive the wicked who have first practised falsehood, is also a kind of justice: —

"It happn'd once, as we find in *Esdras,* and *Josephus,* Authors not less beleiv'd then any under sacred, to be a great and solemn debate in the Court of *Darius,* what thing was to be counted strongest of all other. He that could resolve this, in reward of his excelling wisdom, should be clad in Purple, drink in Gold, sleep on a Bed of Gold, and sitt next to *Darius.* None but they doubtless who were reputed wise, had the Question propounded to them. Who after som respit giv'n them by the King to consider, in ful Assembly of all his Lords and gravest Counsellors, returnd

---

[1]) The frank dismissal of abstractions for facts in these particulars can hardly be understood apart from Macchiavelli. Cf. Dilthey, Ges. Schr. II, p. 33.

severally what they thought.   The first held that Wine was strongest; another that the King was strongest.   But *Zorobabel* Prince of the Captive Jewes, and Heire to the Crown of Judah, beeing one of them, proov'd Women to be stronger then the King, for that he himself had seen a Concubin take his Crown from off his head to set it upon her own: And others besides him have lately seen the like Feat don, and not in jest [1]).   Yet he proov'd on, and it was so yeilded by the King himself, and all his sages, that neither Wine nor Women, nor the King, but Truth, of all other things was the strongest.   For me, though neither ask'd, nor in a Nation that gives such rewards to wisdom, I shall pronounce my sentence somwhat different from *Zorobabel;* and shall defend, that either Truth and Justice are all one, for Truth is but Justice in our know-ledge, and Justice is but Truth in our practice, and he indeed so explaines himself in saying that with Truth is no accepting of Persons, which is the property of Justice; *or els, if there be any odds, that Justice, though not stronger then Truth, yet by her office is to put forth and exhibit more strength in the affaires of mankind. For Truth is properly no more then Contemplation; and her utmost efficiency is but teaching: but Justice in her very essence is all strength and activity; and hath a Sword put into her hand, to use against all violence and oppression on the earth. Shee it is most truly, who accepts no Person, and exempts none from the severity of her stroke. Shee never suffers injury to prevaile, but when falshood first prevailes over Truth; and that also is a kind of Justice don on them who are so deluded.*   Though wicked Kings and Tyrants counterfet her Sword, as som did that Buckler, fabl'd to fall from Heav'n into the Capitol, yet shee communicates her power to none but such as like her self are just, or at least will doe Justice.   For it were extreme partialitie and injustice, the flat denyall and overthrow of her self, to put her own authentic Sword into the hand of an unjust and wicked Man, or so farr to accept and exalt one mortal Person above his equals, that he alone shall have the punishing of all other men transgressing, and not receive like punishment from men, when he himself shall be found the highest transgressor.

We may conclude therfore that Justice, above all other things, is and ought to be the strongest: Shee is the strength, the King-dom, the power and majestie of all Ages.   Truth her selfe would subscribe to this, though *Darius* and all the Monarchs of the World should deny.   *And if by sentence thus writt'n it were my happiness to set free the minds of English men from longing to return poorly under that Captivity of Kings, from which the strength and supreme Sword of Justice hath deliver'd them, I shall have don a work not much inferior to that of Z o r o b a b e l: who by well praising and extolling the force of Truth, in that contemplative*

---

[1]) This sneer at the Queen is frequent with Milton.

strength conquer'd D a r i u s ; and freed his Countrey, and the people
of God from the Captivity of B a b y l o n . Which I shall yet not
despaire to doe, if they in this Land whose minds are yet Captive,
be but as ingenuous to acknowledge the strength and supremacie of
Justice, as that Heathen King was, to confess the strength of Truth:
or let them but as he did, grant that, and they will soon perceave
that Truth resignes all her outward strength to Justice : Justice ther-
fore must needs be strongest, both in her own and in the strength
of Truth.'' (Works (ed. Mitford) III, pp. 516—18). This passage
is curious, also, as showing the conflict of traditional and new
elements in Milton's conceptions. Observe e. g. his beginning with
a formal assertion that justice is not stronger than truth and winding
up with an assertion to the contrary which latter assertion the
whole discourse is intended to make good.

Further to ascertain the position of Milton as constituting
himself one of the few righteous joined in hatred, contempt, and
irresponsibility against the greater part of the English people at
the Revolution, we must read over his words in the preface to the
Eikonoklastes.

"To descant on the misfortunes of a Person fall'n from so
high a dignity, who hath also payd his finall debt both to Nature
and his Faults, is neither of it selfe a thing commendable, nor the
intention of this discourse. Neither was it fond ambition, or the
vanity to get a Name, present, or with Posterity, by writing against
a King: I never was so thirsty after Fame, nor so destitute of
other hopes and means, better and more certaine to attaine it.
For Kings have gain'd glorious Titles from their Favorers by
writing against private men, as *Henry* the 8th did against *Luther;*
but no man ever gain'd much honour by writing against a King,
as not usually meeting with that force of Argument in such Courtly
Antagonists, which to convince might add to his reputation. Kings
most commonly, though strong in Legions, are but weak at Arguments; as they who ever have accustom'd from the Cradle to use
thir will onely as thir right hand, thir reason alwayes as thir left.
Whence unexpectedly constrain'd to that kind of combat, they
prove but weak and puny Adversaries. Nevertheless for their sakes
who through custome, simplicitie, or want of better teaching, have
not more seriously considerd Kings, then in the gaudy name of
Majesty, and admire them and thir doings, as if they breath'd not
the same breath with other mortall men, I shall make no scruple
to take up (for it seemes to be the challenge both of him and all
his party) to take up this Gauntlet, though a Kings, in the behalfe of Libertie, and the Common-wealth.

And furder, since it appeares manifestly the cunning drift of
a factious and defeated Party, to make the same advantage of his
Book, which they did before of his Regall name and Authority,
and intend it not so much the defence of his former actions, as
the promoting of thir owne future designes; making thereby the

Book thir own rather then the Kings, as the benefit now must be thir own more then his, now the third time to corrupt and disorder the minds of weaker men, by new suggestions and narrations, either falsly or fallaciously representing the state of things, to the dishonour of this present Goverment, and the retarding of a generall peace, so needfull to this afflicted Nation, and so nigh obtain'd, I suppose is no injurie to the dead, but a good deed rather to the living, if by better information giv'n them, or, which is anough, by onely remembring· them the truth of what they themselves know to be heer missaffirmd, they may be kept from entring the third time unadvisedly into Warr and bloodshed. For as to any moment of solidity in the Book it selfe, stuft with naught els but the common grounds of Tyranny and Popery, sugard a little over; or any need of answering, in respect of staid and well-principl'd men, I take it on me as a work assign'd rather, then by me chos'n or affected. Which was the cause both of beginning it so late, and finishing it so leasurely, in the midst of other imployments and diversions. And if the late King had thought sufficient those Answers and Defences made for him in his life time, they who on the other side accus'd his evill Government, judging that on their behalfe anough also hath bin reply'd, the heat of this controversie was in likelyhood drawing to an end; and the furder mention of his deeds, not so much unfortunate as faulty, had in tenderness to his late sufferings, bin willingly forborn; and perhaps for the present age might have slept with him unrepeated; while his Adversaries, calm'd and asswag'd with the success of thir cause, had bin the less unfavorable to his memory. But since he himselfe, making new appeale to Truth and the World, hath left behind him this Book as the best advocate and interpreter of his owne actions, and that his Friends by publishing, dispersing, commending, and almost adoring it, seem to place therein the chiefe strength and nerves of thir cause, it would argue doubtless in the other party great deficiencie and distrust of themselves, not to meet the force of his reason in any field whatsoever, the force and equipage of whose Armes they have so oft'n met victoriously. And he who at the Barr stood excepting against the forme and manner of his Judicature, and complain'd that he was not heard, neither he nor his Friends shall have that cause now to find fault; being mett and debated with in this op'n and monumental Court of his owne erecting; and not onely heard uttering his whole mind at large, but answerd. Which to doe effectually, if it be necessary that to his Book nothing the more respect be had for being his, they of his owne Party can have no just reason to exclaime. For it were too unreasonable that he, because dead, should have the liberty in his Booke to speake all evill of the Parlament; and they, because living, should be expected to have less freedome, or any for them, to speake home the plaine truth of a full and pertinent reply. As he, to acquitt himselfe, hath not spar'd his Adversaries, to load them with all sorts of blame and accusation, so to him, as in his Book alive, there will be us'd no more Courtship then he uses; but what is properly his owne guilt, not imputed any more to his evill Counsellors (a Ceremony us'd longer by the Parlament then hee himselfe desir'd) shall be layd heer without circumlocutions at his owne dore. That they who from the first beginning, or but now of late, by what unhappiness I know not, are so much affatuated, not with his person only, but with his palpable faults, and dote upon his deformities, may have none to blame but thir owne folly, if they live and dye in such a strook'n blindness, as next to that of *Sodom* hath not happ'nd to any sort of men more gross, or more misleading.

First then that some men (whether this were by him intended or by his Friends), have by policy accomplish'd after death that revenge upon thir Enemies, which in life they were not able, hath bin oft related. And among other examples wee find that the last Will of *Cæsar* being read to the people, and what bounteous Legacies he had bequeath'd them, wrought more in that Vulgar audience to the avenging of his death, then all the art he could ever use, to win thir favor in his lifetime. And how much their intent, who publish'd these overlate Apologies and Meditations of the dead King, drives to the same end of stirring up the people to bring him that honour, that affection, and by consequence, that revenge to his dead Corps, which he himselfe living could never gain to his Person, it appeares both by the conceited portraiture before his Book, drawn out to the full measure of a Masking Scene, and sett there to catch fools and silly gazers, and by those Latin words after the end, *Vota dabunt quæ Bella negarunt,* intimating, that what hee could not compass by Warr, hee should atchieve by his Meditations. For in words which admitt of various sence, the libertie is ours to choose that interpretation which may best mind us of what our restless enemies endeavor, and what we are timely to prevent. And heer may be well observ'd the loose and negligent curiosity of those who took upon them to adorn the setting out of this Booke: for though the Picture sett in Front would Martyr him and Saint him to befoole the people, yet the Latin Motto in the end, which they understand not, leaves him, as it were, a politic contriver to bring about that interest by faire and plausible words, which the force of Armes deny'd him. But quaint Emblems and devices begg'd from the olde Pageantry of some Twelfe-nights entertainment at *Whitehall,* will doe but ill to make a Saint or Martyr: and if the People resolve to take him Sainted at the rate of such a Canonizing, I shall suspect their Calendar more then the *Gregorian.* In one thing I must commend his op'nness who gave the Title to this Book, Εἰκὼν Βασιλικὴ, that is to say, The Kings Image; and by the Shrine he dresses out for him, certainly, would have the people come and worship him. For which reason this Answer also is intitl'd *Iconoclastes,*

10

the famous Surname of many Greek Emperors, who in thir zeal
to the command of God, after long tradition of Idolatry in the
Church, tooke courage and broke all superstitious Images to peeces.
But the people, exorbitant and excessive in all thir motions, are
prone ofttimes not to a religious onely, but to a civil kind of Idolatry
in Idolizing thir Kings; though never more mistak'n in the object
of thir worship; heretofore being wont to repute for Saints, those
faithfull and courageous Barons, who lost thir lives in the Field,
making glorious Warr against Tyrants for the common Liberty;
as Simon de Momfort, Earle of Leicester, against Henry the
third; Thomas Plantagenet, Earle of Lancaster, against Edward
the second. But now with a besotted and degenerate baseness of
spirit, except some few, who yet retaine in them the old English
fortitude and love of freedome, and have testifi'd it by thir matchless
deeds, the rest imbastardiz'd from the ancient nobleness of thir An-
cestors, are ready to fall flatt and give adoration to the Image and
memory of this Man, who hath offer'd at more cunning fetches to
undermine our Liberties and putt Tyranny into an Art, then any
Brittish King before him. Which low dejection and debasement
of mind in the people, I must confess I cannot willingly ascribe
to the naturall disposition of an Englishman, but rather to two
other causes. First to the Prelats and thir fellow-teachers, though
of another Name and Sect, whose Pulpit-stuffe, both first and last,
hath bin the Doctrin and perpetuall infusion of servility and wretch-
edness to all thir hearers; and thir lives the type of worldliness
and hypocrisie, without the least true pattern of vertue, righteous-
ness, or selfe-denyall in thir whole practice. I attribute it next to
the factious inclination of most men divided from the public by
severall ends and humors of thir owne. At first no man less
belov'd, no man more generally condemn'd then was the King;
from the time that it became his custom to breake Parlaments at
home, and either wilfully or weakly to betray Protestants abroad,
to the beginning of these Combustions. All men inveigh'd against
him, all men, except Court-vassals, oppos'd him and his Tyrannicall
proceedings; the cry was universall; and this full Parlament was
at first unanimous in thir dislike and Protestation against his evill
Goverment. But when they who sought themselves and not the
Public, began to doubt that all of them could not by one and the
same way attain to thir ambitious purposes, then was the King,
or his Name at least, as a fit property, first made use of, his
doings made the best of, and by degrees justifi'd: Which begot
him such a party, as after many wiles and struglings with his
inward feares, imbold'n'd him at length to sett up his Standard
against the Parlament. When as before that time, all his adherents,
consisting most of dissolute swordmen and Suburb roysters, hardly
amounted to the making up of one ragged regiment strong anough
to assault the unarmed house of Commons. After which attempt
seconded by a tedious and bloody warr on his subjects, wherein

he hath so farr exceeded those his arbitrary violences in time of peace, they who before hated him for his high misgoverment, nay, fought against him with display'd banners in the feild, now applaud him and extoll him for the wisest and most religious Prince that liv'd. By so strange a method amongst the mad multitude is a sudden reputation won, of wisdome by wilfullness and suttle shifts, of goodness by multiplying evill, of pietie by endeavouring to root out true religion." (Works (ed. Mitford) III, pp. 329—35)

This passage shows Milton's position Janus-faced, turned, as we said, in contempt, hatred, and irresponsibility not only towards "the rabble" but also towards the King, who here appears as a despicable hypocrite, the prince of lies. This opinion of Milton's has, I think, some curious consequences.

We return for a moment to Milton's "Te, More, ego nefandi illius clamoris vel esse authorem, vel esse pro authore haud injuria habendum statuo."

I think it a rather important point that, in the violent religious contests of the time, it often seemed indifferent to the partisan if the adversaries had really committed the crime imputed or were only thought by him to be capable of it. As far as we have traced the attitude of Milton's mind towards Charles I., we feel persuaded that we here possess a key to the interpolation. Evidently, at the outset of Milton's attack on Charles the latter was outlawed by his adversary, as was More later on. He was believed capable and was accused of anything. Known and commonly estimated even by enemies as strictly moral in his private life, he was by Milton, not only suspected of having, but occasionally without even slight proofs *stated* to have committed most revolting crimes: — "Solomon a meritissimo fratris supplicio regnum auspicatus est: Carolus a patris funere: non dico a nece, quamvis indicia veneni omnia in corpore patris mortui conspecta sint;" (P. W. p. 663); "castimoniam tu ejus et continentiam laudes, quem cum Duce Bucchingamio flagitiis omnibus coopertum novimus? secretiora ejus et recessus perscrutari quid attinet, qui in theatro medias mulieres petulanter amplecti, et suaviari, qui virginum et matronarum papillas, ne dicam cætera, pertractare in propatulo, consueverat?" (P. W. pp. 673—4), such are Milton's assertions in his answer to Salmasius.

The hypocrisy of Charles insisted on by Milton was apparently believed by the latter to admit of unlimited range. When therefore the reported discovery, after the King's execution, of some prayers of his — with Milton's conception of the King as a hypocrite unquestionable manifestations of hypocrisy — and, perhaps, the recent reading of the singularly pertinent Captivity Prayer in the Arcadia, coupled the prayers together in Milton's mind with the worthlessness of the King's worship and suggested its identification with the "trash of heathen and of fiction", it never became to Milton an ethical problem whether it was allowed to tell as a fact what he only thought the King capable — though accidentally and undeservedly innocent — of. We recall his allegations above in the teeth of facts to the contrary. It was rather to him a grim, contemptuous joke deservedly played on both the depraved, hypocritical King and the insipid, despicable, "admiring rabble". At this point too, psychological scrutiny coincides with tradition, as Hills related he had heard Milton joke and laugh over the matter.

Thus, as against the King, Milton's conscience was from the beginning eliminated even to the carelessness of a joke by his identification of crime and supposed criminal disposition. He arrived at the same position as against the people by way of approval of Macchiavelli's opinion that a superior man does not owe truth to the people of whose welfare he takes care.

There has been much discussion about the causes and events that led up to Milton's Latin secretaryship.

It seems certain that, in choosing him for this office, the primary aim of the revolutionaries was not to fill a vacancy or solely to get a person who could write letters in Latin to foreign powers. There was no vacancy because Mr. Weckherlin, the former Latin secretary, continued in his office till he was superseded by Milton, on March 13th, 1649. And he was apparently neither incapable nor invidious to Milton's employers as they appointed him once more, on March 11th, 1652, when Milton had lost his eyesight and could no longer fulfil the tasks imposed upon him. There must apparently be another cause.

In the beginning of February, 1649, Milton had brought forth a pamphlet with the following title: —

"The Tenure of Kings and Magistrates: Proving that it is, Lawfull, and hath been held so through all Ages, for any who have the Power, to call to account a Tyrant, or wicked King, and after due conviction, to depose and put him to death; if the ordinary Magistrate have neglected or deny'd to doe it. And that they, who of late, so much blame Deposing, are the Men that did it themselves."

This book aimed at a justification of the late trial and execution of Charles and was conspicuous even among other publications just then because of its passionate language against the King.

Evidently, the Council must have thought the person who wrote this pamphlet able to answer the "King's Book", in times when invective was the essential means of victory in controversy. Now, I am inclined to think that the primary cause of making Milton Latin secretary was the publication of the Eikon and the necessity of answering it. Some other circumstances seem to point in the same direction.

Milton speaks of his position at the Revolution, his writing the Tenure, his obtaining the secretaryship, and the answer to the Eikon in these words: — "Neque de jure regio quicquam a me scriptum est, donec rex hostis a senatu judicatus, belloque victus, causam captivus apud judices diceret, capitisque damnatus est. Tum vero tandem, cum presbyteriani quidam ministri, Carolo prius infestissimi, nunc independentium partes suis anteferri, et in senatu plus posse indignantes, parlamenti sententiæ de rege latæ (non facto irati, sed quod ipsorum factio non fecisset) reclamitarent, et quantum in ipsis erat, tumultuarentur, ausi affirmare protestantium doctrinam, omnesque ecclesias reformatas ab ejusmodi in reges atroci sententia abhorrere, ratus falsitati tam apertæ palam eundum obviam esse, ne tum quidem de Carolo quicquam scripsi aut suasi, sed quid in genere contra tyrannos liceret, adductis haud paucis summorum theologorum testimoniis, ostendi; et insignem hominum meliora profitentium, sive ignorantiam sive impudentiam prope concionabundus incessi. Liber iste non nisi post mortem regis prodiit, ad componendos potius hominum animos factus, quam ad statuendum de Carolo quicquam quod non mea, sed magistratuum intererat, et peractum jam tum erat. Hanc intra privatos parietes meam operam nunc ecclesiæ, nunc reipublicæ gratis dedi; mihi vicissim vel hæc vel illa præter incolumitatem nihil; bonam certe conscientiam, bonam apud bonos existimationem, et honestam hanc dicendi libertatem facta ipsa reddidere: Commoda alii, alii honores gratis ad se trahebant: Me nemo ambientem, nemo per amicos quicquam petentem, curiæ foribus affixum petitorio vultu, aut minorem conventuum vestibulis hærentem nemo me unquam vidit. Domi fere me continebam, meis ipse facultatibus, tametsi hoc civili tumultu magna ex parte sæpe tetentis, et censum fere iniquius mihi impositum, et vitam utcunque frugi tolerabam. His rebus confectis, cum jam abunde otii existimarem mihi futurum, ad historiam gentis, ab ultima origine repetitam, ad hæc usque tempora, si possem, perpetuo filo deducendam me converti: Quatuor jam libros absolveram, cum ecce nihil tale cogitantem me, Caroli regno in rempublicam redacto, concilium statûs, quod dicitur, tum primum authoritate parlamenti constitutum, ad se vocat, meaque opera ad res præsertim externas uti voluit. Prodiit haud multo post attributus regi liber, contra parlamentum invidiosissime sane scriptus: Huic respondere jussus, Iconi Iconoclasten opposui; non "regiis manibus insultans", ut insimulor, sed reginam veritatem regi Carolo anteponendam arbitratus; immo cum præviderem hanc calumniam cuivis maledico in promptu fore, ipso exordio, et sæpe alias, quoad licuit, a me istam invidiam sum amolitus." (Prose Works, ed. Fletcher, p. 720).

This passage contains several incorrect statements. For the present purpose attention may be drawn to one of them. According to Milton the Eikon appeared some time after his appointment. But the book, as we know, was out early in February and generally talked about within a fortnight. In the middle of March the Council determined to employ Milton as Latin secretary.

"March 13th, 1648.

1. That Mr. Whitlocke, Sir Henry Vane, Lord Lisle (not Present), Earl of Denbigh, Mr. Marten (not Present) Mr. Lisle, or any two of them, be appointed a Committee to consider what alliances this Crown hath formerly had with Foreign States, and what those States are, and whether it will be fit to continue those alliances, and with how many of the said States, and how far they should be continued and upon what grounds, and in what manner applications and addresses should be made for the said continuance.

2. That it be referred to the former Committee to speak with Mr. Milton, to know whether he will be employed as Secretary for the Foreign Tongues, and to report to the Council" (Council Order Book).

Two days later Milton was actually appointed.

"March 15th, 1648.

That Mr. John Milton be employed as Secretary for Foreign Tongues to this Council, and that he have the same salary which Mr. Weckherlyn formerly had for the said service." (C. O. B.)

Not only is Milton's statement so far incorrect that we can prove him to have been appointed after the publication of the Eikon, but it is also doubtful whether the Eikonoklastes was ordered *after* the appointment. Because in the Council Order Book is minutely recorded what each official of the government was directed to do, and there is no trace of an order about the Eikonoklastes, whereas Milton's other pamphlets and Latin letters for the Council after his appointment are mentioned in due place. This seems to suggest that private negotiations between some of the revolutionaries and the author of the "Tenure" about the means of rendering the Eikon harmless preceded the appointment. Remark the word "præsertim", which implies that when the offer of employment was made to Milton there must have been other services discussed than Latin letter-writing though Milton did not care to specify them. That pamphlet-writing was one of these services is evident, because several tracts were ordered within the first weeks. If we consider, too, that Milton's appointment in the middle of March coincides with the measures taken by the government on March 16th and 17th to suppress the current editions of the Eikon and license their own edition, the conclusion is that it was the refutation of the Eikon, in whatever manner intended, that led to Milton's secretaryship.

Milton seems generally to have written the prefaces to his books before he set to work at the subject matter, as, in many cases, a plan is laid down in the preface that is not followed up in the pages ensuing. The preface of the Eikonoklastes similarly seems to have been written earlier than the bulk of the book, because there he says of his present task, "I *take* it on me as a work assigned rather than by me chosen or affected," which ought to imply something to be done rather than ready. Several of the following passages also tell what is going to be done. And, as Milton proceeds by stages, his first chapter corresponding to the first one in the Eikon etc., his preface deals with the folding-plate prefixed to the first chapter in the "King's Book."

Further Milton says in the preface that he is writing to prevent people "from entering the third time unadvisedly into war and bloodshed." As it is known that the Third Civil War was inaugurated by the revolt of the Presbytery at Belfast on the 30th of March, which incident became known in London on April 16th[1]), the Eikonoklastes may (provided the above words really admit of such a temporal location) have been begun at least before the middle of April, that is, within the first weeks of Milton's public career. Other hints at the contemporary state of things point in the same direction, so that Masson thinks that most of the book was ready before Cromwell's departure for Ireland in the first half of July. In fact, if the observations on the last page about Ulster are a safe guide, the book ought to have been finished at least before Jones' victory at Rathmines on Aug 2nd, more than two months before its publication. With these results pointing to an early beginning and finishing, however, Milton's words stand at variance, when he tells us in the preface that he began the book late and finished it leisurely. If Milton really wrote the preface first, this remark must have been put in after the work was done, because, else, Milton could not have known how the work was to be finished. The otherwise striking change of tense also points to a later insertion.

Here are very many inconsistencies. Milton says that the book is urgently needed but none the less leisurely worked out. Internal signs point towards an early beginning and finishing, but Milton says the contrary. He wanted six months to bring out the Eikonoklastes, but wrote and published less urgent treatises within a month or two, e. g. the "Tenure".

If the arbitrary style, the keeping in view of other events than seem implied by the words, and the like do not account for everything, we may conjecture that the refutation was delayed because the interpolation had to work some time and the editions become mixed up so as to defy discovery of the provenience of the prayer. In this place we must recall the recklessness with which Milton maintained a wrong position against people he disdained and hated. Cf. his urging of the King's authorship of the Eikon though his brother-secretary, Frost, brought evidence to the contrary. Another instance is the case of More.

Finally, turning to Hills we remember his testimony that Milton and Bradshaw had joked about their managing the interpolation and that, for this purpose, they had printed the Eikon anew. To this statement fit very closely the facts that on March 16th the Eikon was on the one hand confiscated by the government

---

[1]) See C. S. P.

and on the other licensed for *that* printer who just then did much of the government's printing; that the only "1648" Eikon which has the prayer as an *integral* part of the contents is a close imitation of another edition from which it differs only in having the prayers; and that both these editions are singularly naked and wanting in such characteristics as might betray the printer.

We also recall a supplementary testimony of Hills's that Dugard was caught printing the Eikon and that Milton effected his release on Dugard's promise to add the prayer to his Eikons. Which is verified by the facts that public documents show Milton as supporting Dugard before the government (ante, p. 82); that Dugard must have been seized with his Eikons on March 17th, 1649, but, in spite of the gravity of the offence, was released again without punishment; and that the last two of his six first Eikon editions printed before March 25th, 1649, (which he can have found the time to print in March only), have added a *separately printed appendix with the prayers,* which appendix, on the other hand, must have been printed immediately after March 25th, because, else, these Eikons and appendices would not so regularly have been bound up together.

If, in this way, we find it proved that Milton and the refutation of the Eikon are from the beginning knit together in a much closer manner than Milton himself states; that the words of the witness who testified against him are verified in every detail; and, moreover, that, in the very Eikonoklastes, Milton's mode of thought undoubtedly states the propriety and duty of committing such actions as the present one, under conditions fulfilled in the case of the Eikon Basilike, I am unable to see any possibility of evading the conclusion that he was the author of the interpolation.

Bibliography.

This bibliography does not include 1) quite obvious works of reference such as the Encyclopædia Britannica, the Dict. Nat. Biography, Die Religion in Geschichte und Gegenwart, Herzog-Hauck's Realenzyklopädie, etc; 2) the well-known treatises by Müller, Edmundson, Gosse, Moolhuizen, Pattison, Geoffroy, Telleen, Dunster, Schoembs, etc., considered to be of minor or of no value, at least for the present purpose; 3) the numerous pertinent articles and notes in Notes and Queries, Gent. Mag., the Athenæum, the Academy, Mod. Lang. Rev., Mod. Lang. Notes, Die neueren Sprachen, E. St., Anglia, Revue d. d. Mondes, Archivio Storico, Giornale Storico, etc., 4) the bulk of newspapers, tracts, broadsides, and such like perused or typographically examined in the Thomason Collection, such as "The Man in the Moon", "Impartial Scout", "Mercurius Politicus", "Melancholicus", etc., whose press marks follow here: E. 83—5; E. 359, 367, 369, 379, 383—87; E. 445—460; E. 533, 540, 550, 575—6, 587—97; E. 600—615, 637, 644, 669 f. 10—14; E. 777—80; E. 1098, 1108, 1146, 1188, 1216, 1397; 5) specification of the Eikon editions whose press marks follow here: C. 58. b. 16, C. 59. a. 24, C. 58. b. 14, 8122. a. 7, 8122. a. 9—17, 8122. a. 21, 8122. a. 23, 8122. de. 1—2, 598. a. 32, C. 69. e. 7, 292. a. 45, 294. k. 25, 599, e. 11, 599. e. 15, 807. a. 43, 808. a. 8, 808. a. 16, 8122. a. 22, 8122. a. 25, 8122. bb. 14, G. 1764, G. 11665, G. 11666; and of the Reliquiæ Sacræ Carolinæ 292. b. 5, 599. a. 33, 600. c. 2, E. 1220, 8122. a. 2; 6) the MSS, principally Harleian 4898, 7352; Add. MSS. 29,548—29,596; 36354; the records at Stationers' Hall, etc.

Finally, as the treatise touches on several subjects, it was necessary in many cases to include only some of the most representative works consulted on the matter, so as not to swell this list too much. If the excluded books are directly quoted in the text, full reference is to be found in the same place.

Abetti, A. Galilei in Arcetri. Firenze, 1901.
Addison, J. The Spectator. 4 vols. Everyman.
Aldis, H. G. The Printed Book. Cambridge, 1916.
Allodoli, E. Giovanni Miltone e l'Italia. Prato, 1907.
Almack, E. Bibliography of Eikon Basilike. Lond. 1896.
— — Stuart Series. 7 vols. London, 1902—04.
Ames, P. W. Milton Memorial Lectures, 1908. (Roy. Soc. Lit.).
The Antiquary, 1880.
Bacon, F. Advancement of Learning. Everyman.
Bailey, M. L. Milton and Jacob Boehme. Oxford, 1914.
Bates, G. Elenchus motuum nuperorum in Anglia. London, 1650.
— — Elenchi . . . pars prima. 2nd ed. ibid. 1660.
Bayle, P. Dictionnaire historique. 2nd ed. Tome II. Paris, 1702.
Bayly, L. Practise of Piety. London, 1639.
The Bibliographer, 1883.
Birch, Th. Case of the Royal Martyr. Lond. 1758.
— — Athenian Letters. ib. 1781.
— — Court and Times of Charles I. ib. 1848.
— — Inquiry into the Share Which Charles I. had in the Transactions of Glamorgan. ib. 1747.
Buckle, H. Th. Civilization in England. 3 vols. World's Class.
Burckhardt, J. Kultur d. Renaissance in Italien. 2 vols. Leipzig, 1913.
Burnet, G. History of his own Times. Everyman.
Byse, F. Milton on the Continent. Lond. 1903.
Calendars of State Papers (Domestic) 1640—59. Lond.
Calvin, J. Opera. 59 vols. (Corpus reform.).
Cambridge History of Engl. Lit. Vols. II—VII.
Chauvet, P. La Religion de Milton. Thèse. Paris, 1909.
Chronicles of the Pilgrim Fathers. Lond. n. d.
Cioni, M. Documenti Galileiani del S. Uffizio di Firenze. Fir. 1908.
Cobbett-Howell, Complete Collection of State Trials.
Coleridge, S. T. Essays. Everyman.
Collin de Plancy, J. Dictionnaire Infernal. Brux. 1845.
Cromwell, O. Letters and Speeches. 3 vols. Everyman.
— — Inedited Letters. Lond. 1861.
Cunningham, W. Growth of Engl. Industry and Commerce. 3 vols. Cambr. 1903.
— — Western Civilization. 2 vols. ib. 1902—04.
Cushman, L. W. Devil and Vice in the Engl. Dramatic Literature before Shakespeare (Morsb. Stud.).
Dilthey, W. Gesammelte Schriften, Vol. II, 1914.
Douglas, J. Milton Vindicated. 1756.
Dowden, E. Milton in the 18th Century 1701—50. Oxf. 1909.
Dreyer, M. Der Teufel. Rostock, 1884.
Ellwood, Th. History of Thomas Ellwood. Lond. 1885.
Evelyn, J. Diary. 2 vols. Everyman.
— — ed. Bray. 4 vols. Lond. 1879.

Fischer, W. Aberglaube aller Zeiten. 5 vols. Stuttgart, 1906—07.
Froude, J, A. History of England. 10 vols. Everyman.
Galilei, G. Opere. Ed. nazionale, 20 vols. Firenze, 1890—1909
Gardiner, S. R. History of England 1603—42. 10 vols. Lond.
    1883—4.
— — Hist. of the Great Civil War. 3 vols. Lond.
    1886—91.
— — Hist. of the Commonwealth and Protectorate.
    3 vols. London, 1894—1901.
Good, J. W. Studies in the Milton Tradition. (Univ. Illinois
    Stud.) 1915.
Goodwin, J. Obstructions of Justice. Lond. 1649.
Graf, A. Il Diavolo. Milano, 1889.
Guizot, F. Collection des mémoires relatifs à la révolution d'Angle-
    terre. 20 vols. Paris, 1827.
Hallam, H. Constitutional History of Engl. 3 vols. Everyman.
Harleian Miscellany. 10 vols.
Harrington, J. Oceana. Lond. 1887.
Hatton-Finch Correspondence. Camden Soc.
Herbert, Th. Memoirs. London, 1702.
(Henry Hills) Life of Henry Hills. Lond. 1688.
— — View of Part of the many traitorous, disloyal, and
    turnabout actions of H. H. Lond. 1684.
Hobbes, Th. Leviathan. Everyman.
Hollingworth, R. Defence of King Charles I's Eikon Basilike.
    Lond. 1692.
— — Character of King Charles I. Lond. 1692.
— — Defence of King Charles I Occasion'd by the
    Lyes and Scandals of Many Bad Men of this
    Age. Lond. 1692.
— — Second Defence of King Charles I. Lond. 1692.
— — Death of King Charles I Proved a Downright
    Murder. Lond. 1693.
Hooker, R. Laws of Ecclesiastical Polity. 2 vols. Everyman.
Hutchinson, Lucy. Memoirs of Col. Hutchinson. Everyman.
Hübener, G. Die stilistische Spannung in Miltons Paradise Lost.
    (Morsb. Stud.).
Ilbert, C. Parliament. London. n. d.
Innes, A. D. History of the British Nation. Lond. 1912.
Johnson, S. Lives of the Poets. 2 vols. World's Class.
Journals of the House of Commons, 1640—60.
— — — — Lords, 1640—60.
King Charles I. Reliquiæ Sacræ Carolinæ (see ante).
— — Basilika. Lond. 1662.
— — Works. Lond. 1687.
— — Prayers. Lond. 1649 (Thom. Coll. E. 1317).
— — Certamen Religiosum. Lond. 1649.
— — Eikon Basilike (see ante)

(King Charles I.) Bibliotheca Regia. Lond. 1659.
(—   —)   Hellish Mysteries of the Old Republicans. 1714.
(—   —)   Restitution to the Royal Author. Lond. 1681.
(—   —)   Vindiciæ Carolinæ. Lond. 1692.
(—   —)   Prima et ultima relatione di quanto è successo
            nel regno d'Inghilterra 1649.
(—   —)   Life and Reign of King Charles or the Pseudo-
            martyr discovered. Lond. 1651.
(—   —)   England's Black Tribunal. Lond. 1703.
(—   —)   Εἰκὼν Ἀληθινή. Lond. 1649.
(—   —)   Εἰκὼν ἡ Πιστή. Lond. 1649.
(—   —)   Princely Pelican. Lond. 1649.
(—   —)   Eikon Aklastos. 1651.
(—   —)   Secret History of the Calves-head Club. Lond.
            1709.
Lippi, L. Il Malmantile racquistato. Milano, 1889.
Long, Th. Dr. Walker's true, modest, and faithful account. Lond.
            1693.
Looten, C. Vondel. Lille, 1889.
Louandre, Ch. Le Diable. (Revue d. d. Mondes. 1842)
Lowell, J. R. English Poets. Leipzig, 1912.
Ludlow, E. Three tracts. Lond. 1812.
—   —   Letter to Dr. Hollingworth. Amsterdam, 1691.
—   —   Ludlow no Lyar. Amsterdam, 1692.
—   —   Truth brought to Light. London, 1693.
Macaulay, T. B. History of England. 3 vols. Everyman.
—   —   Essays (Universal Library).
McIlwain, Ch. H. High Court of Parliament. Yale U. P. 1910.
Macchiavelli, N. Opere. Geneva, 1550.
—   —   Il Principe. Milano, 1909.
Maitland, F. Constitutional History of England. Cambr. 1911.
Mantoux, P. La révolution industrielle. Paris, 1905.
Masson, D. Life of Milton. 7 vols. Lond. 1859—94.
Menendez y Pelayo, M. Historia de las ideas esteticas en España.
            Vols. 3, 4, 8. Madrid, 1890—1908.
Michael, W. Cromwell. Berlin, 1907.
Milton, J. Works ed. Mitford. 8 vols. Lond. 1867.
—   —   Prose Works. 1697.
—   —   —   —   ed. Toland. 3 vols. Amsterdam, 1698.
—   —   —   —   ed. Birch. 2 vols. 1738, 53.
—   —   —   —   ed. Symmons. 7 vols. 1806.
—   —   —   —   ed. Fletcher. Lond. 1838.
—   —   —   —   ed. St. John. 5 vols. (Bohn's Library).
—   —   Commonplace Book. Camden Soc.
—   —   Eikonoklastes. Lond. 1649, 1650.
—   —   De Doctrina Christiana. Cambr. 1825.
—   —   Pro Populo Anglicano Defensio. Lond. 1650, 51.

Milton, J. Ready and Easy Way to Establish a Free Common-
    wealth ed. Clark. (Yale Stud. Engl.).
—   — Of Reformation Touching Church-Discipline ed. Hale
    (Yale Stud. Engl.).
—   — Tenure of Kings and Magistrates ed. Allison. (Yale
    Stud. Engl.).
—   — Poetical Works ed. Todd. 3ʳᵈ ed. 1826.
—   —   —   — ed. Masson. 3 vols. 1910.
—   —   —   ... ed. Beeching. Lond. 1913.
Morisot, C. B. Carolus I a securi et calamo Miltonii vindicatus.
    Lond. 1652.
Munk, W. Roll of the Royal College of Physicians of London,
    1878.
Nichols, J. Literary Anecdotes. 1812—15.
—   —   — Illustrations. 1812—58.
Payne-Gallwey, Sir R. Scaffold George of Charles I., Lond. 1908.
Peck, F. New Memoirs of Milton. Lond. 1740.
—   — Memoirs of Cromwell. Lond. 1740.
Pepys, S. Diary. 2 vols. Everyman.
Perrinchief, R. Life and Death of King Charles. 1693.
Pio, F. Den fri konkurrences gennembrud i England. Køben-
    havn, 1902.
Proceedings of the British Academy. 1908.
Publications of the Bibliographical Society. Vol. I. 1893.
Raleigh, W. Milton. Lond. 1915.
Roskoff, G. Geschichte des Teufels. 2 vols. Leipzig, 1869.
Sampson, Alden. Studies in Milton. 1913, 1914.
de Saumaise, C. Defensio Regia. 1649.
Van Schelven, A. A. Nederduitsche Vluchtelingskerken der XVIᵉ
    Eeuw in England. s'Gravenhage, 1909.
Scrocca, A. Studio critico sul Paradiso Perduto del Milton. Napoli,
    1902.
Shakespeare's England. 2 vols. Oxf. 1916.
Stationers' Registers 1554 ff. 8 vols. (1—5 ed. Arber)
Stern, A. Milton u. seine Zeit. 2 vols. Leipzig, 1877—79.
Stow, J. Survey of London. 2 vols. Oxford, 1908.
Symonds, J. A. Renaissance in Italy. 7 vols. Lond. 1906—08.
Taine, H. Littérature Anglaise. 5 vols. Paris, 1885.
Thompson, E. Essays on Milton. 1914.
—   — Controversy between the Puritans and the Stage.
    (Yale Stud. Engl.).
Timperley, Ch. H. Encyclopædia of Literary and Typographical
    Anecdote. 1842.
Todd, J. H. Bishop Gauden the Author of Eikon Basilike. 1829.
Toland, J. Amyntor. 1699.
—   — Life of John Milton. 1761.
von Treitschke, H. Milton. 1865.
Treumann, R. Die Monarchomachen. Heidelberg, 1895.

Troels-Lund, Dagligt liv i Norden. Vols. XIII—XIV.
Troeltsch, E. Die Bedeutung des Protestantismus für die Entstehung
    der modernen Welt. (Historische Bibliothek).
— — Protestantisches Christentum. (Kultur d. Gegenwart).
— — Luther u. d. moderne Welt. (Wiss. u. Bildung).
— — Soziallehren d. Christlichen Gruppen u. Kirchen.
    Tübingen, 1912.
Usher, R. G. Rise and Fall of the High Commission. Oxford, 1913.
— — Critical Study of the Historical Method of S. R.
    Gardiner. Washington Univ. Publ. 1915.
— — Reconstruction of the Engl. Church. 2 vols. Lond.
    1910.
de Visser, J. Th. Daemonologie van het oude Testament. Utrecht,
    1880.
Visser, M. Milton's Prozawerken. Rotterdam, 1910.
Wagstaffe, Th. Vindication of King Charles. 1693, 97, 1711.
— — Defence of the Vindication. 1699.
Walker, Anthony. True account of the author of a Book entituled
    Eikon Basilike. 1692.
Warwick, Sir Ph. Memoirs. 1701.
Weber, M. Protestantische Ethik (Archiv f. Sozialwiss. 20, 21),
    1905.
Whitelocke, B. Memorials. 4 vols.
Windelband, W. Geschichte d. Philosophie. Tübingen, 1912.
— — — d. neueren Philosophie. 2 vols. Leipzig,
    1911.
— — Die neuere Philosophie (Kultur d. Gegenwart).
Winstanley, W. Loyall Martyrology. 1665.
Wood, A. Athenæ Oxonienses. 1691—92.
Wood, L. A. Form and Origin of Milton's Antitrinitarian Con-
    ception. Heidelberg, 1911.
Wordsworth, Chr. Who Wrote Eikon Basilike? 1824.
— — Documentary Supplement. 1825.
— — King Charles I the Author of Eikon Basilike.
    1826.
Zumbini, B. Studi di Letterature Straniere. Firenze, 1907.

Contents.